Edward Meyrick Goulburn

The Holy Catholic Church

Its Divine Ideal, Ministry and Institutions - A Short Treatise

Edward Meyrick Goulburn

The Holy Catholic Church
Its Divine Ideal, Ministry and Institutions - A Short Treatise

ISBN/EAN: 9783337033613

Printed in Europe, USA, Canada, Australia, Japan

Cover: Foto ©Lupo / pixelio.de

More available books at **www.hansebooks.com**

THE HOLY CATHOLIC CHURCH

Its Divine Ideal, Ministry, and Institutions

A SHORT TREATISE

*WITH A CATECHISM ON EACH CHAPTER
FORMING A COURSE OF METHODICAL INSTRUCTION
ON THE SUBJECT*

BY

EDWARD MEYRICK GOULBURN, D.D

DEAN OF NORWICH

NEW YORK
Pott, Young, and Co.
1873

TO THE RIGHT REVEREND

SAMUEL,

Lord Bishop of Winchester,

PRELATE OF THE MOST NOBLE ORDER OF THE GARTER,

ETC. ETC. ETC.

WHOSE DEVOTION, ZEAL, ABILITY, AND

UNWEARIED LABOURS

HAVE CONTRIBUTED MORE THAN ANY OTHER SINGLE CAUSE

TO MAKE THE CHURCH OF ENGLAND

A LIVING POWER AMONG THE PEOPLE OF ENGLAND,

THIS BOOK

IS, BY HIS KIND PERMISSION,

INSCRIBED

WITH SENTIMENTS OF GRATITUDE AND AFFECTION.

PREFACE.

THIS Book is published in obedience to a call, which the Author felt himself unable to resist. So long ago as 1868, several influential clergymen took the opportunity offered them by the Wolverhampton Congress of meeting together to discuss, and consider the remedy for, the ignorance so extensively prevalent on the subject of the Church. It appeared to them that even those who are more or less competently acquainted with the rudiments of the Christian Religion, are often (from want of instruction) lamentably deficient in knowledge respecting the Church,—her claims, her title-deeds, her powers, and the grounds on which she claims the allegiance of her children. They also thought that it might do something towards the removal of this ignorance, if there were a manual, clearly and temperately written, which might meet with something like general acceptance, and might be placed in the hands of school-teachers and others, whose province it was to give instruction on religious subjects. Not wishing their discussion to terminate on itself, without practical issue, they determined to request Dr. Goodwin (then Dean of Ely), and myself, to undertake the task which appeared to them so desirable, indicating a Catechism as the particular form which the work should assume. Dr. Goodwin and I had a meeting, to consider the question of compliance with their wishes; and we both agreed that, though it was an undertaking delicate and difficult, and which of ourselves we never should have sought, yet when it was devolved upon us by several of our brother-clergy, whose opinion we had every reason to respect, it would be hardly proper to decline. We therefore considered the divisions into which the subject would fall, agreed what parts of the joint work each of us should make himself responsible for, and so parted.

Some time after this, Dr. Goodwin, by his elevation to the See of Carlisle (an elevation involving, as such preferment always must, an overwhelming mass of engagements), was obliged to resign partnership. This resignation of course robbed the work of its fairest promise; for Dr. Goodwin had all the qualifications for such an enterprise, and would have been sure to execute his part with vigour, clearness, and acceptance; and, like the king in the parable, I was obliged to consider whether, with my own slender resources, I should not find such a task above my unaided strength. There were three arguments, it seemed to me, for proceeding and doing my best : first, that I had already begun, if not actually to write, yet mentally to construct what was required of me ; secondly, that the same Providence which had in the first instance, without seeking of my own, seemed to summon me to put my hand to such a work, though depriving me of my helpmate, had given no indication that I was to abandon the task imposed on me ; thirdly, that I should hardly be acting up to my idea of my duties, as Dean of a Cathedral Church, if I did not respond to a call made upon me for a work on a theological subject, which it was hoped might be generally useful. So I went on, as I found opportunity to do so, expressing my thoughts first in the shape of Sermons, and then casting them into the mould of Chapters. Had I followed my own inclination, I should have done no more. But I had to consider that I was writing to order ; and therefore, in deference to the recommendations we had received when our task was assigned to us, I have added to each Chapter a Catechism, or (as perhaps in some cases it should be rather called) a dialogue upon it, the object of which is to make clear, to rivet, and occasionally to expand, the lessons contained in it. This has been a work of considerable trouble; but it is trouble which I do not regret. If my Catechisms are useful to no one else, they will at least have been of service to the writer. I have found that the making them has cleared and confirmed my own views. It is easy, in writing an essay, to slur over in one or two hazy sentences the weak points of an argument. But when one sits down to consider what these weak points are, and what answers could be given to a person founding objections on them, and to draw out these answers *in extenso* (and this the compiler of a Catechism must do), the hold one gets of one's own position thereby is far firmer and more satisfactory than before.

If I must be candid about my work, I fear that the views expressed in this Catechism will not meet with sufficiently general acceptance to make it answer the great object which those who suggested it had in view. This I cannot help. It would have been easy to write a quantity of matter on the Ministry, Sacraments, Offices of the Church, and on the relation which in our own country she holds to the State, while blinking the delicate question as to her real essence and constitution. But this would have been neither clear in theory, nor brave in practice. For my own part, *I cannot understand how the Ministerial Succession can be otherwise than essential to a rightly constituted Church;* and, as I entertain this conviction deeply, I have announced it fearlessly, while earnestly endeavouring, at the same time, both to hold and to speak " the truth in love." I am quite aware, of course, that this feature of it must preclude the general acceptance of my work. But for this failure I submit that my employers, more than myself, must be held responsible. They should have intrusted the task to another hand.

One observation, however, I may make, by way of preventing the reader from turning away at the outset, upon finding a Scriptural interpretation in which he cannot concur. In the first Chapter I have assigned that meaning to our Lord's great promise to St. Peter, which seems to me the most simple and suitable of any I have met with. I am not unaware that both ancient and modern

Doctors of the Church, of the greatest theological eminence, interpret the promise differently. The passage being a fundamental one, I was obliged to consider it; and in doing so, I have expounded it in the way which most approves itself to my own mind. But I am anxious to point out that *the possible incorrectness of my exposition does not affect my argument.* Granting that ἐπὶ ταύτῃ τῇ πέτρᾳ does *not* mean St. Peter in any sense, still it is as a fact indisputable that he took the prominent part in commencing the superstructure of the Church, whereof his Master had laid the foundations, and that by wielding the keys of the Word and Sacraments he first unlocked "the kingdom of heaven" to penitent and believing souls. That is all that is necessary for the argument;—a certain fact, not a questionable interpretation.

It remains to acknowledge my heavy debt to the Reverend Dr. Irons, and to the late Professor Blunt, in the three last Chapters. I have not read Dr. Irons's most valuable Essay[1] on the Interpretation of the Bible, since it was first published; but my strong impression is, that nearly

---

[1] THE BIBLE AND ITS INTERPRETERS. By William J. Irons, D.D., etc. London, 1865.

Preface. xiii

all the thoughts contained in Chaps. VIII. and IX. are originally his, sown in my mind by his Essay, and now reproduced in my own language. To the late Margaret Professor at Cambridge[1] my obligations are even greater and more conscious (alas! when shall we look again upon a divine so learned, so acute, so in harmony with both elements in our Communion?); and the latter part of the last Chapter is, as will be seen, only an expansion of one of his terse eulogies of the Book of Common Prayer. If I have in any way contributed to the wider knowledge of his works, and their greater appreciation by English Churchmen, I shall not have written altogether in vain.

E. M. G.

AYNHOE RECTORY, BANBURY, *Oct.* 9, 1872.

---

[1] FIVE SERMONS PREACHED BEFORE THE UNIVERSITY OF CAMBRIDGE IN 1845, AND FIVE OTHERS IN 1851 Cambridge, 1847 and 1852.

Contents.

CHAPTER I.

What the Church is, and when and how it was founded.

'*And I say also unto thee, That thou art Peter, and upon this rock I will build my church.*'—ST. MATT. XVI. 18.

PAGE

General need of methodized instruction on the subject of the Church—'The invisible Church' an unscriptural phraseology—Etymology and signification of the word 'Ecclesia'—Distinction drawn by our Lord between the 'called' and the 'chosen'—The man without the wedding garment, the representative of the called who are not chosen—Why the chosen are represented as many, and the called as only one—Call for the present treatise—Scriptural warrants for a treatise on the Church—Its close union with Christ—The Acts of the Apostles an inspired history of the Church—The fundamental Church truth—First announcement of our Lord's purpose of building the Church—Reason why our Lord's disciples (while He was upon earth) were not a Church—Difference between an aggregation and a body—St. Peter's part in the proceedings of the day of Pentecost—His admission of the Gentiles to the Church in the person of Cornelius—The two predictions respecting St. Peter's ministry, and their fulfilment—Meaning of the name 'Peter,' and probable reason of its being changed into the feminine form, in the celebrated promise to St. Peter—St. Paul, and all the Apostles, as well as St. Peter, were layers of foundations—St. Peter the earliest layer of the foundation—Bengel's distinction between being 'built' and being 'founded'—Why Christ founded a Society, as well as taught a religion—Risk of corruption in forming a society—God's purpose of renewing man, not of reconstructing him—Society man's earliest want—Instincts of human nature which have no meaning except on the hypothesis of his being a social creature—Instincts of love and friendship—Another issue for each of us, besides the question whether we receive the truths which Christ taught—A man cannot make himself a member of a society, but must be admitted by others—Necessity of admission into the Church—Necessity of an historical continuity to the identity of societies—Difference of appearance not incompatible with identity—Illustration from architecture—Importance of the Ministerial Succession—The Roman Communion in England a schismatical intruder—The debt which the Church owes to the Reformers—The due moral effect of the advantage of our position, as a Church at once Scriptural and Apostolical—The Church's spiritual lineage independent of State Patronage, ... 1

CATECHISM ON CHAP. I., . . 22

CHAPTER II.

Duty of the Church towards those who hold to the Apostles' doctrine, in separation from the Apostles' fellowship.

'*And John answered him, saying, Master, we saw one casting out devils in thy name, and he followeth not us: and we forbad him, because he followeth not us. But Jesus said, Forbid him not: for there is no man which shall do a miracle in my name, that can lightly speak evil of me. For he that is not against us is on our part.*'—ST. MARK IX. 38, 39, 40.

'*They continued stedfastly in the apostles' doctrine and fellowship.*'—ACTS II. 42.

The balance of forces a law of Nature—Religious truths are moral forces—The balance of truths a law of Grace—Both the Apostles' doctrine and their fellowship to be continued in—N 'nes 'fellowship' to be created, but the old one to be adhe In the infancy of Christianity the 'doctrine' and 'fellow ensive —How the two came to be separated—Perplex the ex rom this separation—How this perplexity was   warks,' etc. Other countries not as highly favoured; and   ed before the in such countries—The earliest idea of a Chris   ord framed Rapid propagation of the idea—The Founde   iely marred—Spiritual life visible, and spiritual age   rk, outside the Apostles' fellowship—How we are to   k of and deal with such phenomena—The man who cast out devils in Christ's name, but did not follow with the Apostles—Why he must have been a sincere believer—His probable independence of spirit—How much he lost by not following in the train of the Lord Jesus—High privilege of association with the Apostles, even after Christ had left them—The Apostolic Fellowship is still in the world—Loss suffered by separation, however conscientious—England has preserved both Christianity and the Church—Universal Christian sympathy to be cultivated along with Church principles—Spiritual history of many a separatist—His experience of the power of the Name of Jesus—His impulse to make known to others the power of this Name—His impatience of restraint—Success of his ministry, and the effect of such success upon himself—How we are to deal with such persons—Neither the State, nor the Church, are to forbid them—We must acknowledge his work as from God, and be thankful for it—Church principles by no means inconsistent with Christian sympathy—Appearance of saintliness and high prophetical gifts in the schismatical kingdom of the Ten Tribes—Schismatical Communions which preach Christ, like the 'little ships' in the wake of the vessel which bore the Person of Christ, ... 38

CATECHISM ON CHAP. II., . . 55

CHAPTER III.

The Unity of the Church, and its Disruption.

'*Neither pray I for these alone, but for them also which shall believe on me through their word; that they all may be one; as thou, Father, art in me, and I in thee, that they also may be one in us: that the world may believe that thou hast sent me.*'—ST. JOHN XVII. 20, 21.

The divisions of the Church made tolerable to us only by our familiarity with them—Unity Christ's design for His Church, however extensive it might in course of time become—Unity of the Church recognised in the same parables which predict its spread—Unity of the Church designed to be an instrument in the conversion of the world—Departure of the Church from the Founder's ideal—Origin of the ——cost—— the schism between the East and West—Its ground——nad—— and ceremonial—The schism at the Reformation and difficulties——it—Schism between the Reformed Churches parties with —— to propagate itself—Drawbacks of the Reformation ——dowme—— thought between the Unity of the Church and t—— of Saints,—exposed by the words of the Apostle, a—— analogy drawn from the body—The guidance given us by ho—— Scripture under the present circumstances of the Church—The establishment of the Israelitish monarchy—The causes which led to it, the misconduct of the rulers, and of the people—How the same causes have operated to produce schism in the Church—A second disturbance of God's plan for the government of His people, by the schism of the Ten Tribes, which might have been averted by a conciliatory policy on the part of Rehoboam—The secession received the Divine sanction, and the seceding tribes, even in their lowest moral condition, received the recognition of Almighty God—Law of the Divine administration, which God's sanction, first of the Monarchy, and then of the Schism, exhibits—Application of the narrative to the Christian Church, in its present divided state—The ideal of the Church, and its original constitution, shattered by the schism, and by the organization of new ministries—Our duty under these circumstances : 1. To recognise sin in the Church as the source of schism—The sin in our own Communion which led to dissent ; 2. To recognise our divisions as 'penal' in their character, and humble ourselves accordingly, and avoid those sins, which drew down the chastisement,—ambition, the lust of the eyes, and the attaching importance to trifles—Prospect of the unity of Christendom, very much like the prospect of the cessation of war, impossible of realization by mere human effort—Ezek. xxxvii. 22, 24 ; 3. Never to deny the working of the Spirit of God in schismatical Communions—Fullest acknowledgment of this compatible with the denial of any due authorization for their ministry—God does not confine His graces and gifts even to the channel of His own appointment—The Unity of the Church to be sued for in earnest prayer—The guarded terms in which our own Church teaches us to pray for it, ... 66

CATECHISM ON CHAP. III., . 85

CHAPTER IV.

The survey of Zion's towers, bulwarks, and palaces.

'*Walk about Zion, and go round about her : tell the towers thereof. Mark ye well her bulwarks, consider her palaces ; that ye may tell it to the generation following.*'—Ps. XLVIII. 12, 13.

The probable date of the forty-eighth Psalm—The confederacy referred to in it—Miraculous defeat of the confederacy—Security of the City of God against hostile invasion—Spiritual meaning of the exhortation to 'tell the towers of Zion, and mark well her bulwarks,' etc.—In the natural creation, the body of man was framed before the breath of lives was breathed into it—Similarly our Lord framed the structure of His Church before the Holy Spirit descended at Pentecost to animate it—The significance of the great Forty Days—Their evidential significance—Their constructive significance—The germs of Church institutions, Church offices, and Church seasons, laid during this period—Subsequent development by the Apostles of the Ministry of the Church, and of her legislative powers—St. Matt. xviii. 15-21—The Saviour's promise to be in the midst of the two or three gathered together in His Name, and the context preceding and leading up to it—Literal fulfilment of the promise during the great Forty Days—Ordinance of United Prayer—Ground on which the blessing covenanted to that Ordinance rests—The promise to 'the two or three' is the charter of the Christian Society—Christ's example social, while His doctrine was that of mutual love—Question raised as to how the Christian Society was to be extended and replenished—Self-admission to any society an impossibility—St. Matt. xxviii. 16 to end—Probable reference of St. Paul to this interview of Christ with the Eleven—Presence of many others at the interview—The deed of gift referred to in Ps. ii., under which Christ sends His Gospel to the heathen—Suitability of the scene to the commission—The Ordinance of Missionary Preaching instituted—Mode of formally admitting new converts to the Christian Society—Instruction required subsequently to Baptism—Recognition in the Baptismal Service of the necessity of such instruction—Ordinance of Preaching to Christians instituted—The different kinds of teaching which are required previously and subsequently to Baptism—Popular contempt for Preaching condemned by our Lord's institution of it—Ordinance of Christian Education—How this is to be found in the words, 'Teaching them to observe all things,' etc.—Close and vital connexion of Christian Education with Baptism—Christ's solemn charge respecting each baptized infant—How Christian Education is recognised in the restoration of St. Peter to the Pastoral Office—Hence it follows that Education apart from Religion, or even apart from the authority of the Church as a teaching Society, is condemned by Christ's Commission to His Church—The Commission to be perpetuated to the successors of the Apostles—Deep significance of the 'Amen' at the close of it—Christ's Presence with His Church in the darkest periods of her existence, shown by the vigour with which she shook off her corruptions—Baptism the divinely instituted form of admission to the Church—The signing with the sign of the Cross merely an assent to that admission on the part of the Christian Society—The outward visible sign of Baptism (where it may be had) shown to be essential to the remission of sins by Ananias's exhortation to St. Paul—Saul, though repentant and believing, not forgiven till he was baptized—Testimony of the Nicene Creed to the necessity of Baptism—Objection arising from the case of the penitent malefactor answered—Full Christian Baptism not in existence till after the day of Pentecost—God dispenses with His Ordinances, where they cannot be had—Double aspect of the Church of England, and the perils and difficulties entailed by it Aggravated struggle of the two great parties within the Church—The cry for disestablishment and disendowment—Scepticism within the Church, undermining the faith of her children—The clergy should teach the people to appreciate the advantages of their position as English Churchmen—The laity should study more deeply and compare Bible and Prayer-Book, and seek to understand their mutual relations; and all should implore the great Head of the Church to make our candlestick a burning and a shining light, ... 98

CATECHISM ON CHAP. IV., . 120

CHAPTER V.

The Institution of the Ministry, and its relation to the Church.

'Walk about Zion, and go round about her: tell the towers thereof. Mark ye well her bulwarks, consider her palaces; that ye may tell it to the generation following.'—Ps. XLVIII. 12, 13.

PAGE

The walk about the spiritual Zion resumed—The word 'Church' only used in the Gospels on two occasions: in the promise to St. Peter; and in the direction how to deal with a trespassing brother—Remarkable coincidence between our Lord's directions for excommunication and the record of St. Paul's practice of it—The parties which must concur in inflicting, and in relieving from, a sentence of excommunication—The moral power of excommunication exhibited, on a small scale, in the expulsion of mischievous members from Schools and Colleges—The power of binding and loosing lodged at one time with the whole Church, at another with a single Apostle—The meaning of 'binding' and 'loosing:' 1st. Excommunication, and relief from it; 2dly. Censure, followed by temporal judgments, and relief from it; 3dly. Authoritative prohibition and permission; 4thly. The withholding or granting of Sacraments; Or 5thly. Of any appointed means of grace, or even of any rite of the Church—Christ's Institution of the Ministry on the evening of the Resurrection Day—Broad sense of the words, as meaning that the Ministry of the Apostles, and every other Ministry, so far as it is a reproduction of theirs, is the appointed medium through which forgiveness, and all other blessings of the Christian Covenant, flow forth to men—With whom is the power of binding and loosing really lodged, with the Society or with its officers?—Christian Ministers the organs of the Church—Illustration from the natural body, the whole of which is endowed with sensation, while at the same time there are special organs, through which sensation is exercised—Christian Ministers representatives of the Church—Representative character of the Jewish priesthood—The angels (or bishops) of the Seven Asiatic Churches, addressed in the Revelation as representatives of the Churches over which they presided—Representative character of the Christian clergy recognised by the word 'Parson'—Political representatives derive their power from the people, and yet have prerogatives which the people may not usurp; and so the clergy, who are representatives of the Church—Korah spoke the truth in asserting that all the congregation were holy; but argued wrongly thence that he might assume sacerdotal functions—Encroachment upon ministerial functions condemned by this narrative, and by that of Uzziah's leprosy, ... 140

CATECHISM on Chap. V., . . 158

CHAPTER VI.

The Holy Eucharist at its successive stages.

'*Being seen of them forty days, and speaking of the things pertaining to the kingdom of God.*'—ACTS I. 3.

PAGE

Threefold purpose of the great Forty Days, which elapsed between the Resurrection and the Ascension of Christ—Recapitulation of the several Church Institutions, the germs of which were laid during this period—One would expect to find some reference to the Lord's Supper during this period, although it had of necessity, and in conformity with its character, been instituted previously—And we find that the very day of the Resurrection was not allowed to close without such a reference—The journey to Emmaus, and the conversation on the road—Sameness of the phraseology with that in which St. Matthew and St. Mark record the institution of the earlier part of the Eucharist—Attention specially called to the action of breaking the bread—The 'breaking of the Bread' the term used by the Primitive Church to denote the celebration of the Eucharist—Immediate appearance of the Eucharist on the very birthday of the Church—Privacy of primitive celebrations—Christ's design of disentangling the Ordinance from its sentimental relation to the Apostles, made manifest by what passed at Emmaus—In St. Luke's narrative of the Institution, our Lord holds out hope of again eating and drinking with His disciples, when the kingdom of God should have come—Words of similar general scope uttered shortly afterwards—Remarkable difference of the two sayings, while their general tenor is the same—The Emmaus Supper the earliest fulfilment of the promise to eat and drink with them again, after the setting up of the kingdom—This supper not an actual Communion, but a prelude to Communion—and so also every occasion of eating and drinking with them, after He rose from the dead—When the kingdom of God had more fully arrived at Pentecost, the Lord's Supper, in common with other parts of the Church system, received a glorification, becoming the great medium of His spiritual Presence, and of the closest communion with Him, which can be enjoyed on earth—Yet still its early associations are not dropped; and the dropping of any of them hazards an obscuration of the Ordinance—The Church still waits for the final arrival of the kingdom of God, which will be ushered in by the marriage-supper of the Lamb—That marriage-supper is the point of sight, for which our Communion Feasts are rehearsals and preparations—Diffusion of life represented by Baptism, concentration of life by the Lord's Supper—The Lord's Supper the Sacrament of perpetual re-union with Christ, and with His members, and therefore, as one of its conditions, demands a gathering of two or three in Christ's Name, and should be celebrated in a spirit of mutual love, . . 175

CATECHISM ON CHAP. VI., . 190

CHAPTER VII.

On the powers of the Church in Council.

'*It seemed good to the Holy Ghost, and to us.*'—ACTS XV. 28.

A later period of New Testament history brought under review in the present Chapter—The authority claimed for the decree of the first Christian Council—The natural means by which the conclusion had been arrived at—The decree founded on principles previously admitted—St. Peter builds his argument on God's previous dealings with himself and with the Gentiles; St. James on the same dealings, of which he finds a prediction in the book of the prophet Amos—The sanction of the Holy Ghost claimed for a decision so arrived at, on the ground of the Lord's own promises of guidance by the Spirit of truth, which Spirit had been given at Pentecost, and had flowed down upon the Church through various channels of Ministry — Being endowed with the Spirit, as well as with the Word of God, the Church might be left to legislate for herself in such emergencies as might arise; nor did our Lord give to His Apostles, nor His Apostles to their successors, any definite directions as to the method of meeting such emergencies—The Apostles bequeathed to the Church their inspired writings, in which are laid down the principles on which every controversy must be decided—Objection raised against two co-ordinate authorities in the government of the Church—Complexity of the finer organizations in Nature—The Church's legislative power: how far it extends—In the decree of the Council of Jerusalem we find an exercise of it—The modern Church might exercise the same power in matters ritual or ceremonial, though even then under a check from God's Word written—The Church's judicial power of declaring, in controversy, by a reference to Holy Scripture, what the true doctrine is, just as a judge expounds and declares, though he does not make, the Law—The Church has also a power of organizing herself, which is not noticed in Art. xx., but exhibited in Acts vi.—The new organization was in conformity with principles laid down by Christ; and with what had been done in the Old Testament Church—Points of the narrative which should be borne in mind in proposed new organizations for Church help—The legislative and judicial powers of the Church are, in our own Communion, in abeyance—Need of new Services, to meet new forms of religious activity—Need of a properly constituted Church tribunal—Reasons why neither Convocation, nor the Judicial Committee of the Privy Council, meet these needs—The Judicial Committee not a court of heresy—But if it must be admitted that the Church of England has its defects, so have all other Communions—The question is, Where can we find the fewest defects?—The shortcomings of the Roman Communion—The shortcomings of the Christian sects—Long usage may pos-

Contents. xxiii

PAGE

sibly sanction irregularities in the sight of God—We may reasonably hope that our defects are in process of being remedied; and certainly the Ministries of our Church show greater vitality than ever, and religious activity is everywhere abroad within her pale—All is well, if our Lord be with us, ... 203

CATECHISM ON CHAP. VII., . 224

CHAPTER VIII.

The Church presenting, exhibiting, and defending the Truth.

' *The house of God, which is the church of the living God, the pillar and ground of the truth. And without controversy great is the mystery of godliness: God was manifest in the flesh, justified in the Spirit, seen of angels, preached unto the Gentiles, believed on in the world, received up into glory.*'
—I TIMOTHY III. 15, 16.

Relations of the Church to the Truth, exhibited in St. Paul's designation of the Church—Desirableness of consulting the Epistles as well as the Gospels and the Acts, on the subject under consideration—Possible allusion, in the term 'Church of the living God,' to the idol in the Ephesian temple—Support of the Truth, one notion yielded by the word 'pillar'—Guidance and illumination a second notion—Three different modes in which the Church upholds the Truth—By presentation and recommendation—The Jewish Church intrusted with the Old Testament, the Christian Church with the New—The Church the appointed keeper of Holy Writ—Analogy between the history of the world and that of the individual, in that the Church was before the Bible in the world's history, and that to the individual it is the Church who presents the Bible—The spoken Word must exist before the Church, though the Church existed before the written Word—Christian parents are the Church's earliest agents—Sponsors are bound officially (and not by mere natural affection) to see that each child receives instruction in the Truth—It is the business of the Church to place Holy Scripture in the hands of her children, and call their attention to it—The Church maintains the Truth by exhibition of it—The principle of our nature on which this exhibition is made to the eye—Truths represented in Baptism, and in the Lord's Supper —The representation a living and effectual one, making a conveyance of the grace represented—The symbolism of Public Worship, Confirmation, and Absolution—Possibility of arriving at the Truth by an analysis of the rites embodying it—The Church maintains the Truth by vindicating and defending it—New heresies necessitated the expansion of early Creeds—Usefulness and necessity of fortifications, however little attractive they may be—The Church would betray her trust, if she protested not against heresies—Clearness of mind on subjects of Faith, the gain which believers derive from the Church's definitions—The definition of the two natures and one Person in Christ, an instance of this—Helpfulness of that definition—Its source, the Athanasian Creed—Creeds, in their origin, were not defensive—Before there was a Scripture, there was a Truth—What the Truth was in Patriarchal times—Earliest shape in which the Truth appeared in New Testament times—What St. Paul meant by 'the Truth,' in the passage under consideration—Why he calls 'the Truth' 'the mystery of godliness'—Contrast between 'the mystery of godliness' and heathen mysteries—'The mystery of godliness' a fragment of an early Creed—Comprehensiveness of this short doctrinal summary—A triumph-song rather than a fortification—Jubilant aspect of the Christian Creeds may well drown in our minds, when we use them, their polemical associations—Creeds are better sung than said, ... 241

CATECHISM ON CHAP. VIII., . . . 256

CHAPTER IX.

The Church guiding into and illustrating the Truth.

'And the Lord will create upon every dwelling place of Mount Zion, and upon her assemblies, a cloud and smoke by day, and the shining of a flaming fire by night.'—ISAIAH IV. 5.

Possible reference of the words 'pillar of the truth' to the pillar of fire and of the cloud—Restoration of the pillar of fire and of the cloud predicted by Isaiah—The guiding and illuminating functions of the Church a partial fulfilment of this prediction—Objection raised that, in order to understand Holy Scripture, we want no guidance save that of average education and intelligence—A crucial experiment proposed, by way of testing this hypothesis—Let a child be brought up without any religious instruction, and whose mind shall be left a blank as to any religious ideas—Let him be of ordinary ability, and receive a good secular education; at the age of twenty-one let the Bible be placed in his hands, and let him be exhorted to ascertain from it all religious Truth—Certainty that he will fail to do this, even on the more important doctrines—The very first verse of the Bible assumes previous knowledge, not to be gained from the Bible itself—The sources from which we derive our idea of the existence of God—That all the doctrines of the Faith are to be found in Holy Scripture, does not imply that they can be found there without a guide—Fruitless search for a great work in a vast library, unless we have guidance and help—Whence did we obtain the information that the serpent in Gen. iii. is the devil?—St. John, the only Scriptural writer who gives a hint of it; and yet surely the Church must have possessed the information before his time—Usual interpretation of the Prophecy respecting the Seed of the woman, not obtained from the Bible itself; nor could a person deriding the usual interpretation be convicted of error from the Scriptures—The typical relation of the sacrifice of Isaac to the sacrifice of Christ must be denied, if the Bible is to be strictly self-interpreting—St. Paul's direct assertion that the old patriarchs looked not for transitory promises—They had nothing in the Old Scriptures to ground their hopes upon—Insufficiency of the history of Enoch for a well-grounded hope in the case of others—Absence of the doctrine of eternal life from the Pentateuch, a postulate of Warburton's argument—Though the New Testament needs explanation less than the Old, yet in many points we are obliged to call in the tradition of the Church, in order to interpret it—The substitution of the Lord's Day for the Sabbath, and its sanctification, nowhere expressly prescribed in the New Testament—Infant Baptism also rests not on express New Testament prescription, but on traditional usage, tracing back to the earliest times—No one really reads Scripture without borrowing something from an hereditary transmitted interpretation—Office of the Church fulfilled by St. Philip to the Ethiopian, when he complained that he could not understand what he read, except some man should guide him—In what sense Holy Scripture is, in its turn, the pillar and pedestal of the Church—The office, authority, history, and existence of the Church can only be ascertained from Holy Scripture—The Holy Scriptures and the Church mutually necessary to one another—Exclusive prerogative of the Holy Scriptures above the Church—Subject of the final Chapter introduced, . . . 274

CATECHISM ON CHAP. IX., . . . 290

CHAPTER X.

On the Prayer-Book as a Commentary on the Bible.

'*Therefore, brethren, stand fast, and hold the traditions which ye have been taught, whether by word, or our epistle.*'—2 THESS. II. 15.

The necessity of some help from traditional sentiment and observance, for the full understanding even of the New Testament—In the absence of such help, the most well-intentioned man might find himself at a loss in many points—What he would find about the Church in the New Testament—What he would not find there:—a definitive prescription on the subject of Infant Baptism;—a direction how our Lord meant His example and precept about the foot-washing to be understood—The inquirer would wish to know how these and similar points were understood by the first Christians—Reference to traditional rules and observances in the Epistles of St. Paul; in 2 Thess. ii. 15; in 2 Tim. i. 13; in 2 Thess. iii. 6, 10; in 1 Cor. vii. 12, 17; in 1 Cor. xi. 2; in 1 Cor. xi. 16; and in 1 Cor. xi. 34—The being possessed of these traditions would be a great help to the right understanding of the New Testament—Such knowledge can only be obtained by ordinary Christians through the Book of Common Prayer—Qualifications for their work of the compilers of this Book—Why the Prayer-Book is probably a unique book of its kind—Deformed condition of the old Service-Books, when they fell into the hands of the Reformers—Tests employed by them to discriminate the valuable from the worthless: 1. Holy Scripture—The devotions which would not stand this test; 2. Primitive Antiquity—Certainty that the mind of the Apostles would express itself in the traditional usages of the Churches founded by them—Professor Blunt's panegyric on the Prayer-Book—Necessity of admitting that the Prayer-Book gives a certain tone to the Holy Scripture, and insinuates a certain view of it—No devotional form, whether for private or public use, could help doing this; for forms of devotion inevitably convey doctrine—An atmosphere essential to the life and beauty of things on the earth; while, in certain conditions, the atmosphere may be charged with death rather than life—Noxious ecclesiastical atmosphere which wrapped round the Scriptures at the time of the Reformation—Object of the Reformers to purify the atmosphere, not to dispense with it—The five helps which the Prayer-Book gives to the full interpretation of the Bible: 1st. Expressing what is there hinted—Question of the propriety of Infant Baptism decided by the Prayer-Book in the affirmative, on the ground of primitive usage—Justin's testimony to the Baptism of children in his days makes it almost certain that the practice must have had the sanction of the Apostles; 2. Enlarging what is there succinct—The priesthood of the Christian Laity recognised by St. John, St. Peter, and also by St. Paul—These intimations expanded by the Prayer-Book, which assigns to the Laity a distinct part in the Services of the Church, sometimes by directing them to join audibly with the Minister in the recital of Prayers, sometimes by putting responses into their mouth—The light thrown upon an incidental expression of St. Paul's Epistles by the fact that all the ancient Liturgies assign a part to the people in the celebration of the Holy Communion; 3. Illustrating what is there obscure—Obscurity of the text about the 'Amen at thy giving of thanks' cleared up by Justin's account of a primitive celebration—Particulars of this account—'Eucharist' a primitive name to denote the Holy Communion—The order of our Communion Service very similar to that which is described by Justin; 4. Concentrating what is there dispersed—The doctrine of the Holy Trinity gathered from several places of Holy Scripture, which the Church has collected into one focus; 5. Organizing what is there promiscuous—The testimony of 'ancient authors' to the existence of a threefold Ministry—The Scriptural warrant for which is to be sought in different connexions, in the Inspired Volume—The practical advice which flows from the consideration of the whole subject—Let an end of Controversy be sought by accepting the Prayer-Book as the interpretation of the Bible—Questions, which this acceptance does not set at rest, may safely be left open for the present—Desirableness of an end of Controversy—Danger of being drawn off by speculative and controversial from personal and practical questions, enforced by the story of the woman of Samaria—Let us put away controversies, and address ourselves to the task of growing in grace and knowledge, ... 308

CATECHISM ON CHAP. X., . . 326

CHAPTER I.

WHAT THE CHURCH IS, AND WHEN AND HOW IT WAS FOUNDED.

"And I say also unto thee, That thou art Peter, and upon this rock I will build my church."—St. Matt. xvi. 18.

"I BELIEVE in the holy Catholick Church." How many thousands of persons are there, who recite these words glibly Sunday after Sunday in the Creed, who nevertheless do *not* believe in the holy Catholick Church, and in whose mouths therefore this Article of Faith is an idle word! And their unbelief is due in great part, if not entirely, to ignorance. They have been fairly well instructed in those religious truths which have to do with the individual soul; a good deal of information has been communicated to them at various times about the duties, the privileges, and the hopes of the Christian. Nay, more than this: they have learned something respecting the Heavenly Father, the Saviour, the Comforter; they know what are the offices of the three Divine Persons in the scheme of Human Redemption, and they could quote several texts in illustration of those offices. But anything like methodized instruction respecting the Church they never re- *General need of methodized instruction on the subject of the Church.*

ceived in their youth; and maturer years have not supplied the deficiencies of early training. This being the case, they become the easy victims of any popular error on the subject of the Church, which may happen to be floating about in their theological atmosphere. One of these errors—a very mischievous one, and the more likely to mislead because it is patronized by persons who have a reputation for piety, and because it wears a specious appearance—confounds the Church with God's elect people, whom only He Himself can for certain know and see. Hence springs the erroneous and unscriptural phraseology, "The invisible Church." There is properly no such thing. The Church of Holy Scripture, whether under the Old[1] or New Dispensation, is always a visible body, which may be known and seen, established in the earth to bear testimony to God's Truth, and intrusted with the ministration of His Word and Ordinances. And the distinction between the Church and God's elect people (which is what is meant by "the invisible Church") is clearly drawn by our Lord Himself. I should say that the word Church, in the original Greek of the New Testament, means "a body *called* out." It is derived from a compound verb; that is, from a verb with a preposition prefixed; and the verb means "to call," and the preposition means "out." The

marginalia:
'The invisible Church' an unscriptural phraseology.

Etymology and signification of the word 'Ecclesia.'

---

[1] It is strictly Scriptural to speak of the Church under the Old Dispensation. St. Stephen does so: "This is he, that was in *the church* in the wilderness with the angel which spake to him in the mount Sina, and with our fathers: who received the lively oracles to give unto us" (Acts vii. 38).

words of our Lord which I refer to are as follows—
"For many are *called*, but few are *chosen out*[1] (or elect)." They occur in a connexion which throws great light upon them, immediately after the Parable of the Wedding Garment, upon which they form our Lord's comment. A great number of people out of the highways, of all characters and circumstances, had been *bidden* to the wedding; these are the called ones, the members of the Church, or body *called*. One man in the story, the representative of a great multitude, had not on a

Distinction drawn by our Lord between the 'called' and the 'chosen.' St. Matt. xx. 16, and xxii. 14.

St. Matt. xxii. 14.

The man without the wedding garment, the representative of the called who are not chosen.

---

[1] The distinction between "calling" (κλῆσις) and "election" (ἐκλογή), "the called" (κλητοί) (who, as collected and organized into one body, are the ἐκκλησία or *called out Society*) and "the elect" (ἐκλεκτοί), is carefully observed in the New Testament, even in passages where the two might seem to a superficial observer to be confounded. It is to be remembered that "calling" has a certain affinity with "election," all the "elect" being "called," though by no means all the "called" are "elect." In St. Peter's Second Epistle we find "calling" and "election" side by side: "Wherefore the rather, brethren, give diligence to make your calling and election sure" (σπουδάσατε βεβαίαν ὑμῶν τὴν κλῆσιν καὶ ἐκλογὴν ποιεῖσθαι). It might be inferred hence that "calling" and "election" are the same thing; but Holy Scripture, which is spare rather than lavish of words, never uses two words to express the same idea. The warning of the passage is that both "calling" and "election," through the perversity of the human will, may fail. Judas was (like St. Paul) a *called* Apostle (κλητὸς ἀπόστολος); for our Lord, in appointing him, "called unto Him whom He would" (προσκαλεῖται οὓς ἤθελεν αὐτός), St. Mark iii. 13, 19; and he was also a *chosen* Apostle, for our Lord says, including him, "Did I not *choose* you twelve?" and yet his "calling" and "election" failed; he was "a devil," St. John vi. 70. See the two words in juxtaposition in Rev. xvii. 14. "He" (the Lamb) "is Lord of lords, and King of kings; and they that are with Him are *called*, and *chosen*, and faithful" (κλητοὶ καὶ ἐκλεκτοὶ καὶ πιστοί); not *called* and *chosen* only, but such as had made their calling and election sure, having been *faithful* unto death, and

wedding garment, that is, though a called one, a member of the Church, he had not that spirit of holy joy[1] and love, which harmonizes with the great solemnity of the marriage supper of the Lamb. He stands for those who, though *called*, are not *elect* or chosen, and who would probably have been represented as the majority of the company, if the propriety of the story had admitted of such a representation. But the presenting oneself at an Eastern wedding without that costume, which it is the part of the giver of the entertainment to

Why the chosen are represented as many, and the called as only one.

therefore inheriting "the crown of life" (Rev. ii. 10). The "elect" are not "called" merely, but "the called according to God's purpose" (Rom. viii. 28), to whom "all things work together for good." We hear of them under another attribute in Acts ii. 47, where they appear as in course (or process) of salvation : "And the Lord went on adding to the Church" (*i.e.* to the visible society) "daily those who were in process of salvation" (for such is the exact rendering of the words, 'Ο δὲ Κύριος προσετίθει τοὺς σωζομένους καθ' ἡμέραν τῇ ἐκκλησίᾳ,—one of the many passages in which our translators have hardly been observant enough of the force of the tenses). The evidence of "election" seems to be the Gospel's coming to a man "in power, and in the Holy Ghost, and in much assurance" (1 Thess. i. 5). The "call" is seconded in such cases by an inward experience of the kind described. And yet this inward experience does not necessarily involve "faithfulness unto death," or secure the person undergoing it for eternal life. We may be both "called" and "chosen," and yet not "faithful." My only aim in these observations is to give consistency and harmony to the phraseology of the New Testament on this difficult subject, and I trust I have not stumbled in the attempt. At all events this is certain, that Ἐκκλησία (Church) means, according to its etymology, a *body called out ;* and that the idea conveyed by it is entirely distinct from that of *people chosen out* (ἐκλεκτοί).

[1] This is Professor Archer Butler's interpretation of the Wedding Garment in his magnificent sermon on that Parable ; and I have never seen any which so much approved itself to my mind.

provide for his guests, would be quite an exceptional case; and our Lord's parables describe only such cases as have a certain amount of verisimilitude, and might have actually happened.[1]

It appears to me, then, that a short and simple treatise, setting forth in a methodical manner the doctrine of Holy Scripture respecting the Church, may be useful, under God's blessing, in filling up a gap in the faith of some, and in bringing out into the clearer consciousness of others, and giving a logical consistency to, truths which are at present held by them with somewhat of confusion and vagueness.

Call for the present treatise.

---

[1] The other connexion in which the same words occur should not be overlooked. It is at the close of the Parable of the Labourers in the Vineyard. St. Peter had asked the Lord what he and his colleagues should have for the sacrifices they had made in order to follow Him. The Lord answered by assuring them of an over-abundant recompence; but at the same time said much to correct the state of mind out of which the question had grown. The questioner must be warned first that others called later into the vineyard, and serving there a much shorter time (as was the case with St. Stephen) should be as munificently recompensed as he, God's recompences being of grace, and not mere mercenary equivalents of the service rendered. This teaching is conveyed by the story of the labourers hired at the eleventh hour, who received the same wages with those sent into the vineyard early in the morning. Secondly, it is just to be insinuated to St. Peter that, notwithstanding all the sacrifices made by him, he may fail still (for has not Iscariot made the same?), and come short of the glory of God altogether. "Know ye not that they which run in a race run all, but *one* receiveth the prize?" "*Strive* to enter in at the strait gate; for many, I say unto you, will seek to enter in, and shall not be able." So our Lord closes the parable with the maxim, "So the last shall be first, and the first last; *for many be called, but few chosen;*" almost as if the earlier-called labourers *had been mulcted altogether of their wages*, on account of their churlish murmuring.

Scriptural warrants for a treatise on the Church.

And here methinks it is quite possible that the reader, who has proceeded only thus far, should be whispering to himself—"Better write about Christ, than write about the Church." Indeed! but I was under the impression (and I imagined that I had Scripture for it) that in doing the one I was doing the other. I thought that Christ and the Church were one—so entirely one, that He is called the head and she the body, He the vinestock and she the branches, He the bridegroom and she the bride—so entirely one, that He feels and resents as inflicted upon Himself any injury done to her, according to that word of His own to Saul of Tarsus—"Saul, Saul, why persecutest thou *Me?*" I thought I had read also that our Lord and His apostle Paul went about "preaching *the kingdom of God;*" and I supposed that part of the meaning (if not the whole meaning) of that term was the Church. And tell me, moreover, my reader, whether you desire me to speak to you faithfully the whole of God's Word, or only such parts of it as you fancy most, and as jump with the religious views which you have been led to form. I hope you will say, "I desire you to give me the *whole;*" but, whether you desire it or not, I am solemnly bound to do it. And I find in the Scriptures of the New Testament not only four most precious books descriptive of Christ, but one book, in the nature of an appendix, devoted to the history of that Church, which Christ in the passage now before us proposes to build. The Book of the Acts of the Apostles describes the foundation, development, progress, and spread of the Christian

Its close union with Christ.

The Acts of the Apostles an inspired history of the Church.

Church; nor does the inspired historian lay down the pen, till he has brought St. Paul, the great preacher of God's Kingdom among the Gentiles, to Rome, which was then the mistress of the civilisation of the world. Where the Holy Spirit devotes one whole book to the history and fortunes of the Church, can a Christian minister, who desires to declare *all* the counsel of God to his hearers or readers, be justified in ignoring the subject? Let us then open in the present Chapter the subject of the Church.

In all subjects of human knowledge a right grounding is of the utmost importance. A right grounding makes a safe superstructure. Nay, more than this. A correct fundamental principle on any subject, once seized by the mind, is often more correctly likened to a seed than to a foundation. A foundation is not a house, and can never of itself become one; but a seed *is* a plant in embryo; it will become a plant, when the germ is disentangled and developed. A whole host of popular misapprehensions about the Church is put to flight, and a right direction is given to all thoughts upon the subject, by simply embracing the fundamental Church truth, which is, that *our Lord came not simply to teach certain religious doctrines, but to found a society;* and that He did what He came to do,—left behind Him, and bequeathed to the world, not only a large amount of precious truth, which is preserved in the volume of the New Testament, but also a great Divine world-embracing Society, having (as human so-

The fundamental Church truth.

cieties have) its officers, its rules, its rite of admission, its power of expulsion, its solemn meetings or assemblies. Grant this, and grant it with a living conviction, prepared to accept all the legitimate consequences which it draws after it in its train, and you have already mastered a great part of the truth respecting the Church. And grant it you must, if you desire to be guided by God's Word. In the passage which stands at the head of this Chapter, our Blessed Lord announces His intention of building a Church, and of building it, in some sense (to be presently explained), upon the apostle Peter. "I say also unto *thee*," (St. Peter had just confessed our Lord to be "the Christ, the Son of the living God;" and now our Lord is about to confess *him* before His Father and the holy angels,—to tell St. Peter what *he* is) "That thou art Peter, and upon this rock I will build my Church." In which words we observe first, that the Church was not actually built when the words[1] were spoken—an observation which may throw some light upon its character. For why does not our Lord recognise the little group of disciples, who gathered round Him in the days of His earthly pilgrimage, as in itself a Church? Did not the Apostles and holy women, and all those who during our Lord's

First announcement of our Lord's purpose of building the Church.

Reason why our Lord's disciples (while He was upon earth) were not a Church.

---

[1] The same fact—that the Christian Church was not in existence in our Lord's own time—might be inferred from the scanty mention of it in the Gospels,—this and St. Matt. xviii. 17 being the only places where the word occurs. In the Acts it occurs twenty-one times, and in St. Paul's Epistles and the Revelation frequently. The thing represented by it was then in existence.

life were attracted by His miracles and teaching, and who with Peter confessed Him to be the Christ the Son of God, of themselves constitute a Church? Not in strictness of speech. And why not? Because a number of believers in Christ, not gathered into one society, wanting organization and mutual interdependence, are not a Church. A Church is not an *aggregation* of believers, but a *body* (or society) of believers. There is a great difference between an aggregation and a body. A body is not a heap of members (if foot, and hand, and eye, and ear, were fashioned separately, without any coherence or common principle of life, this would not be a body); but it is a system of members knit together into one organism, and pervaded by one life. Or (to borrow an illustration from the vegetable world), if you severed, and placed together in a heap, the stock, the branches, the leaves, and the clusters of a vine, this would not be a vine. A vine is a tree, through whose stem the sap rises in spring, and circulates through the branches, and pours itself in rich luxuriance through every tendril and sucker. Now, like a body, and like a tree, the Church is a living organism, deriving from Christ (who is its Head, if we regard it as a body; its Root, if we regard it as a tree) the life of the Holy Ghost. And the vitalizing, organizing, cementing power of the Holy Ghost came down into the community of the disciples on the feast of Pentecost, ten days after their Master's ascension into Heaven, forming them into what they had never been before—one Body, the Body of Christ, or the Church.

Difference between an aggregation and a body.

If then the Church was built for the first time, or rather *began to be built,* on the feast of Pentecost, is there any allusion to the transactions of that day in the words before us? Most assuredly there is. Certainly Scripture hangs together with Scripture, all Scripture having been given by inspiration of God, with a wonderful coherence.

<small>St. Peter's part in the proceedings of the day of Pentecost.</small>

Who was the prominent character—who took the leading part—in the proceedings of the day of Pentecost? Clearly St. Peter. It was he who preached the first Christian sermon, —a sermon attended with marvellous effects, for it was the instrument of converting three thousand souls. It was he, under whose sanction (and probably in many cases by whose hand) "they that gladly received his word were baptized."

<small>His admission of the Gentiles to the Church in the person of Cornelius.</small>

Again, it was he who admitted the Gentiles to the Church in the person of Cornelius and his near friends. The proceedings on that occasion were of much the same character. A simple sermon from St. Peter, bearing brief testimony to the character, life, death, and resurrection of Jesus, was the first of these proceedings. Then the Holy Ghost fell on the hearers, with precisely the same effect as at Pentecost,—the speaking with tongues. But the ordained form of admission to the Church, the form which our Saviour before His ascension had solemnly enjoined, had yet to be complied with, and was complied with; for they who had received the inward spiritual grace of the Sacrament of Baptism could not with propriety be denied its outward sign. "Can any man forbid

THE¹ water, that these should not be baptized, which have received the Holy Ghost as well as we?" So St. Peter "commanded them to be baptized in the name of the Lord." By these great acts of the ministry of St. Peter two predictions of our Lord respecting the future of that Apostle were fulfilled. The one was uttered immediately after the first miraculous draught of fishes; "Fear not; from henceforth thou shalt catch men." (Was it not indeed catching men in the Gospel net, when by one act of his ministry he converted three thousand souls?) The second prediction is in the words before us, and it is quite as personal to St. Peter,—has quite as little to do with any official successors (or imagined official successors) of the Apostle, as the earlier one. The word Peter in the original language of the New Testament means a stone, while the feminine form of the word, which is used in the latter clause, means a rock. What our Lord declares is that St. Peter's work should agree with his name; and doubtless the words would have been, "Thou art Peter, and upon this *stone* I will build my Church," if this would not have violated the propriety of the figure. Houses never are built upon a single stone; but they may be built upon a rock. Therefore our Lord changes the word into the feminine, while He retains the play upon it.

The two predictions respecting St. Peter's ministry, and their fulfilment.

Meaning of the name 'Peter,' and probable reason of its being changed into the feminine form, in the celebrated promise to St. Peter.

---

¹ It is much to be regretted that in the Authorized Version of Acts x. 47, our translators have neglected to represent the definite article. Cornelius and his friends had received the "inward spiritual grace" of the Sacrament of Baptism. St. Peter's argument is, "Can any one refuse them THE water —the outward visible sign?"

(And, if our Lord did not speak in Greek, but in Aramaic, this remark will equally well apply to St. Matthew's version of His words, which of course was given by inspiration.) The meaning is, that St. Peter was destined, in the order of God's Providence, to lay the first foundation of the Church. I say the *first* or *earliest* foundation. Others laid foundations as well as he.

St. Paul, St. Paul did so, and says he did so. "As a wise master-builder, I have laid the foundation, and another buildeth thereon." Any man who is the first to preach Christ, and win souls to Christ in a particular district, lays the foundation in that district. As it is said in the Epistle to the Romans, "Yea, so have I strived to preach the

and all the Apostles, as well as St. Peter, were layers of foundations. gospel, not where Christ was named, lest I should build upon *another man's foundation.*" All the Apostles laid foundations, each in his own sphere, and are recognised as having done so in that noble passage of the Epistle to the Ephesians; "Ye are . . . . . . fellow-citizens with the saints, and of the household of God; and are built upon the foundation of the apostles and prophets, Jesus Christ himself being the chief corner-stone." And in the Book of the Revelation this fundamental character of the work of the Apostles is exhibited symbolically in the description of the New Jerusalem, which represents the Church triumphant. "And the wall of the city had twelve foundations, and in them the names of the twelve apostles of the Lamb." But St.

St. Peter the earliest layer of the foundation. Peter laid the earliest foundation (in point of time) which ever was laid; and it need not therefore surprise us to hear Christ announcing that He intends to build His Church upon Peter, that is, upon Peter's ministry, his ministry having been the earliest Christian ministry ever exercised. If it be desired further to obviate any erroneous inference which might be drawn from the words, and any trenching upon the prerogatives of the Blessed Saviour, (though why should we be so afraid of the plain sense of God's Word misleading? is God unable to guard His own phraseology? must we for ever be putting forth our hands, Uzzah-like, to the sacred ark, as if He who sitteth between the cherubim were not able to protect it, when the blundering oxen stumble?) we may remark, with Bengel (though perhaps it is a little too subtle), that the Church is not said to be *founded* upon Peter, but *built* upon him. Christ is the only foundation for trust and reliance; and, in this aspect of the subject, Peter is one of the living stones built upon Christ. But all that the text implies is, that St. Peter was the prominent human minister in the Church's beginnings. And the Book of the Acts shows most clearly that he was so.

Bengel's distinction between being 'built' and being 'founded.'

But a truce to interpretations. Let us contemplate calmly for a time the position which we have arrived at from the study of this fundamental passage, compared with other parts of Holy Scripture. It is this: Christ proposed to found, and did found, by the ministry of St. Peter originally, a certain organized society, called the Christian Church, which "all nations" were invited to join, and which is therefore called Catholick or universal—a society having, as every other society has, its officers, institutions, rite of admission, and rules. Why, we may be permitted to ask, did He do so? Why should the Son of God appear as the Founder of a society no less than as the Teacher of a religion? Was there not something grand and high-sounding in the professions of Socrates, that he would not found a school at all, or attempt to perpetuate his doctrines by committing them to the guardianship of men, and trying to win adherents to them, but simply set forth the truth and expose error, and throw his arguments upon the world, to commend themselves as they might to the minds and consciences of the hearers? Truth may be spoken pure and without alloy (you have it in this form in the Holy Scriptures); but it is impossible to form a society of men, which shall be always pure and true to the principles of its foundation; for men are fallen creatures, and will bring their evil with them sooner or later into a society formed for the best ends. Then, this being the case, why did our Lord found a society at all, at the risk of having His work marred and disfigured (as it often has been grievously marred and disfigured) by men? The reason no doubt is, that it is His good pleasure to sanctify and save man *as he is*, to build the new man upon the same platform as the old,—not to construct another creature, but to raise up and reform the creature which had fallen. Now there can be no doubt that man, as he came from his Creator's hands, was social and made for society. Society was the first want experienced by man, and it was experienced while yet he was

[margin notes: Why Christ founded a society, as well as taught a religion. — Risk of corruption in forming a society. — God's purpose of renewing man, not of reconstructing him.]

in a state of innocence, so that the instincts which draw men to one another in no way came in with the Fall. "It is not good that the man should be alone," was the first observation made by the wise Creator upon the rational creature whom He had introduced into Paradise as its lord. And accordingly, even in the Paradise state, marriage was found to be a necessity, and instituted. And what is marriage but the rudiment of all societies, itself the first society, from which all others spring, out of which all others are developed? For this society of two is the means of continuing our race; so that round the parents there speedily springs up a group of children. Then, in the relation between the parents and the children, you discern (in its earliest form) law, subjection, discipline—the bonds these by which society is held together. The parents are to be honoured and obeyed; for a time they are in the place of God; their will is to be the child's law. When the children grow up, they too marry, and form separate households; and then speedily, in the multiplication of families, mutual need (as also the desire of security) draws men together, one man producing by his work what his neighbour wants, and taking his neighbour's produce in exchange for his own. And thus is gradually formed a state, which is only the family developed; the king or chief magistrate representing the parent or patriarch, and ruling and punishing, of course on a larger scale, but on much the same principle, as a father does. And that this living together in community is the true natural state of man—

Society man's earliest want.

the state for which he was originally designed—you may see not only from the inspired account of his creation, and from the necessities which draw men together, but also from some of the strongest instincts and passions of our nature, which have no meaning except in reference to society. Why was benevolence, why was compassion given us, except on the supposition that there would be those around us, to whom they would need to be exercised? why the instincts of love and friendship, unless we were designed to be drawn together into one body?

Instincts of human nature which have no meaning except on the hypothesis of his being a social creature.

Instincts of love and friendship.

This then being the original nature and constitution of man, it pleases God to accommodate Himself to this nature in redeeming, sanctifying, and saving him. He is to be saved, not as an independent member of the human family, but in combination with others. And therefore not only has the Lord Jesus given him a supernatural and revealed truth (in His own teaching), by the action of which upon his conscience he is to be sanctified, but has founded for him also a supernatural Society, into which He brings him by one Sacrament, and continues him by another Sacrament, conferring supernatural grace,—a Society which has officers divinely commissioned, institutions divinely ordained, and a law divinely given. And this Society is the Church, or kingdom of Christ upon earth.

Upon the subject thus expounded a great many thoughts arise, fatal to certain popular views of Religion, which nevertheless have obtained a very wide currency. For what has been said raises another and distinct issue for each one of us, in addition to the question whether we are receiving into our hearts and minds the truths which Christ taught, whether we are real believers in those truths, so as to be living under their influence. Another question we must now ask ourselves, hardly less important, perhaps, than the one just stated,— whether we are members of the Society which Christ founded. It is easy to see how different this is from the foregoing. A man believes Christ's truth by the action of his own mind and heart, under the influence of the Holy Ghost, quite independently of any other person's agency. It is a matter wholly between himself and God. But no man, by the action of his own mind and heart, can make himself a member of any society. I do not become a member of a society by sympathizing with the objects of the society, nor even by doing its work. A man does not become a member of the Gospel Propagation Society, because he feels a warm interest in spreading the Gospel, nor even because he does his best to spread the Gospel at home and abroad. A man does not become a member of a Cathedral foundation, because he likes Cathedral Service, or thinks that Cathedrals may do a very good work for religion and the Church. The Gospel Propagation Society (like every other society) has certain rules about the qualification and admission of its members; and nothing else but compliance with those rules can make any one a member. The various members of Cathedral bodies are appointed and admitted in different ways; and unless a man has been ap-

Another issue for each of us, besides the question whether we receive the truths which Christ taught.

A man cannot make himself a member of a society, but must be admitted by others.

pointed and admitted in one of these ways, the utmost sympathy with Cathedrals, and the utmost interest in their work, will not put him on a Cathedral foundation. And, in like manner, the fact of a man's loving and prizing the holy truths which our Redeemer taught, and even trying to bring other people under their power, by no means proves that he belongs to the Society which Christ founded. That Society must take him up, must engraft him into its bosom, must adopt and admit him according to its own rules, before he can become a member of it.

Necessity of admission into the Church.

But possibly my reader thinks that there is no doubt at all about his own membership in this Society. You belong, if not to the Church of England, yet to what is called a Christian denomination; and you were baptized when an infant,—is not that enough to make you a member? Suffer me still to ask whether you are well assured that the religious community to which you belong—be it the Church of England, or any other—is indeed the very Society which Christ founded by the ministry of St. Peter? For myself, I am utterly at a loss to see how this can be, unless your community can trace historically back to the ministry of St. Peter. Remember there must never be any new beginning made, if it is to be Christ's own Society. A society may have altered very much in many respects, and yet be the same (just as the body of a grown man looks very different from, but yet is identical with, that which he had as a child); but it cannot be the same, if a new foundation is made. The Society for the Propagation of the

Necessity of an historical continuity to the identity of societies.

Difference of appearance not incompatible with identity.

Gospel is in many respects very different from what it was when it first started; it has a vastly greater number of members; it has modified some of its laws, repealed others, perhaps added others; but it is still the Gospel Propagation Society, incorporated by Royal Charter. But if a good man, thinking there is not now enough of missionary agency in the world, should set up another missionary society, and *call* it the Society for the Propagation of the Gospel, and adopt the same rules and the same terms of admission, and construct everything on much the same plan, only without procuring a Royal Charter of Incorporation, this, while there might be ever so much *outward* resemblance, would be another society altogether. An old Gothic tower, some part of which has been dilapidated by lapse of time, and which the ivy has overgrown, flaunting down over the windows, and shutting out the blessed light of heaven, does not become a new tower by having the ivy cut away and the dilapidations repaired; it is the same tower still, only different in appearance. But if the proprietor should go to another part of his estate, and there should build another tower of exactly the same size and architecture with the former—that is, strictly speaking, a new tower, and not the one which he inherited from his old feudal ancestor. And, in like manner, no man can, in a late period of the world's history, set up a new Christian communion independent of, and not deriving from, that founded by the ministry of St. Peter, which shall have any sort of claim to be the Christian Church. The mere fact of its

Illustration from architecture.

being *like* the Christian Church, and doing the the things the Christian Church does,—the fact of its preaching, and circulating the Scriptures, and baptizing, and administering the Communion, —cannot make it the Church. The question is, How was the appointment of ministers (or Church-officers) made in that communion? A man cannot possibly appoint himself a minister, any more than he can baptize himself. Previous ministers must make him a minister, and they in their turn must have been ordained by those before them, and they again by earlier ministers, and so on till we come to St. Peter, St. Paul, St. John, and the other Apostles, who by the Lord's own Royal Charter of Incorporation, and as it were under His hand and seal, were the first to send forth ministers into the Lord's vineyard.

Importance of the ministerial succession.

The only Reformed Communion in England, which can found any claim to the Ministerial Succession from Christ and His Apostles is our own Church of England at present by law established, but which would be the only true Church of Christ in England, if she were disestablished. (As for the Roman Church in England, while we do not deny it the Succession, yet we may truly say that it is an intruder, foisted in by the Bishop of Rome, contrary to the first principles of Church Discipline, upon Dioceses the Bishops and Clergy of which, at the Reformation, threw off the yoke which he had imposed upon Christendom, and rejected the superstitions which he still countenanced.) She and she alone is the ancient tower of Christ's foundation; but at the time of the Reformation she

The Roman Communion in England a schismatical intruder.

had become obscured and dilapidated by the ivy of old superstitions and abuses, which in the long lapse of ages had grown over her, and which had shut out the blessed light that beams forth from the pages of God's Word. Then arose those wise, holy, and dutiful men, the English Reformers, who, without building on another foundation, or in any way disconnecting the Church with its spiritual ancestry and antecedents, pruned away the flaunting, disintegrating, mischief-working ivy, and allowed the light of heaven to stream into the building once more. Let this great advantage of our position, as members of a communion built on the foundation of the Apostles and Prophets, and yet scriptural and pure in its doctrine, breed in us, not an arrogant censure of others less favoured than ourselves, but rather a deep humiliation for our own shortcomings among so many great privileges, and a humble thankfulness to God, whose Providence has placed us where we are. And while we never presume to judge other Communions, nor forget what our Lord said in reference to the man who cast out devils in His name, and yet followed not with the Apostles—"He that is not against us is on our part,"—let us maintain our own connexion with the foundation of Christ's laying as being unassailable, through whatever storms our Church may be destined to pass. Even should State Patronage be withdrawn, her high spiritual lineage cannot fail her, and fidelity to her principles will insure her the presence and protection of Him, who was in the Apostles' fishing-boat, though

The debt which the Church owes to the Reformers.

The due moral effect of the advantage of our position, as a Church at once Scriptural and Apostolical.

The Church's spiritual lineage independent of State Patronage.

asleep, when the winds raved and the waves surged around her.

"God is our refuge and strength, a very present help in trouble. Therefore will not we fear, though the earth be removed, and though the mountains be carried into the midst of the sea; though the waters thereof roar and be troubled, though the mountains shake with the swelling thereof. . . . God is in the midst of her; she shall not be moved: God shall help her, and that right early."

Catechism on Chap. E.

1. *Catechist.*—The Church is to form the subject of instruction in this Catechism. How may we know that it is a subject of great importance?

Answer.—Because belief in the Church is a part of the Christian faith. In the Apostles' Creed we say, "I believe in the holy Catholick Church;" in the Nicene Creed, "I believe one Catholick and Apostolick Church." These Creeds are very short summaries of the things to be believed by Christians, in which only the most important matters are touched upon, and many truths, clearly laid down in Holy Scripture, are not at all alluded to.

2. *Catechist.*—Give me some other reasons for thinking the subject of the Church to be one of great importance.

Answer.—Because one whole book of the New Testament, the Acts of the Apostles, is devoted to the history of the Church, beginning with its foundation by the ministry of St. Peter, and ending with its plantation in Rome, the capital of the world, by the ministry of St. Paul.

3. *Catechist.*—This is a good reason, as far as it goes. But give me a better reason still.

Answer.—The near relation of the Church to Christ makes the Church a subject of the highest importance. This relation is so intimate that He is called the Head, and the Church His body (Eph. i. 22, 23; Col. i. 18, 24); He the Vine-stock, and she the vine (St. John xv. 1, 2, 5); He the Bridegroom, and she the bride (Eph. v. 25-32; 2 Cor. xi. 2; Rom. vii. 4; St. Matt. xxv. 1, 2; Rev. xix. 9).

4. *Question.*—Where does our Lord Himself recognise the truth that He and His Church are one?

Answer.—In His words to Saul of Tarsus, of which we have three reports in Holy Scripture, one from the pen of St. Luke (Acts ix. 4), and two from St. Paul's own mouth (Acts xxii. 7 and xxvi. 14). The words are, "Saul, Saul, why persecutest thou me?" Saul had not persecuted the Lord Jesus Himself; probably had never seen Him while He was upon earth. But he had persecuted bitterly the members of the Christian Church (Acts ix. 1, 2; xxii. 4; xxvi. 10, 11). And, because Christ is one with His Church, whatsoever is done to the least member of His body He counts as done to Himself (see St. Matt. xxv. 40, 45). For indeed, as St. Paul says in his Epistle to the Ephesians, where he compares the union betwixt Christ and His Church to that between man and wife, who "are no more twain, but one flesh" (St. Matt. xix. 6), "We are members of his body, of his flesh, and of his bones" (Eph. v. 30).

5. *Question.*—But did the Apostles and early missionaries make the Church a subject of their preaching?

Answer.—They did. The twelve Apostles were originally sent "to preach the kingdom of God;" and so were the seventy disciples (St. Luke ix. 2, and x. 9). St. Philip the Deacon preached "the things concerning the kingdom of God" (Acts viii. 12). St. Paul describes his whole ministry at Ephesus as a "preaching" of "the kingdom of God" (Acts xx. 25. See also ch. xix. 8). At Rome, too, he "expounded and testified the kingdom of God," and "preached" it for "two whole years" (Acts xxviii. 23, 31). Now, although the kingdom of God has yet to be developed *in glory*, and some things said of it in the New Testament refer to this future developement (as, for instance, "Flesh and blood cannot inherit the kingdom of God" (1 Cor. xv. 50), and "Know ye not that the unrighteous shall not inherit the kingdom of God?" (1 Cor. vi. 9)), yet is the kingdom of God amongst us *in grace* at present; God "hath translated us into" it (Col. i. 13); and it is like a "net cast into the sea that gathered of every kind," "the wicked" as well as "the just," who, however, "at the end of the world" shall be "severed" and "cast away" (St. Matt. xiii. 47, 48, 49, 50).

6. *Catechist.*—You have proved that the subject under consideration is one of great importance, and such as people, who profess and call themselves Christians, ought to be carefully and methodically instructed in.—Now, to begin at the beginning, can you tell me what the word "Church" means?

Answer.—The Greek word, translated "Church" in the New Testament, means a *body called out*. It was a word used to denote the political assemblies (or, as we might say, Parliaments) of the ancient Greeks, and indeed is so used in the nineteenth chapter of the Acts of the Apostles, where the tumultuous assembly in the theatre of Ephesus is twice called *ecclesia* (Acts xix. 32, 41), and where the town-clerk uses the same word of the regularly constituted assemblies of the people, held for the purpose of carrying on the local government (Acts xix. 39).

7. *Catechist.*—You say that the word "Church" means a *body called out*. What class of persons is often erroneously confounded with this *body called out*, by persons who are not apt at seizing distinctions?

Answer.—The elect people of God,—"those whom He hath chosen in Christ out of mankind" "by his counsel secret to us" (Art. xvii.)

8. *Question.*—How does our Lord distinguish between " the chosen out " (or elect ones), and those who are merely *called out?*

Answer.—He says, " Many are *called*, but few are *chosen*,"—a sentence which occurs twice in St. Matthew's Gospel, and each time at the end of a parable; once at the end of the Parable of the Labourers in the Vineyard (xx. 16), and again at the end of the Parable of the Wedding Garment (xxii. 14).

9. *Catechist.*—Illustrate from the latter parable the difference between the "called " and the " chosen."

Answer.—The man who " had not on the wedding garment," and who was eventually " taken away " and " cast into outer darkness," was " called " (or invited). The other guests, who appeared at table clad in the wedding garment, represent the elect (or " chosen ") people of God, who (by His grace) have a spirit of joy and praise, in harmony with the solemnities of the Gospel festival.

10. *Catechist.*—But if this is the meaning of the parable, why are the guests who have the wedding-garment represented as many, and he who has it not as a single individual? For you said that our Lord warned us that the chosen were few, but the called many; whereas it would seem from the representation in His parable as if the chosen are many, and the called few.

Answer.—This arises from the necessity under which a person who teaches by parables lays himself. Our Lord's parables are all drawn from nature or from human life, and represent things which do or might happen. Now, no such thing ever could happen at an Eastern wedding as that the greater number of the guests should sit down without wedding garments. For it is the part of the host at such entertainments to provide wedding-garments for his guests, so that there can be no excuse for appearing without one.

11. *Catechist.*—You have now explained and illustrated the difference between the *called out body*

(or Church) and the *chosen out people* (or the elect). "The elect" are not merely "the called," but the "called according to God's purpose" (Rom. viii. 28). What unscriptural and misleading phraseology is often employed by those who confound the two things?

Answer.—They speak of "the invisible Church," whereas the Church spoken of in Holy Scripture is always a visible body, which may be seen and known.

12. *Catechist.*—Mention some passages of Holy Scripture in which "the Church" *must* mean a *visible* body.

Answer.—St. Matt. xviii. 17, "And if he shall neglect to hear them, tell it unto *the church*: but if he neglect to hear *the church*, let him be unto thee as an heathen man and a publican." Acts viii. 1, 3, "At that time there was a great persecution against *the church* which was at Jerusalem. . . . As for Saul, he made havock of the *church*." Acts xiv. 27, "When they were come, and had gathered the *church* together, they rehearsed all that God had done with them." Acts xv. 22, "Then pleased it the apostles and elders, with the whole *church*, to send chosen men of their own company to Antioch." 1 Cor. xiv. 23, "If therefore the *whole church* be come together into one place, and all speak with tongues, . . . will they not say that ye are mad?" 1 Tim. v. 16, "If any man or woman that believeth have widows, let them relieve them, and let not the *church* be charged." 3 John 5, 6, "Beloved, thou doest faithfully whatsoever thou doest to the brethren, and to strangers; which have borne witness of thy charity before the *church*." Only a visible body can have reports made to it of the bad or good conduct of its members; or can have persecution directed against it; or can be called together to receive tidings, or offer worship; or can depute members on a certain mission; or can be taxed for charitable purposes.

13. *Catechist.*—You have now shown that the Church is a visible *body called out* of the world, and that

it must not be confounded with the smaller invisible body (contained within it) of the elect people of God. Now, can you tell me what is the fundamental Church truth,—the earliest fact, out of which all other truths about the Church grow?

Answer.—It is that our Lord came not merely to teach religious doctrines, but to found a Society, and that He did the last as well as the first.

Catechist.—Yes; if a man really believes that our Lord founded a Society as well as taught a religion, he has learned the rudiment of all Church truth, and the whole science may in due time grow out of this rudiment. But how do you prove from Holy Scripture that our blessed Lord founded a Society?

Answer.—Because He said, while on earth, that He would do so; and He, the Truth, cannot fail of keeping His word. "Hath he said, and shall he not do it? or hath he spoken, and shall he not make it good?"

14. *Question.*—What words of Christ's do you allude to?

Answer.—To those which are found in St. Matt. xvi. 18: "And I say also unto thee, That thou art Peter, and upon this rock I will build my church."

15. *Question.*—Is there any force in the "also" in these words?

Answer.—Yes; it refers to what had gone before. St. Peter had just confessed the Lord Jesus in these remarkable words; "*Thou art* the Christ, the Son of the living God." Our Lord proceeds to confess St. Peter, to tell him what *he is;* "And *I* also say unto *thee,* that *thou art* Peter."

16. *Question.*—What does our Lord's use of the future tense in this passage imply? Why does He say, "I *will* build"?

Answer.—Because the Church was not yet built.

17. *Catechist.*—But how is it that the disciples of Christ were not a Church, while their Master was

upon earth? In several respects they looked like one. They had their Master visibly in the midst of them, as He has promised to be in the midst of the two or three gathered together in His Name (St. Matt. xviii. 20). He taught them the Truth, and sent the twelve Apostles and seventy Disciples to preach that Truth to others (St. Luke ix. 1, 2; x. 1, 9). Nay, we find that they admitted people to their Society by baptism; for we are told that "Jesus made and baptized more disciples than John, (though Jesus himself baptized not, but his disciples)." St. John iv. 1, 2.

Answer.—There was not a Church, strictly speaking, before the day of Pentecost, because before that time the disciples were not organized into one body. They were like separate leaves and branches of a tree laid in a heap, which would not be a tree; or like severed limbs of a body piled upon one another, which would not be a body. A number of people, even if they have the same hopes, views, and sentiments, do not constitute a society or corporation. A corporation is a system, the different parts of which are connected together by mutual dependence, and work together for one end.

18. *Catechist.*—You have mentioned trees, and the natural body of man, as instances of an organized system. What is the principle of unity which holds together the different parts of a tree, or the different members of the body?

Answer.—It is called life.

19. *Question.*—What is the Church's life, which holds all its members in unity, and makes them one body?

Answer.—The Church's life is the Holy Spirit of God, who took up His abode in her on the day of Pentecost, and, proceeding from Christ, her risen Head, shed His gracious influences through her whole frame.

20. *Catechist.*—Quote some passages of Scripture which speak of the Church as an organized body.

Answer.—Rom. xii. 4, 5, "As we have many members in one body, and all members have not the same office : so we, being many, are one body in Christ, and every one members one of another." And 1 Cor. xii. 12, 13, "For as the body is one, and hath many members, and all the members of that one body, being many, are one body: so also is Christ. For by one Spirit are we all baptized into one body, whether we be Jews or Gentiles, whether we be bond or free; and have been all made to drink into one Spirit." And the whole of the chapter, from which this last text is taken, is devoted to the exposition of this one subject, the Church as an organized body.

21. *Catechist.*—Quote a passage of Scripture, to show that the Church is knit together in one body by the life which she derives from Christ, her risen Head.

Answer.—Eph. iv. 10-16, "He that descended is the same also that ascended up far above all heavens, that he might fill all things. And he gave some, apostles; and some, prophets; and some, evangelists; and some, pastors and teachers; for the perfecting of the saints, for the work of the ministry, for the edifying of the body of Christ: till we all come, in the unity of the faith and of the knowledge of the Son of God, unto a perfect man, unto the measure of the stature of the fulness of Christ: that we henceforth be no more children, tossed to and fro, and carried about with every wind of doctrine, by the sleight of men, and cunning craftiness, whereby they lie in wait to deceive; but speaking the truth in love, may grow up into him in all things, which is the head, even Christ: from whom the whole body, fitly joined together and compacted by that which every joint supplieth, according to the effectual working in the measure of every part, maketh increase of the body unto the edifying of itself in love."

22. *Catechist.*—You have said that the Church was founded on the day of Pentecost. How was St. Peter connected with its foundation?

Answer.—It was he who took the prominent part in it. For he preached the first Christian sermon, by which three thousand souls were converted. And afterwards "they that gladly received his word were baptized" (Acts ii. 14, 37, 41).

23. *Catechist.*—This was the foundation of the Church among the Jews. Did St. Peter take any part in its foundation among the Gentiles?

Answer.—Yes. It was he whom Cornelius, the Roman centurion and a Jewish proselyte, was directed to send for, that he might "hear words of" him. St. Peter, when he arrived, spoke the word of God to Cornelius and his kinsmen and near friends. The Holy Ghost fell on the hearers; and St. Peter, seeing that they had received the inward spiritual grace of the Sacrament of Baptism, could not refuse them the outward visible sign. So "he commanded them to be baptized in the name of the Lord" (Acts x. 5, 6, 22, 34, 44, 47, 48). When St. Peter rehearsed these circumstances to the Jews at Jerusalem, the conclusion they gathered from it was: "Then hath God *also to the Gentiles* granted repentance unto life" (Acts xi. 18).

24. *Question.*—What two predictions of our Lord respecting St. Peter were fulfilled by these incidents of his history?

Answer.—First, that which we find in St. Luke v. 10: "And Jesus said unto Simon, Fear not; from henceforth thou shalt catch men." Secondly, that which we find in St. Matthew xvi. 18: "I say also unto thee, That thou art Peter, and upon this rock I will build my church."

25. *Question.*—What is the meaning of the name *Peter* or *Petros?*

Answer.—It means *a stone.*

26. *Question.*—If our Lord, then, meant that He would build His Church upon St. Peter, why did He not say, "Upon this *stone* I will build my Church?"

Answer.—Because houses are never built upon single stones. They may however be built upon a *rock*, and the word for *a rock* in Greek is the same word as that for a *stone*, only with a feminine termination—*Petra* instead of *Petros*.

27. *Question.*—What did our Lord mean by saying He would build His Church upon St. Peter?

Answer.—It was merely a prophecy that St. Peter should lay the earliest foundation of the Church both among the Jews and Gentiles, as we have seen that he did.

28. *Question.*—But did no other Apostle lay foundations of the Church but St. Peter?

Answer.—Certainly. They all did so; inasmuch as all of them preached Christ to nations to whom He had never been preached before. St. Paul more especially laid foundations, and speaks of himself as having done so. He was the first to preach the gospel at Corinth, and other ministers carried on his work; in allusion to which he says: "According to the grace of God which is given unto me, as a wise master builder I have laid the foundation, and another buildeth thereon" (1 Cor. iii. 10). And he seems to recognise the laying of foundations as his special work in Rom. xv. 20: "Yea, so have I strived to preach the gospel, not where Christ was named, lest I should build upon another man's foundation."

29. *Catechist.*—You have said that the Apostles are spoken of as *laying* foundations. But this is rather different from *being* foundations. Are there any passages of Scripture, in which they are spoken of in the latter point of view?

Answer.—Yes. Eph. ii. 19 to end: "Now therefore ye are no more strangers and foreigners, but fellow-citizens with the saints, and of the household of God; and are built upon the foundation of the apostles and prophets, Jesus Christ himself being the chief corner-stone; in whom all the building fitly framed together groweth unto an holy temple in the Lord: in whom ye also are builded together for an habitation of God through the Spirit." And in the description of the heavenly Jerusalem which is given in Rev. xxi., and which is an allegorical representation of the glorified Church, we read, "The wall of the city had twelve foundations, and in them the names of the twelve apostles of the Lamb" (ver. 14).

30. *Catechist.*—But does not St. Paul say, in the context of one of the passages you have quoted, that *Christ* is the foundation of the Church; "Other foundation can no man lay than that is laid, *which is Jesus Christ*" (1 Cor. iii. 11)? How then can St. Peter or any of the Apostles, or all of them together, be called "foundations" of the Church?

Answer.—The Apostles are foundations in a different point of view, and in a different sense, from our Lord Himself. He is the soul's only rock of trust and confidence, and in this sense the *only* foundation, beside which no man can lay another. His Apostles are foundations of the Church, because the Church took its rise from their ministry. And when they are spoken of as a foundation, their Master is represented as the "chief corner-stone," which locks the building together (as a keystone does an arch), and in which all the lines of it meet (Eph. ii. 20).

31. *Question.*—But suppose we do not accept the interpretation you have given of St. Matt. xvi. 18, and prefer (with many learned commentators) to consider our Lord Himself, or the confession of faith, which St. Peter had just made, as the "rock" of which Christ spoke,—does what you have said about the Church fall to the ground in consequence?

Answer.—By no means. It is certain from the Acts of the Apostles that Christ did found a Divine Society in the earth, and that St. Peter was the first to call into this Society Jews and Gentiles.

32. *Catechist.*—You have shown that our Lord founded a Society, as well as taught a religion. What

objection might seem to lie against this method of proceeding?

Answer.—The objection that truth may be taught purely and without alloy, and, when committed to writing, handed down in its purity. This is the case with the volume of the Holy Scriptures, which contains pure truth, without the smallest admixture of error. But a society, being made up of men, is always liable to be corrupted and perverted from its original design. And this has happened to the Church, which has often been grievously corrupted, and into which error found its way, even when inspired Apostles were watching over it. Witness St. Paul's Epistles to the Corinthians, Galatians, Thessalonians, and the letters in the Revelation, which St. John is commissioned to write to the Seven Churches of Asia.

33. *Question.*—If then a Church is liable to be corrupted, what good reason may we suppose moved our Lord to found one?

Answer.—Because He had made man for society originally; and it was His gracious intention to sanctify and save the nature which had fallen, not to create a new nature.

34. *Question.*—How can you show from Scripture that man is made for society?

Answer.—Because God said in the beginning: "It is not good that the man should be alone; I will make him an help meet for him" (Gen. ii. 18).

35. *Catechist.*—That was said in allusion to marriage. But how does it bear upon the question of man being made for society?

Answer.—Because marriage is the earliest society, and the foundation of every other. Families spring from marriage; and a group of many families forms a state or nation.

36. *Question.*—Is there any evidence in our nature itself that man was made for society?

Answer.—God has endowed us with several passions or affections, which have no meaning except in reference to our fellow-creatures. His having implanted in us, for example, benevolence and compassion, is a clear proof that we were destined to live in the midst of objects which would draw out these feelings.

37. *Catechist.*—Man, then, having been made for society originally, this constitution of his nature was to be recognised in Grace; and accordingly a Society was founded by Christ, in which men were to be one body, and into which all nations were to be called. And this Society is the Church, or Kingdom of Christ upon earth.—What question is it every man's duty to ask himself in reference to this Society?
Answer.—Whether he belongs to it.

38. *Question.*—But if a man prizes the holy truths which Christ taught, and strives to guide himself by them, and to live under their influence, is not that enough, without his troubling himself with anything further?
Answer.—No; because Christ did not only teach a Religion, but founded a Society; and we have a duty towards the Society which He founded, as well as towards the Religion which He taught.

39. *Question.*—What is the great difference between the duty we owe to the Religion, and that which we owe to the Society?
Answer.—That the first may be done by the action of our own minds, without anything between us and God. But we cannot admit ourselves into a Society. We must be admitted into it, according to its own rules, and by its own officers. Nothing we can do ourselves will make us members of it.

40. *Question.*—Can you illustrate this by a reference to our Church Societies?
Answer.—Yes. A man does not become a member of the Society for Propagating the Gospel, because he takes a great interest in spreading the Gospel in our colonies, and in mission work generally. He must comply with the rule about membership, whatever

that rule may be, before he can become a member. Christ's rule about membership in His Church is, that it shall be given by Holy Baptism; and unless a man is baptized (which he cannot be without some one to baptize him), no amount of Christian feeling or Christian conduct will make him a member of Christ's Church.

41. *Question.*—But, as you were baptized when an infant, what doubt can there be that you are a member of Christ's Church?

Answer.—There still remains the question, by what community of Christians I was baptized. For there are many such communities, which do not profess to trace up their descent historically to the Apostles of Christ, to whom He gave the commission to baptize and preach the Gospel. These communities were mostly founded in the sixteenth century, or have been founded since, by good men who thought they saw errors in the old Church, or could not get Holy Orders in it, and therefore took upon themselves to preach the Gospel, and administer the Sacraments, without any regular commission. Their Sacraments may outwardly be like the Sacraments of the Church; but they must be wanting in authority.

42. *Question.*—How do you prove that in this country the Church of England is the only Church, which holds Christ's commission to preach, and administer the Sacraments?

Answer.—Because it can trace up the descent of its ministers to Augustine, who was sent over to this island to convert the Saxons by Pope Gregory; and the descent of Pope Gregory may be traced up in the same way to the times of the Apostles.

43. *Question.*—But did not the Church of England become frightfully corrupt before the time of the Reformation?

Answer.—Doubtless it did. And because it was at that time so corrupt, that it could hardly have been recognised as the Church which Christ planted, God raised up our Reformers to prune away its abuses and superstitions, and to let in once more the light of the Gospel of Christ, which had been greatly obscured. But they did not presume to make a new foundation; nor indeed was there any call for them to do so. The Bishops and Clergy, with very few exceptions, came round to the Reformation; and thus the old Society of the Church of Christ was preserved, while it was purified.

44. *Question.*—Can you illustrate this by a comparison?

Answer.—Yes. An old Gothic tower, founded centuries ago, might in lapse of time be so overgrown with ivy, and choked with rubbish, as to have all its original features concealed. If the ivy were pruned away, and the rubbish removed, it would not be a newly founded tower, but the old one restored. But if the proprietor should build a new one on some other part of his estate, digging new foundations and raising new walls, this would be another tower, however closely it might resemble the old one in its outward features.

45. *Question.*—Is the descent from Christ and His Apostles, and the inheritance from them of the commission to preach the Gospel and administer the Sacraments, all that is necessary to make a Christian Community to be a Church?

Answer.—Yes; it will be a Church, if it have received this commission, though by no means necessarily a pure or a Scriptural Church.

46. *Question.*—Then why have the priests of the Church of Rome, who hold this commission as well as our own ministers, no lawful authority to preach the Gospel or administer the Sacraments in this country?

Answer.—Because it is a principle of Church order that there cannot be in any diocese two Bishops. Our own Bishops have been in possession, since the Church was first planted in this country, and are in possession now. The Pope's Bishops are a new colony sent into this country, to invade the rights and usurp the office of the old Bishops, because they are not willing to acknowledge his supremacy,—a doctrine which cannot be proved either by Scripture, reason, or primitive antiquity.

47. *Question.*—But is not the recognition and acknowledgment of the State necessary to the existence of the Church?

Answer.—It is the duty of civil rulers to recognise and support the true Church, and to make themselves "nursing fathers" to her. And no doubt nations from this acknowledgment of God reap many great blessings. But even if this recognition were withheld, the Church would lose nothing of her authority, though she would be deprived of many advantages for doing her work. Her commission is derived from Christ, and not from the powers of this world; and none but He who gave it can take it away.

CHAPTER II.

DUTY OF THE CHURCH TOWARDS THOSE WHO HOLD TO THE APOSTLES' DOCTRINE, IN SEPARATION FROM THE APOSTLES' FELLOWSHIP.

"And John answered him, saying, Master, we saw one casting out devils in thy name, and he followeth not us: and we forbad him, because he followeth not us. But Jesus said, Forbid him not: for there is no man which shall do a miracle in my name, that can lightly speak evil of me. For he that is not against us is on our part."—ST. MARK IX. 38, 39, 40.

"They continued stedfastly in the apostles' doctrine and fellowship."—ACTS II. 42.

The balance of forces a law of Nature.

THE world of Nature seems to be governed by a system of forces, which counterbalance and hold one another in check. The planet is kept in its orderly course, partly by the original impulse which launched it into space, partly by the power of gravitation, which draws it towards the sun. Without the former of these impulses, it would simply fall into the sun and be dashed to pieces or consumed; without the latter of them, it would travel on for ever in the line in which it was originally projected. Another familiar instance of the same law in the animal world is, that certain tribes are a restraint upon one another. Kill all the small birds, because they are mischievous to the fruits, and you will soon find yourself plagued with a swarm of insects, still more mischievous to the roots. Nature exhibits in all her departments a balance of forces.

Now the God of Nature is the God of Grace also; and we should therefore expect to find in God's Word the same principles which regulate His hand in His works. The forces of God's Word are truths. What are the great truths of Religion but moral forces—forces operative upon the conscience, the heart, the will? And these truths are not unfrequently forces acting in opposite, or apparently opposite, directions, and holding one another in check. God's election of certain persons to eternal life is a great truth. So is man's entire and exclusive responsibility for a failure in winning eternal life. The necessity of God's grace to our salvation is a great truth. So, on the other hand, is the perfect freedom of the human will. It is easy to seize upon one of these principles, and make it the keystone of our whole religious system, without taking much account of the other. But the really sound and Scriptural divine will attempt to lose sight of neither, and to give its due weight to each. He will try to reconcile the two truths,—in theory, if they admit of such a reconciliation,—in practice, at all events, if their theoretical reconciliation should be a problem beyond the powers of the human mind. Professor Archer Butler, in a sermon from which I shall presently make a further extract, says as follows: "The most important steps in

Religious truths are moral forces.

The balance of truths a law of Grace.

every part of moral science consist in the adjustment of rival truths; it being always far more easy to see the force of a great principle than to see its limits."

Both the Apostles' doctrine and their fellowship to be continued in.

Now, I am about to apply these remarks to the great and somewhat difficult subject opened in our first Chapter—the subject of the Church. It is said of the early Christians in the Acts of the Apostles, that "they continued stedfastly in the apostles' *doctrine*"—here is Christian Truth, one of the great forces in the spiritual system,—and in the apostles' "*fellowship*"—here is the Christian Church, another great force. To this latter subject we devoted our attention exclusively in the last Chapter. We showed that the Church was a society planned by our Blessed Lord, and built by the ministry of St. Peter and the other Apostles, and that, though the old building may be cleared of corruptions which have gathered over it in course of time (which in fact was done at the Reformation), no other building can be reared, which shall not be a new foundation, wanting the Divine authority and sanction of the old, and quite distinct from "the Apostles' fellowship," or, in other words, from the Church which Christ by the ministry of His Apostles founded. It was then stated that all dissenting communities in this country were in fact such new foundations (not one of them dating four hundred years back), having many of them striking features of outward resemblance to the Christian Church—the same Sacraments (to the eye), the same form (or very much the same) of administering Holy Orders, and much

No new 'fellowship' to be created, but the old one to be adhered to.

the same doctrine and teaching,—but that all this superficial resemblance did not, and could not, really connect them with the Church of the Apostles, any more than if a private individual should set up a mint against the Queen's mint, and coin and distribute gold pieces stamped with the Queen's effigy, those sovereigns would be the real currency of the realm, authorized by the Government.

That was one side of the question, and I trust I stated it bravely and fairly, and that, in what follows of the same argument, I shall not shrink from any consequences of the position which I have taken up. But the question has another side; and the due consideration of that other side is all the more binding upon us, because it will lead us, while holding fast our own principles, to hold them in love. At the earliest commencement of Christianity, the Apostles' doctrine and fellowship were co-extensive. God's Truth was in the Church, and the Church stood fast in God's Truth. But this happy state of things was not to last long. Very speedily errors and corruptions began to show their head, and run their mischievous course. Many of them were condemned by Church Councils; but there were others which Councils could not, or did not, reach; and little by little, one innovation after another being introduced, one deviation after another from primitive faith and practice being first excused, then allowed, then adopted, and the Bishop of Rome pushing in by degrees his monstrous usurpations over the conscience, and his

In the infancy of Christianity the 'doctrine' and 'fellowship' co-extensive.

How the two came to be separated.

claim to overrule the authority of kings, the Church became quite altered from the primitive model, and retained but few features of resemblance to (though it was *historically* the same body, having come down in lineal succession from) the Church which Christ founded by the ministry of the Apostles. Then what was to be done, when the Apostles' doctrine was no longer held in its purity by the Apostles' fellowship? God's Truth was just as precious as God's Church; was certainly more reliable, because the Truth cannot be corrupted, but the Church may. In England, through God's great mercy, the case presented but little difficulty. The great majority of the existing Bishops and Clergy came round to the principles of the Reformation; so that there was no difficulty for us in maintaining the Apostles' doctrine without departing from the Apostles' fellowship. In other countries people were not so highly favoured. The Bishops, who alone could confer Holy Orders, and thus continue the Apostles' fellowship, were too often found to be inveterate maintainers of the old abuses, and showed no sympathy whatever with that awakening of mind on religious subjects, which had been brought about by the freer circulation of the Holy Scriptures.—Again, I ask what was to be done, where it happened to be so? What *was* done in some places—often reluctantly, sometimes (no doubt) where violence characterized the leaders, with heat, and coarse, foul language—done surely not without such excuse as we may well hope palliated the act in the eyes of the Divine Founder,—

Perplexity which arose from this separation.

How this perplexity was solved in England.

Other countries not as highly favoured; and

what had to be done in such countries.

was to cling to the Apostles' doctrine, and let go the Apostles' fellowship—to maintain Christian Truth, but not in connexion with the old foundation. And thus came in the first idea of what is called a Christian denomination,—that is to say, a community teaching the leading truths of the Gospel, and professing to administer the Holy Sacraments, yet without deriving any authority to do so from the Church which Christ built by the ministry of the Apostles. At first the doing this was thought, even by those who acknowledged the necessity of doing it, somewhat of an audacious and perilous step, to be taken only under severe pressure of circumstances. But the example once set became, as such examples are apt to do, contagious. The independence gained by secession from the Church made secession popular, especially in England, where the national mind is always impatient of control. And thus it comes to pass that Christians in this empire are broken up into I know not how many sects, and present a most melancholy contrast to the Founder's ideal, which was that there should be but one body, even as there is but one Spirit; "Neither pray I for these alone, but for them also which shall believe on me through their word; that *they all may be one;* as thou, Father, art in me, and I in thee, that *they also may be one in us:* that the world may believe that thou hast sent me" (St. John xvii. 20, 21). *The earliest idea of a Christian denomination.* *Rapid propagation of the idea.* *The Founder's ideal completely marred.*

I have said enough to show that, whatever may be alleged in favour of certain separatists at the Reformation, nothing can justify a refusal in this country to join the Church of England, pure as she is in doctrine, no less than apostolic in discipline. And yet it must be admitted, because it is a simple fact, which it would be closing our eyes to the light to refuse to see, that in other Christian communities many brilliant examples of godliness are to be found, and that souls are really won to Christ by ministers who do not stand upon the old foundation, and do not derive from the Church, on which the Spirit came down at Pentecost, their authority to minister the Word and Sacraments.

Spiritual life visible, and spiritual agencies at work, outside the Apostles' fellowship.

How are we to feel towards, and deal with, such phenomena, without, on the one hand, disguising the plainest facts of experience, and, on the other, without for a moment justifying (or even excusing) secession from a branch of the Church which is doctrinally pure? Holy Scripture, which was written in the foresight, on the part of the Spirit, of the Church's future history, has provided for this as for all other emergencies, and gives an answer which probably will not satisfy the violence of prejudice on either side, but will none the less approve itself to the calm wisdom of the man of God. Let us inquire reverently and prayerfully what that answer may be.

How we are to think of and deal with such phenomena.

I. While our Lord Jesus Christ was upon earth, one man at least (perhaps several) was found, who, without any recognised connexion with Him, went about casting out devils in His Name,—not merely *endeavouring* to confer that benefit on suffering humanity, but actually doing it. "Master, we saw one" (*somebody*—with a touch

The man who cast out devils in Christ's Name, but did not follow with the Apostles.

of disdain, which the Master in His answer does not fail to correct by expressing His esteem for the man), " casting out devils in thy name, and he followeth not us" (St. Mark ix. 38). A singular phenomenon indeed! For no doubt this man was a real believer in Christ. No virtue would have followed upon his exorcisms, had he merely, parrot-like, taken up into his lips a name, to the power of which his own heart was a stranger. We know from another part of Scripture that the issue of such a procedure would have been utter discomfiture and dismay. For when the " seven sons of one Sceva, a Jew, and chief of the priests" at Ephesus, " took upon them to call over them which had evil spirits the name of the Lord Jesus, saying, We adjure you by Jesus, whom Paul preacheth," " the evil spirit answered and said, Jesus I know, and Paul I know; but who are ye? And the man in whom the evil spirit was leaped on them, and overcame them, and prevailed against them, so that they fled out of that house naked and wounded" (Acts xix. 13-16). Very different must have been the spirit of this man from that of the sons of Sceva. Doubtless he recognised Jesus as the Messiah, who should come into the world, and as the hope and consolation of Israel. It does not appear, however, that Christ had called him. Nor does it appear that he troubled himself to get called. Perhaps his want of humility, which called itself (as want of humility often does) independence of mind, made him unwilling to go to the disciples in the regular way, and seek from them baptism in the name of

Why he must have been a sincere believer.

His probable independence of spirit.

Jesus. As for himself, he may have thought, he would not adjure the spirits by Jesus, whom Peter and John preached, and into whose Name they baptized;—he had much better ground to go upon in his own convictions;—he felt sure that God had sent the great message of salvation into the world, and he believed that this message was free as the wind which careers over the open down, and he would go forth with the message upon the wings of the wind,—a self-elected missionary.

How much he lost by not following in the train of the Lord Jesus.

Now I suppose that few people will have the hardihood to say that he was no loser by this course of proceeding. No one surely will presume to assert that, although not following with the Apostles in the train of the Lord Jesus, he enjoyed the privileges and advantages which they enjoyed. As regards religious belief, he doubtless had the root of the matter in him; but he hung not upon those lips, so full of grace; he heard not those prayers, so simple and yet so unfathomably profound, in which the Son of Man poured out his soul before his Father; he did not enjoy the opportunities of having his sentiments momentarily inspected and corrected by the Divine Wisdom Incarnate.

High privilege of association with the Apostles, even after Christ had left them.

That, you will say, is true; but when the Lord's bodily Presence was withdrawn, how was he the worse for not following with the Apostles? Surely much the worse in every way. The words, the sentiments, the precepts, the institutions of their Master lived in them. They represented Him by His own appointment,—a position surely not to be despised. Upon them, as they were sitting in the one house, fell the Holy Spirit at Pentecost. And the new band of believers baptized on that day, felt that not only was the message of the Apostles to be received, but that their Society, no less than their message, had the Divine sanction. For "they continued stedfastly," not "in the apostles' doctrine" only, but "in their fellowship" also.

Now we believe that Apostolic Fellowship or Society to be still in the world. We believe that there is a Church, legally inheriting all the institutions and privileges of, and dating up historically to, the company assembled in the one house, when the Holy Spirit made His august descent on the day of Pentecost. We maintain not only the present ever fresh vitality of Christian doctrine, but the existence of an institution framed to give that doctrine a local habitation and a name, and being the very pillar and ground of the truth; an institution now hoary with the antiquity of eighteen centuries, resting ultimately upon the foundation of the apostles and prophets. It is true, indeed, that this noble column became overgrown in the course of time with parasitical weeds, and covered with the ivy of manifold superstitions and abuses, which, as ivy does to every structure, threatened the very existence of the building over which they had crept. But to us in this favoured country that matters little. We have had our Reformation, which without removing, or even disturbing the foundation of, the column, entirely cleared it of all the rank

The apostolic fellowship is still in the world.

vegetation which concealed its fair and majestic proportions. And in conformity with these principles, we believe that there is no separatist in the world who does not suffer loss by separation. We believe separation to be a very hardy act, which must have very clear grounds in conscience, before it can even justify itself to the good sense and candour of those who resort to it. Suppose we had lived in the island of Crete, at the time when a bishop presided over the Church there, whom Titus had consecrated by laying on of hands. Would not any candid person regard that ordination as a very important sanction of the bishop so ordained, and feel that he must have perfectly overwhelming grounds, before he could reject the authority and separate from the communion of that bishop? Yet the only difference between such a separation, and that of modern dissenters, is made by the many more links of the chain which are interposed between the Apostles and ourselves. Timothy, though appointed by St. Paul, was no more inspired than is a modern bishop. And that the charter and privilege of the visible Church is not injured by transmission, even to the latest age, may be gathered with certainty from our Lord's parting charge: "Go ye, . . . and teach all nations, baptizing them in the name of the Father, and of the Son, and of the Holy Ghost: teaching them to observe all things whatsoever I have commanded you: and, lo, *I am with you alway, even unto the end of the world.* Amen." The late King of Prussia is said to have observed that

Loss suffered by separation, however conscientious.

in Rome you see a Church without Christianity; in the sects Christianity without a Church; but that in England an attempt was made to maintain both—Christianity and the Church together. We are thankful for such a testimony from a foreign sovereign. Why are we to slight the Apostles' fellowship, because we are resolved to maintain, as dearer than life, their doctrine?

England has preserved both Christianity and the Church.

II. But our narrative teaches us, not only (by implication) the privilege of fellowship with the visible body which our Lord founded, but also (directly) the duty of cultivating, along with our Church principles, a spirit of universal Christian sympathy. "But Jesus said, Forbid him not: for there is no man which shall do a miracle in my name, that can lightly speak evil of me."

Universal Christian sympathy to be cultivated along with Church principles.

There is many a man in modern times, who, like the man before us, unable to see and recognise the blessing of fellowship with the Church of Christ, has yet felt deeply in his own soul the saving power of the Name of Jesus. He has felt that, just as in the sun is wrapped up all the physical virtue which pervades the realm of the universe (for the rain, which is a great principle of fertility, comes from exhalations which the sun draws up), so in the Name of Jesus Christ, that is, in His revealed character and attributes, all *spiritual* virtue resides,—a balm to heal every heartache, a consolation to soothe every trouble, and a sweet relief under the galling consciousness of guilt. The discovery of the hidden virtue of this precious Name fills him with joy and peace, and with that gush of spiritual emotions, which

Spiritual history of many a separatist.

His experience of the power of the Name of Jesus.

God mercifully grants, by way of lifting His children over the difficulties of an early stage of their religious career. He is impelled by an irresistible impulse to try upon others—his relatives, friends, neighbours, dependants—the powers of that Name, which has already wrought such wonders in his soul, and to which (as his conscience now responds, re-echoing the words of Inspiration) "all things in heaven, in earth, and under the earth, do bow and obey." A soul chafed with religious emotion is naturally impatient of restraint—he cannot wait, he thinks, for the tedious processes by which, in the ordinary course, the surplice and the academical hood are made, like the prophet's mantle, to fall upon a man's shoulders. What matter those or any other forms? (I am representing his sentiments, not expressing my own concurrence in them.) Souls are perishing all around him. He "believes" (with the Apostles), and therefore with the Apostles will he "speak." And very often (may we not say always, more or less? for zeal has a marvellous self-propagating power) he not only speaks, but speaks with the best effect. Other hearts vibrate as he sounds forth the Name, which is the alone key-note of all spiritual harmony. Then follows a reflex action upon his own mind. He is amazed, or rather awe-stricken, at the effect which he has himself produced. "There is no man which shall do a miracle in my name, that *can* lightly speak evil of me." Lightly speak evil of Christ! No; that is indeed for such a man a moral impossibility. He is far too solemnly impressed with the reality of the power, which the great Name exercises. When Frankenstein in the fiction had completed the fabric of a human body, having curiously compounded the materials which go to make up our animal frame, and prepared the internal system of bones, muscles, arteries, ducts, and glands, he was overwhelmed with an ecstatic awe, when he perceived symptoms that the vital spark had descended into this dead machinery, when the chest began to heave, and the pulse to throb, and the eye to flash, and the rigid muscles of the countenance to relax into play of feature, and to dawn into expression. And a similar, though a far deeper, sensation of awe creeps over a man when he becomes aware that, in obedience to his proclamation of the gospel of Christ, a dead soul is being quickened, a mouth which before was mute is beginning joyfully to articulate the praises of God, and a heart which before was of stone is now changing its nature to throbbing palpitating flesh. That man has proved by experiment in his own soul, and in the souls of others, the power of the Name of Jesus. And is not that Name the great secret of success, by which alone souls can be won, whether in or out of the Apostles' fellowship? For what end does the Church herself exist, but to win and edify souls? The case then stands thus; that a man who follows not with the Church, has stolen the Church's secret, and finds it as operative in his hands as it is in hers.

How then does the Lord of the Church instruct us to deal with such persons, and to regard them? Does He say to His Apostles that His doctrine

How we are to deal with such persons.

was the only thing they need regard, and that His fellowship was nothing? Does He say, "It would be no advantage to that man, if he did company with you all the time that I, the Lord Jesus, am coming in and going out amongst you"? Does He say, "Do not imagine that you are any gainers by being in My company, or that you would be any losers by forsaking it"? I hear nothing of the kind from Him; and if men will pervert His blessed words to this meaning, they must take on themselves the responsibility of wresting the Scriptures to their own one-sided views. "Jesus said, Forbid him not." Happy, thrice happy England, in which the law of the land echoes back this precept of the Church's Head, "Forbid him not;" in which any and every man who has a secret, whereby he considers that his fellow-creatures may be benefited, is at full liberty to announce it, even should it go the length of fanatical extravagance. Let all religionists say their say, of whatever sect and creed,—nay, let them say it, even should they discard and refuse to recognise the wonder-working Name, from the use of which alone spiritual results will flow.— But these heavenly words of Christ are not to be emptied of their force, by being regarded as a mere precept of legal toleration. Oh no! Not only is the State not to forbid, but the Church (the one Apostolic Fellowship) is not to forbid those, who, by a believing use of the Name of Jesus, convert and edify the souls of men. And more than this: "He that is not against us" (or, according to the much better reading of several excel-

[margin: Neither the State,]

[margin: nor the Church, are to forbid them.]

lent manuscripts), "He that is not against *you* is on your part." The man is actually doing your work, and furthering your end. For what is the work of the Church? Is it not the salvation of souls? And what is the end of the Church? Is it not that glory of God, which is most strikingly illustrated by the salvation of souls? Then, if this man is to all appearance saving souls, and bringing men to live soberly, righteously, and godly in this present world,—if he is really exorcising from the souls of this crooked and perverse generation the demons of sensuality, covetousness, and earthly-mindedness, which have entrenched themselves there,—you may indeed, and should, grieve for the loss and forfeiture which he sustains by his separation from the lineal succession; but, so far from forbidding him, you must acknowledge his work as from God, and be sincerely thankful for its progress, and say, as the Apostle born out of due time said, who did not indeed hear the Lord's words on this occasion, but doubtless *did* hear *of* them, "Notwithstanding, every way, whether in pretence, or in truth, Christ is preached; and I therein do rejoice, yea, and will rejoice" (Phil. i. 18).

We must acknowledge his work as from God, and be thankful for it.

We do not believe that the strictest maintenance of Church principles is inconsistent with universal Christian sympathy. While, in deference to truth, we cannot recognise that schismatical societies have the divine sanction, or are built upon the divine ground-plan, we do not feel ourselves precluded from recognising eminent saintliness, and eminent efficiency for good, in

Church principles by no means inconsistent with Christian sympathy.

many individuals belonging to such societies. It is a very observable fact, on which we propose to dwell further in the sequel, that although the kingdom of Jeroboam was a schismatical polity, certainly not contemplated in the original draught of the Hebrew monarchy, which was to be one, and always to run in the tribe of Judah and in the royal line of David, yet the representative of all the Prophets, and the only man (except Enoch) whose saintliness was crowned with an assumption to glory, was born a subject of the schismatical kingdom, and ministered not in Judah but in Israel. Who, on the one hand, will dare to dispute that Elijah was a true prophet? Who, on the other hand, will presume to deny that the royal family of David had a claim upon the allegiance of every Hebrew, in virtue of the Divine charter made to him and his heirs, and that the lamp of promise and covenant was handed down exclusively in that line, until at length it rested on the head of Messiah? And as I have thus brought into the argument what (strictly speaking) the passage of Scripture on which I am dwelling does not lead me to the consideration of,—the case of schismatical *Communions*, as distinct from that of *the individuals found in their bosoms*,—I will close this Chapter with the striking words of one who, had he lived, would probably have been at present a foremost divine of our Church. After vindicating in a masterly argument (worthy of his namesake, Bishop Butler) the claims of the Church upon the allegiance of all good Christians, as being lineally the fellowship of the

Appearance of saintliness and high prophetical gifts in the schismatical kingdom of the Ten Tribes.

Apostles, he adds this image of the relation borne to the Church by the orthodox religious communities of this country.

"When our Lord was in that ship in the tempest, which all ages have agreed in employing as a type of His Church, St. Mark alone of the Evangelists, as it were incidentally, observes— 'And there were also with Him other little ships.' Nothing more is said through the narrative of these '*little* ships.' Yet they, doubtless, enjoyed a share in the blessing of calm obtained by the ship that bore Jesus Christ. I have sometimes thought that they picture vividly the fortunes of those societies, which in these later ages have moved in the wake of the ancient Apostolic Church; which are with it forced to endure the storms of a world impartially hostile to every form of religious effort; and which are not without participating in the blessings of the holy Presence abiding in that Church, as long as in sincerity of heart they endeavour to keep up with the Master in His course."—(*Professor Archer Butler's Sermons.*)

Schismatical Communions which preach Christ, like the 'little ships' in the wake of the vessel which bore the Person of Christ.

Catechism on Chap. II.

1. *Catechist.*—In your former examination you stated that Christ had founded a great world-embracing Society, and had commissioned His Apostles to call all men into it. This is the great Church truth of God's Word. What other great truth is there, which must be held fast at the same time, and with equal earnestness?

   Answer.—That Christ taught, and commissioned His

Apostles to teach, certain doctrines; and that these doctrines must be maintained and clung to.

2. *Catechist.*—This is a truth which might lead us in a direction contrary to the former. For if the Society founded by Christ should happen at any time not to hold the doctrines which He taught, a question would arise whether we should hold to the Society or to the doctrines. Can you give any other instances of two rival truths of God's Word, which lead in opposite directions?

Answer.—Yes. It is a truth, on the one hand, that some persons are chosen by God to eternal life. "But we are bound to give thanks alway to God for you, brethren beloved of the Lord, because God hath from the beginning chosen you to salvation through sanctification of the Spirit and belief of the truth" (2 Thess. ii. 13). And it is a truth, on the other hand, that, if we fail to attain salvation, the failure is to be set down entirely to our own fault. "Why will ye die, O house of Israel? For I have no pleasure in the death of him that dieth, saith the Lord God: wherefore turn yourselves, and live ye" (Ezek. xviii. 31, 32). Again; it is a truth of God's Word that salvation is by grace. "By grace are ye saved through faith; and that not of yourselves: it is the gift of God" (Eph. ii. 8). But it is equally a truth of God's Word that our will is free to work out, or not to work out, our own salvation. "Work out your own salvation with fear and trembling" (Phil. ii. 12); "Let us labour to enter into that rest" (Heb. iv. 11); "Giving all diligence, add to your faith virtue; and to virtue knowledge," etc. (2 Pet. i. 5, etc.) Though indeed there is no need to prove that the human will is free; for every precept of the Bible proves it, unless we suppose that God mocks mankind by giving them commands which they are unable to fulfil.

3. *Question.*—Do you find anything in Nature which resembles these rival truths of Holy Scripture?

Answer.—Yes: we find in Nature a balance of

forces, and a system of checks. The centrifugal power in astronomy counteracts the centripetal, and the two together keep the planet in its orbit. And many tribes of animals keep one another in check. The small birds destroy certain tribes of insects which, if they were allowed to multiply without restraint, would be mischievous to vegetation.

4. *Catechist.*—You speak of these things as *forces* and *checks* in Nature. What are the forces and checks in the spiritual system called?

Answer.—Religious truths; which are forces operative upon the heart and will of man, and several of which hold one another in equipoise, and keep him who observes them in a right path, steering him clear of opposite perils.

5. *Catechist.*—Repeat once again the rival truths now under consideration.

Answer.—That we must continue in the Church which Christ and His Apostles founded, and also maintain as dearer than life the truths they taught.

6. *Question.*—In what words are we told that the early Christians did both of these things?

Answer.—It is said that "they continued stedfastly in the Apostles' doctrine and fellowship" (Acts ii. 42).

7. *Question.*—What soon made it difficult for Christians to continue in both?

Answer.—The novelties and errors which crept into the Church; the superstitions and abuses which grew up in it; and, in process of time, the unscriptural doctrines and practices which were not only maintained but sanctioned.

8. *Question.*—Did these corruptions take their rise very early?

Answer.—Yes. We find that even in the days when inspired Apostles ruled the Church, serious errors began to show their heads. Thus there were "some among" the Corinthian Christians, who said that there was "no resurrection of the dead" (1 Cor. xv. 12); some at

Ephesus who said that "the resurrection" was "past already" (2 Tim. ii. 18). And St. John tells us that in his time there were "many Antichrists" (1 John ii. 18 and iv. 3), and St. Paul that "the mystery of iniquity" was already working, but under a hindrance, the removal of which should be followed by the revelation of the Man of Sin (2 Thess. ii. 3, 7, 8).

9. *Question.*—If God's Truth and God's Church were so utterly at variance that we could not abide by both, what reason might justly move us to abide by the Truth in preference to abiding by the Church?

Answer.—That the Truth, as given in the Holy Scriptures, is entirely pure, and cannot be corrupted; but the Church is composed of sinful and fallible men; and it was predicted by our Lord that there should be in it the tares of error and evil; and these tares actually appeared even in the days of His Apostles.

10. *Question.*—How did it come to pass that in England there was no difficulty in abiding both by the doctrine and by the fellowship of the Apostles, whereas, in other less highly-favoured countries, good men were driven to leave the old Church, and form new Communions of their own?

Answer.—Because in England by far the greater number of the Bishops and Clergy came round to the side of the Reformation, and thus there was no difficulty in continuing the Church upon its old foundation, while abuses and corruptions were swept away; but in other countries, the Bishops (who alone can continue the ministerial succession by conferring Holy Orders) maintained the old abuses, and refused to consecrate or ordain any one who sympathized with the new movement.

11. *Question.*—What do you mean by a Christian denomination?

Answer.—A body of professing Christians who receive the Creeds and leading truths of Religion, but who have separated from the Church, and assumed to themselves an authority to administer the Holy Sacraments, not derived from the Apostles of Christ. This definition holds good of most denominations. The Quakers, however, have no Sacraments, and disparage all outward ordinances.

12. *Question.*—Quote some passages of Holy Scripture, which strongly condemn the division of Christians into several bodies.

Answer.—St. John xvii. 20, 21, " Neither pray I for these alone, but for them also which shall believe on me through their word; that they all may be one; as thou, Father, art in me, and I in thee, that they also may be one in us: that the world may believe that thou hast sent me." Eph. iv. 4, " There is one body, and one Spirit." Rom. xvi. 17, "Now I beseech you, brethren, mark them which cause divisions and offences, contrary to the doctrine which ye have learned; and avoid them." 1 Cor. i. 10, 11, 12, 13, " Now I beseech you, brethren, by the name of our Lord Jesus Christ, that ye all speak the same thing, and that there be no divisions among you; but that ye be perfectly joined together in the same mind and in the same judgment. For it hath been declared unto me of you, my brethren, by them which are of the house of Chloe, that there are contentions among you. Now this I say, that every one of you saith, I am of Paul; and I of Apollos; and I of Cephas; and I of Christ. Is Christ divided? was Paul crucified for you? or were ye baptized in the name of Paul?"

13. *Question.*—But, although separation from the Church of Christ's foundation cannot be justified (more especially in a country like our own, where the Church holds and teaches God's Truth), is it not a fact that many members of dissenting bodies, as also many foreign Protestants, are eminently holy and devoted men, and that many souls are won to Christ by the ministrations of those who have never been lawfully or regularly ordained?

Answer.—Most assuredly. God's Grace may often

be found flowing outside the channels of His own appointment.

14. *Question.*—What sort of sin would it be to deny the working of God's Hand, where spiritual good is manifestly done, and where the proper evidences are given of piety and devotion?

Answer.—A very grave sin, resembling in kind (if not in degree) that of the Pharisees, who ascribed our Saviour's miracles to Beelzebub, and are censured for "blasphemy against the Holy Ghost," *i.e.* a sinning against the evidences of His power, and a perverse denial of the convictions wrought in the heart by those evidences.

15. *Question.*—If then we cannot, on the one hand, justify or excuse separation, nor, on the other, deny the good manifested and done by many separatists, in what light are we to regard such of them as manifest and do good?

Answer.—We are to regard them much as the Apostles were directed to regard the man who cast out devils in the Lord's Name, but did not follow with them (St. Mark ix. 38, 39).

16. *Question.*—In the case you refer to, how is it evident that the man himself was a sincere believer in Christ?

Answer.—Because, had he tried the power of Christ's Name upon others, without experiencing it in his own heart, it would not have had any effect.

17. *Question.*—How do you know that?

Answer.—From Acts xix. 13-16, where we read that the "seven sons of one Sceva, a Jew, and chief of the priests, . . . took upon them to call over them which had evil spirits the name of the Lord Jesus, saying, We adjure you by Jesus, whom Paul preacheth." But these vagabond Jews were repulsed by the evil spirit whom they sought to expel. They "acknowledged" the authority of Jesus, and "knew"[1] Paul as His faith-

---

[1] The distinction between γινώσκω and ἐπίσταμαι in ver. 15 must not be overlooked.

ful servant and Apostle, but neither acknowledged nor knew these pretenders. "The man in whom the evil spirit was leaped on them, and overcame them, and prevailed against them, so that they fled out of that house naked and wounded."

18. *Question.*—But if this man, who actually cast out devils in the name of Jesus, was a sincere believer, in what respects was he wrong?

Answer.—In not following Christ in the regular and appointed way. It does not appear that he had been called by Christ, as the Apostles had. Doubtless he had been impressed by the miracles and discourses of our Lord, but it does not appear that he had gone to the Apostles and sought baptism from them, as he might have done; for we are told that, during our Lord's ministry, He baptized (by the hands of His Apostles), and that multitudes flocked to His baptism (St. John iv. 1, 2, and iii. 26). Thus he had no call to preach the Gospel; and he does not seem himself to have received the Gospel in the regular way.

19. *Question.*—Must he have been a great loser by "not following" Jesus?

Answer.—Doubtless. Our Lord's words and example must have been of unspeakable advantage to those, who had daily opportunities of observing Him.

20. *Question.*—But, after our Lord's bodily presence was withdrawn, would he have been a loser by "not following with" the Apostles?

Answer.—Certainly; for their Master had given them the words which God had given Him (St. John xvii. 8); had made known unto them all things that He had heard of His Father (St. John xv. 15); had moulded them by His example and influence into the character which He approved; and, to crown all, sent down upon them the Holy Ghost on the day of Pentecost, to guide them into all the truth (St. John xvi. 13), and to set up in the earth the "Apostles' fellowship," "the household of God," which is "built upon the foundation of the apostles and prophets, Jesus Christ himself being the chief corner-stone" (Eph. ii. 19, 20).

21. *Question.*—Does this "fellowship of the Apostles" still exist in the world?

Answer.—Certainly. The Apostles consecrated Timothy, and Titus, and other Bishops, to superintend the different Churches founded by themselves; and these Bishops, according to the instructions given them, handed on to others their doctrine, their commission, and the grace of Ordination (see 2 Tim. ii. 2, and i. 6, 7; and 1 Tim. iii. 2, 5, 6; and Titus i. 5, 6), and these again, in their turn, sent other labourers into the Lord's vineyard, until the commission came down in regular course to our present Bishops and Clergy.

22. *Catechist.*—St. Paul consecrated Titus to be Bishop of Crete. It is easy to understand, then, that a Christian in the island of Crete, who set up a different Communion from that of which Titus was the head, and took upon him to consecrate or ordain, though he had never received the commission to do so from Titus, would be acting wrongly and presumptuously. What is the difference between his case and that of a man who in our days sets up a division, and assumes authority to minister the Word and Sacraments?

Answer.—The only difference is, that there is but one Bishop intervening between St. Paul and the supposed Christian in Crete; whereas between St. Paul and the modern separatist there are very many links of the Episcopate intervening.

23. *Question.*—And does not this circumstance of the many links through which the ministry is derived (several of those links having been profligate, superstitious, or even unbelieving Bishops), somewhat invalidate the commission?

Answer.—By no means. If a Society is founded by Royal Charter, and regularly continued by the lawful admission of members, no negligence or misconduct of the members can annul the Charter, or make it need renewing.

24. *Question.*—How does it appear from our Lord's

commission to His Apostles that He designed it to be carried onward by future generations to the end of time?

Answer.—Because, though He must have known that His Apostles would not live to the end of the world, He says that He will be "with" them "alway, even unto the end of the world." By "them," therefore, he must have meant not only themselves personally, but all who in future generations should represent them.

25. *Question.*—But what is the direct lesson taught us by the narrative of the man who cast out devils in the Lord's Name, and whom He would not have His Apostles forbid?

Answer.—That of cultivating, besides Church principles, a spirit of universal Christian sympathy.

26. *Question.*—Who in these days seems to correspond to the man in the narrative?

Answer.—Those who, having felt the power of Christ's Name in their own hearts and consciences, are impelled to communicate to others the secret, which has brought peace, and joy, and victory over besetting sin to themselves.

27. *Question.*—What mistake is such a person apt to make?

Answer.—The mistake of not waiting till he is called in a regular way to preach, and of putting himself into the Ministry, instead of being put there by the Church.

28. *Question.*—But is it often found that, notwithstanding this great mistake, the ministry of such a man is a success?

Answer.—It is. The Name of the Lord Jesus, than which "there is none other Name under heaven given among men, whereby we must be saved" (Acts iv. 12), has such marvellous and potent virtue that it cannot fail, when proclaimed by one who has experienced its virtue, to carry grace and power with it. Dead souls are quickened by the proclamation.

29. *Question.*—What effect has this success upon the man who is instrumental in achieving it?

Answer.—While, on the one hand, it flatters his natural vanity, on the other, it certainly tends to deepen the impression already made on his own heart. It solemnizes his mind, and brings into it a feeling of awe in connexion with Divine Truth, so as to make it an impossibility for him "lightly to speak evil" of Christ.

30. *Question.*—How does our Lord instruct us to deal with such persons?

Answer.—He bids us simply "not forbid them" to act as they are doing.

31. *Question.*—And why are we not to forbid them?

Answer.—Because they are really on the Church's side, and furthering (though in an irregular way) the Church's work. "He that is not against you is on your part."

32. *Catechist.*—What is the Church's work?

Answer.—The salvation of souls by the power of the Name of Jesus.

33. *Question.*—Do we find that the Apostles rejoiced in the announcement of this Name, even when it was announced in a vexatious and unloving spirit, because they knew it to be the only instrument of sanctifying and saving souls?

Answer.—Yes. St. Paul says (Phil. i. 15-18), "Some indeed preach Christ even of envy and strife; and some also of good will: the one preach Christ of contention, not sincerely, supposing to add affliction to my bonds: but the other of love, knowing that I am set for the defence of the gospel. What then? notwithstanding, every way, whether in pretence, or in truth, Christ is preached; and I therein do rejoice, yea, and will rejoice."

34. *Question.*—But is our Lord's precept, "Forbid him not," to be understood as authorizing or sanctioning an uncommissioned Ministry, or as making light of the "Apostles' fellowship?"

Answer.—No. To understand it so would be to "add unto" the words of God, which we are forbidden to do under a threat of fearful plagues. (See Rev. xxii. 18, 19.)

35. *Question.*—Is there any ground in the narrative of the Old Testament for thinking that great spiritual good may be done by Communions of separatists?

Answer.—The appearance of Elijah and other great prophets in the kingdom of the ten schismatical tribes, which had thrown off their allegiance to the royal family of David, seems to show that God does not always limit His graces to the regular channel. Elijah was the greatest of all the prophets; but the scene of his ministry was schismatical Israel.

36. *Question.*—Can you point out, however, why this argument, good as far as it goes, must not be pressed too far?

Answer.—Because the cases are not exactly parallel. God did explicitly, and in so many words, sanction the schismatical kingdom of the Ten Tribes, nay, cause it to be set up (see 1 Kings xi. 31, 35, 38); but He has never given His sanction to a schismatical Christian Communion (otherwise than by crowning its ministry with success).

37. *Question.*—Has any Scriptural image been suggested for the orthodox religious communities of this country, which represents their position in a very favourable light?

Answer.—Yes. They have been compared to the "other little ships" which St. Mark tells us (iv. 36) were in attendance on the larger boat, which bore the Saviour Himself. Similarly these "other little ships" have been supposed "to picture vividly the fortunes of those societies, which in these later ages have moved in the wake of the ancient Apostolic Church; which are with it forced to endure the storms of a world impartially hostile to every form of religious effort; and which are not without participating in the blessings of the holy Presence abiding in that Church, as long as in sincerity of heart they endeavour to keep up with the Master in His course."

CHAPTER III.

THE UNITY OF THE CHURCH, AND ITS DISRUPTION.

> "Neither pray I for these alone, but for them also which shall believe on me through their word; that they all may be one; as thou, Father, art in me, and I in thee, that they also may be one in us: that the world may believe that thou hast sent me."—ST. JOHN XVII. 20, 21.

The divisions of the Church made tolerable to us only by our familiarity with them.

THERE is nothing to which habit of long standing will not inure us. There are certain abuses and anomalies which, if we were not accustomed to see them every day, we should cry out against as altogether flagrant and intolerable; but which, as our eyes are always resting upon them, we accept as part of the normal condition of things. One of these grievous abuses and anomalies is the want of unity in the Church or Christian Society.

Unity Christ's design for His Church.

The Church has, at many periods of her history, departed, both in doctrine and practice, from the original design of her Founder, but perhaps in no point so strikingly as in this of unity. The dying prayer of our Lord for His disciples (I call it His dying prayer, because it was offered on the night before His death) solicits for them an union as intimate, as dear, as profound as that which knits together the Persons of the Blessed Trinity in Unity; "Holy Father, keep through thine own name those whom thou hast given me, that *they may be one, as we are.*" And lest it should be thought that such an unity might indeed be more or less practicable, so long as the Church was a small and numerically insignificant body, held together by external pressure from the unbelieving world, but would become impossible of realization, as soon as Christianity had spread itself over the face of the world, and boasted disciples in every nation under heaven, our Lord distinctly contemplates, in our text, an indefinite increase of believers, and prays, in the same terms, that, under the circumstances of that increase, they may still be one. "Neither pray I for these alone, but for them also which shall believe on me through their word; *that they all may be one; as thou, Father, art in me, and I in thee, that they also may be one in us.*" An intimation of the rapid and extraordinary *growth* of His Church He had already given in the parables of the Mustard-seed and the Draw-net. The tiny mustard-seed was to become a tree, so that the birds of the air should come and lodge in the branches thereof. The draw-net, empty at first, was ultimately to gather of every kind. But in both these figures of the extension of the Church, the idea of her *unity* is carefully preserved. The mustard-tree, however many branches it may have, is one tree, developed out of one seed. The draw-net, however many meshes it may have, is but one net.

however extensive it might in course of time become.

Unity of the Church recognised in the same parables which predict its spread.

More than this. It would appear from the words which stand at the head of this Chapter that the great instrument, in the design of Christ, for the conversion of the world, was not so much the preaching of the Gospel as the spectacle of a Church united in the Truth; "that they also may be one in us: *that the world may believe that thou hast sent me.*" The perfect union and love subsisting among believers was to be a standing *moral* miracle for the conviction and conversion of the sceptic, even when *natural* miracles had passed away.

Such, then, was the ideal in the Founder's mind and intentions, of what the Community which was to take its name from Him should be; the Christian Church was to be a thoroughly united body, "perfectly joined together in the same mind and in the same judgment," even as the Persons of the Blessed Trinity are—co-operating, moreover, as those Persons do, for the same great ends of God's glory and man's salvation. But in the lapse of time it is a common thing for institutions to depart far away from the mind and intention of their founders. And the Christian Church has been guilty, more than almost any other institution, of this departure from its original idea. Sanctity may be seen here and there in all parts of it; the Sacraments are all but universally retained, and are everywhere salient features of the Christian Religion; the Gospel is preached in every community of professing Christians, with more or less fidelity to the original message; the Scriptures are spread in all parts. But of whatever treasures it may be the depository, of whatever mercies it may have been the instrument to mankind, the Church has not retained in any sort or shape the feature of unity; it does not present, and it has not for many centuries presented, one front to the unbelieving world. This want of union among Christian churches, and even among different theological schools of the same Communion, would, as I said, if we had not been inured to the spectacle of it from our earliest days, create in us a painful revulsion of feeling. Jews are a far more united body, Mahometans (to our burning shame be it said) are a far more united body, than Christians.

How came about this lamentable state of things? To omit all minor separations from the Christian body, there was in the first place the great schism between the East and the West, which, after being threatened and more or less carried into effect long before, was finally consummated in A.D. 1054. Its origin was a difference of opinion on the question whether the Holy Ghost proceeded only from the First, or also from the Second Person of the Trinity, a question which, probably, is as much philosophical as theological. This, and some other perfectly trifling and purely ceremonial differences (such as a variety in the time of keeping Easter, and the usage of leavened bread in the Communion by one party, of unleavened by another), first set up an alienation, the hostility, rivalry, and anathemas of which are not yet extinct. *Origin of the Divisions. The schism between the East and West. Its grounds, philosophical and ceremonial.*

Then came the schism at the Reformation, in

which the Reformed Communions had to allege, in justification of the step taken by them, the grievous corruptions, both in faith and practice, of the mediæval Church, the unscriptural terms of communion insisted on by Rome, and the absolute refusal (in most countries) of the Bishops to consecrate those who did not accept such terms. And if, after their separation on these grounds, the reformed Churches could have shown an unbroken and undivided front among themselves, it would have been much in their favour, and would have been an undeniable token that God was with them; but alas! the case was the very reverse. Formal schism, once engendered, is sure to put forth, like the Hydra, a hundred heads. Protestantism, so far from being a bond of union among Protestants, is simply a negative denomination, which shows the person claiming it to be *not* a Roman Catholic, or, in other words, not to hold with the abuses and corruptions of the mediæval Church; but it pledges him to nothing positive; and members of our own Communion are comprehended under the name of Protestants with a number of other sects, with some of whom they have nothing, or scarcely anything, in common, either in doctrine or discipline;—with Socinians, for example, and Unitarians, and Mormons. We owe a deep debt to the Reformation; and we should be deeply thankful to Almighty God for the share in its blessings which He has allowed to the Church of England; but its blessings were all on the side of truth, not on the side of unity; and its whole

The schism at the Reformation, and the grounds of it.

Schism between the Reformed Churches.

Tendency of schism to propagate itself.

Drawbacks of the Reformation.

tendency has been towards disintegration and the multiplying of schisms.

But I seem to hear some of my readers saying that the unity of the Church of Christ is spiritual, and in no sense visible or external; and that therefore these lamentations over its visible and external ruptures are groundless, and based upon a false assumption. You are thinking that, however much Churches and theological schools may ostensibly differ, and however loudly they may anathematize one another, all devout and good Christians in the several Communions, be they Church of England people, or Greeks, or Russians, or Quakers, or Baptists, or Romanists, —all who are, not influenced merely, but *led* by the Spirit of God,—*do* substantially agree in the hidden ground of the heart, rest upon the same Saviour, derive support and comfort from the same promises, approach the same Father through the same Mediator, are animated by a common hope of glory. You are thinking, I dare say, that this is all the unity which Christ ever designed for His disciples; and that, as all good Christians all over the world are knit together by this invisible bond, the Founder's ideal has not been really frustrated or broken. If this is your view, you are running away with a half truth; and half truths not unfrequently prove, if insisted upon without reference to the corresponding half, the most mischievous of falsehoods. It is true, no doubt, perfectly true, and it is a beautiful, consolatory, and edifying truth, that all the true servants of God have this unity of the Spirit, this

<small>Confusion of thought between the Unity of the Church and the Communion of Saints.</small>

community of hopes, interests, and prayers, for which you give them credit; nay, it is a truth so important that it forms an article of the Faith; for what else than this spiritual union is meant by "the Communion of Saints," in which we all daily profess our belief? But what was St. Paul's view of the unity which was intended to subsist among Christians? He speaks indeed of there being "one Spirit;" but does he speak of nothing else?

Exposed by the words of the Apostle, These are his words: "There is *one body, and one Spirit*, even as ye are called in one hope of your calling,"—not "one Spirit" only, knitting together the elect in one hidden communion and fellowship, but "one body" also; yea, one body primarily and in the first instance; for the body (or community) of Christ's disciples *and by an analogy drawn from the body.* existed, before the Spirit came down at Pentecost to inhabit and organize it, just as the body of Adam was first framed, before the breath of life was inbreathed into his nostrils. Now a body, observe, is something visible and external, something which may be handled and seen, something which has locality,—which takes up a definite room in space. A body, and the life which animates it, are two distinct things, not to be confounded. And what St. Paul says is, not only that Christians, however separated from one another by tracts of time and space, are animated by one common spiritual life, but also that they all belong to one and the same visible society; "There is one body, *and* one Spirit."

We have seen, then, that Christ designed unity—

visible unity—for his Church; designed that Christians all over the world should have one profession of Faith, one Baptism, one Ministry, as well as one hope, and one source of consolation and strength. And we have also seen how far this is from being the case, and how Christendom is broken up into a hundred different sects, many of them actuated by such hostility to rival sects, that to kneel down together to receive the one Sacrament of the Body and Blood of Christ would be for both an impossibility. Now what, under these circumstances, should be our views and feelings, and consequently our conduct? Does Holy Scripture leave us without any guidance, in view of the sad divisions of Christendom? Or, on the contrary, does it give us a clue as to our sentiments and line of action, in the midst of these immense and perplexing difficulties? We believe that it does the latter, not perhaps obviously, but by implications, which the wise and thoughtful student will not miss. *The guidance given us by Holy Scripture under the present circumstances of the Church.*

Consider, then, what occurred under the old Dispensation, in respect of the establishment and the disruption of the Israelitish monarchy. Human affairs, we know, though more fluctuating and variable than natural phenomena, are on the whole governed by certain fixed laws, which yield a similarity of results, when the circumstances are in the main similar, and produce what the philosopher calls historical cycles. With wonderful accuracy the fortunes of the Jewish monarchy have been reproduced on the grander arena of the Church or Kingdom of Christ. Every one re- *The establishment of the Israelitish monarchy.*

members the story. Originally, the Israelites were never intended to be under a king at all. They were to be a peculiar people in many respects, and in this more particularly, that the unseen God was to be their king, who should issue His commands to them through the prophet or person at the head of the nation for the time being. But they were dissatisfied with this arrangement; and their dissatisfaction seems to have had two grounds. It arose first from the mal-administration of persons in authority. When the pious Samuel was growing old, his sons who tried causes for him, "turned aside after lucre, and took bribes, and perverted judgment." But there was a fault in the people as well as in the judges. They did not in the least appreciate the wonderful privilege of having God for their king; they desired to be put on a level with other nations in respect of their form of government. The unseen made a demand upon their faith, which their faith was not strong enough to meet. They liked to look upon the pomp and insignia of royalty, and to have an embodiment of it in their midst; "Nay; but we will have a king over us; that we also may be like all the nations; and that our king may judge us, and go out before us, and fight our battles."—Now, it is certainly a very observable fact that the more recent divisions in the Christian Church may all be traced up to the attempt (made in the arrogance and ambition of man's natural heart) to establish a visible monarchy called the Papacy. As Christ had founded the Church, He and He alone was to be her Head,—the chief

The causes which led to it, the misconduct of the rulers,

and of the people.

How the same causes have operated to produce schism in the Church.

pastors consecrated by the Apostles and their successors being all of co-ordinate authority, and standing all of them in much the same relation to the Christian Church which Samuel held towards the Jewish. But ecclesiastical ambition in Church-rulers, and desire among Church-people to walk by sight rather than by faith, to have the chief Church-ruler a great monarch, like the monarchs of the world, robed and sceptred and tiaraed, and installed in a palace, and surrounded by soldiers, to have a visible representative of the King in His resurrection beauty (oh, what a lowering of the great idea, to imagine that any earthly ruler can represent *Him!*)—this it was which struck the note of discord and faction in the Church, and prepared the way for secession, or, in other words, for revolt against the usurpation of the throne of Jesus.

But the erection of a monarchy in Israel is by no means the only point in Israel's history typical of the fortunes of the Christian Church. The monarchy having been established (although no such arrangement was in God's original design, and although the request for it in the first instance called down His anger), received His gracious sanction. He did not leave His people, but dealt with them under the forms of monarchy as He had dealt with them under the forms of theocracy. But there soon appeared (such is the perversity of man's heart) another disturbance of the plan of government. There was one grand ideal of the Jewish monarchy, formed in the Divine mind, and developed and divulged in due season; the

A second disturbance of God's plan for the government of His people.

centre of it was to be the throne of David, august beyond all thrones, because on it Messiah, the desire of all nations, was in course of time to sit. Every true Israelite owed allegiance and homage to this throne, if it were only that the national hopes and the national glory were all bound up in its future occupant. In the darkest days of political depression, this one throne of David was designed to be the pole-star and rallying point of Israel. But alas! the unity of David's throne was to be the boast of the nation only for a very short time. Solomon's degeneracy from the faith and worship of his father called down upon him the chastisement of Heaven; and Jeroboam was raised up, in the providence of God, to divide the empire, and to rule over a numerical majority of its subjects. An opportunity, indeed, was offered of averting the schism, and retaining the allegiance of the Ten Tribes, as well as of Judah and Benjamin. If Rehoboam had been guided by the counsel of the older courtiers, and had announced a conciliatory policy as the basis of his administration, the people, who only asked for the alleviation of his yoke, and probably were animated by no hostility to his person, would have been his "servants for ever." But his reply to their petition, suggested by the younger courtiers, was insolent and arrogant in the extreme, and could not fail to alienate the petitioners. He was their lawful master, he told them, and he meant to show it. "My father," said he in an evil hour for the integrity of his empire, "made your yoke heavy, and I will add to your yoke: my father also chastised you with whips, but I will chastise you with scorpions" (scourges with metal points inserted into their lashes, to make them sting more severely). This most wrong-headed and unfeeling answer to a petition, urged (it would appear) quietly, and without any threats, led immediately to the secession of all but the two tribes more immediately connected with the royal family. The heir of David, indeed, reigned still over these two tribes; and his metropolis was that of the Church as well as of the State of Israel; but the glory of his empire was greatly diminished, and the numbers who paid homage to it were miserably reduced. And it must be remarked, as a most essential feature of the case, that, under the circumstances, the secession received the Divine sanction, and that its throne, had its occupant only remained in allegiance to the Invisible Sovereign, would have been by Him maintained and upheld. For thus spake the prophet Ahijah, in God's name, to Jeroboam: "Thou shalt reign according to all that thy soul desireth, and shall be king over Israel. And it shall be, if thou wilt hearken unto all that I command thee, and wilt walk in my ways, and do that is right in my sight ... as David my servant did; that I will be with thee, and build thee a sure house, as I built for David, and will give Israel unto thee." Jeroboam, indeed, did not comply with this condition of faithful allegiance to the Divine Sovereign; and accordingly his house, so far from being sure, was entirely extirpated by Baasha, who commenced a new dynasty. And thenceforth

The secession received the Divine sanction,

unsettling dynastic changes, and violent transfers of the sovereignty into other hands, became common things in the kingdom of the Ten Tribes. But that, even when their moral and spiritual character was at its lowest ebb, and their sovereign had entirely ceased to regard himself in his true character as God's delegate and viceroy, God did not forsake, but still recognised them, is clearly shown by the fact, that in the reign of Ahab and Jezebel, the prophet Elijah, the representative of all the prophets, and in deed, if not in word, the mightiest of all of them, appeared in their midst, and was succeeded by the prophet Elisha, whose career was hardly less marvellous, and whose Divine mission was even more strongly attested by miracle than that of Elijah. The throne of the Ten Tribes was a schismatical throne; and the names of its occupants have no place in the august line of succession from David to Christ; yet, though it was a departure from the primitive ideal and constitution of the monarchy, it was expressly and solemnly sanctioned by God, who, in His wise providence, made it the instrument of chastising and humbling the Davidical family. The whole narrative exhibits a great law of the Divine administration, which is, that *when a primitive ideal is hopelessly frustrated, and the first best thing made impracticable by human sin and perverseness, God introduces a second best thing, and endows it with (at all events) a temporary sanction.* That second best thing is not constituted according to the original design; the unruly wills and affections of sinful men have prevented its being so; but its constitution seems taken up into the grand, comprehensive scheme of Divine providence, and made "to work together for good" to those who live under it.

Now, this Old Testament narrative offers at once lessons of consolation, guidance, and charity, under the miserable divisions of the Church of Christ. *Application of the narrative to the Christian Church, in its present divided state.*

The Church has departed widely from the primitive ideal traced out for it, and the primitive constitution given to it, by its Founder. The ideal was, that Christians, however remotely separated by tracts of space, should all be one by adherence to one Faith, and to one visible Society, organized at Pentecost, and called the Apostles' Fellowship; that this community should embrace and fuse together all races and conditions of men, Jew and Greek, barbarian, Scythian, bond and free. The constitution was, that Apostles should appoint and consecrate (as we know they did appoint and consecrate) bishops to succeed them in all such parts of their office as were transmissible, and that these bishops should appoint others, so continuing down to the last day the commissioned line, to which the Lord had said, "Lo, I am with you alway, even unto the end of the world." *The ideal of the Church, and its original constitution.*

But the ideal was shattered by the schism of the Greeks and Latins, which was established on either side by mutual anathemas. And the constitution was shattered at the Reformation, when the Protestant sects, full of zeal (as we have *shattered by the schism, and by the organization of new ministries.*

admitted) for God's Truth, organized their own ministries, on platforms altogether different from "the Apostles' fellowship." Now, under these most unhappy circumstances, what is to be felt and done?

Our duty under these circumstances:
1. To recognise sin in the Church as the source of schism.

First; sin in the Church must be duly recognised, and, in our prayers to God for unity, acknowledged as the origin of schism. It was partly Solomon's lapse into idolatry, and partly Rehoboam's intolerable arrogance, which brought about the secession of the Ten Tribes. And it was partly the deep degeneracy of the mediæval Church, its corruptions in faith and practice, its saint-worship, its image-worship, its relic-worship, its trafficked indulgences; partly the insolent and arrogant pretensions of the Bishop of Rome, who claimed lordship over God's heritage, and forgot that he was set to be a pattern to the flock,—which alienated Continental Protestants from the Apostles' Fellowship, and placed a vast numerical proportion of the sheep of Christ under other and irregularly constituted ministries. And in our own Communion, some half-century ago, it was the secularity of the clergy, their pluralities and their sinecures, the active opposition which many of them offered to anything like earnest spiritual life, their sneers at what was good in Methodism, and their persistent standing upon their rights, rather than upon the conscientious fulfilment of their pastoral duties, which raised up in many a parish a meeting-house, and organized a schism, the heart-burnings of which are not yet extinct, though the original fomenting cause of it—indif-

The sin in our own Communion which led to dissent.

ference and neglect in the lawful pastor—has long ago subsided.

Secondly; the present divided state of the Church is in the nature of a punishment; just as the rending away of the Ten Tribes from the house of David was the divinely inflicted penalty of Solomon's apostasy, and was announced as such, before it was brought about by the unruly wills and affections of sinful men. I ask particular attention to this point, because it seems to me to be generally overlooked. There is a considerable movement in our Church just now towards union with foreign Churches; and it has taken strong hold of the public mind that the isolation of the several Communions of Christendom, and their standing aloof from one another, is what ought not to be, is a wrong and a sin. Be it so; but this is only half the truth; *it is a punishment also,—possibly, as regards our own responsibility in the matter, more of a punishment than of a sin.* The withdrawal of great part of Christendom from the Apostles' Fellowship, the divisions and dissensions in the Fellowship itself, are part of the chastisement of the Church's unfaithfulness. It is not therefore in our power entirely to alter the state of things. That state must continue, until the chastisement has done its work, and God removes His Hand. I do not say that we must not pray and strive for another and happier condition of affairs; but only that the most effectual mode of securing the happier condition would be by thoroughly repenting of and avoiding the sins that called down the chastisement,—superstitions,

marginalia: 2. To recognise our divisions as 'penal' in their character, and humble ourselves accordingly, and avoid those sins, which drew down the chastisement, arrogance, indolence, unfaithfulness, and so forth. It was ambition in Church-rulers, and leaning on sense rather than on faith, which brought the Papacy into the Church. Let Church-rulers be ambitious of nothing but to do good; let the people eschew the guidance of the lust of the eyes; and let all be contented with simplicity in the externals of Religion.—It was a question of forms and ceremonies, as to the time of keeping Easter, and as to the use of unleavened bread, which contributed to the split between the Eastern and Western Church. Let modern Churchmen beware how they attach too much importance to the question of the vestment or the posture to be used in the celebration of the Holy Communion, lest such trifles should again work an equally disastrous result.—In this and similar ways we shall be striking at the root of the evil of schism, and so really promoting the unity of the Church. But the actual realization of this unity, very much like the cessation of war in the world, is in its full extent a millennial prospect, impossible to be realized under the present condition of things. With all your doing, and all your communications with foreign prelates, and all your proposals for adjustment of differences, do not suppose you can do very much in the matter till God gives the word, and,

> "Like a bell with solemn sweet vibrations,
> We hear once more the voice of Christ say, 'Peace.'"

Then, and not till then, will be fulfilled to the spiritual Israel of God, the Holy Catholic Church, that glorious prophecy which, in its earliest application, has reference no doubt to the Jewish people; "I will make them one nation in the land . . . . . ; and one king shall be king to them all: and they shall be no more two nations, neither shall they be divided into two kingdoms any more at all . . . and David my servant shall be king over them; and they all shall have one shepherd." *Ezek. xxxvii. 22, 24.*

Thirdly; let us never omit to acknowledge in the fullest way the working of the Spirit of God in schismatical bodies. Remember what has been said about God's extending His sanction to second best things, when first best things have been rendered impracticable by human sin. For my own part, I quite believe that in many parishes, where the lawful pastor has been slothful, or even (alas!) scandalous in his life and conversation, the ministry of dissenters has been God's highly honoured instrument for keeping alive in that parish the sparks of His Grace. Do not imagine that, in saying this, I yield to such a ministry any right or truly derived authority whatsoever. My argument does not in the least require such a concession. I will show all love to schismatics, and most readily admit that many of them God loves; but I will show them no liberalism; because liberalism is always found to mean the compromise of a principle for the sake of conciliating an adversary. I will compromise no principle, but on the contrary, proclaim my principles on the house-top. There is, and can be, no real and true Church apart from the one Society which the

3. Never to deny the working of the Spirit of God in schismatical Communions.

Fullest acknowledgment of this compatible with the denial of any due authorization for their ministry.

Apostles founded, and which has been propagated only in the line of the Episcopal Succession. There is no regular authority or right for the ministry whatsoever, but only in this one line. But, on the other hand, there have been many great saints, and many great teachers, eminent for learning and piety, not at all connected with this line. God has a regular channel in which His graces ordinarily run; but I do not find that He limits either His gifts or His graces to that channel. There was no saint, and no prophet, among the subjects of David's kingdom, so illustrious as were Elijah and Elisha in the kingdom of the Ten Tribes. And there have been at various times among Nonconformists splendid instances, not only of a spiritual walk, but of spiritual power for good over others, such as have never been surpassed, perhaps in some instances never equalled, in the Church. Probably, in his own peculiar line of argumentative eloquence, no minister of our own Church, be he bishop, priest, or deacon, has ever excelled Robert Hall, the Baptist minister, as a sacred orator. Horsley probably exceeded him in learning, but surely was exceeded by him in the oratorical gift.

God does not confine His graces and gifts even to the channel of His own appointment.

In conclusion; we shall not leave this subject without deriving some profit from it, if we are led by what has been said to make the unity of the Church in the avowal of the Truth a subject of much more real hearty prayer than we have hitherto done. And we cannot do this in words more exactly to the point than those with which our Church supplies us—" Beseeching thee to

The Unity of the Church to be such for in earnest prayer.

inspire continually the universal Church with the spirit of truth, unity, and concord: And grant, that all they that do confess thy holy Name may agree in the truth of thy holy Word, and live in unity and godly love;" or, as it is expressed in the Daily Office; "We pray for the good estate of the Catholick Church: that it may be so guided and governed by thy good Spirit, that all who profess and call themselves Christians may be led into the way of truth, and hold the faith in unity of spirit, in the bond of peace, and in righteousness of life."

The guarded terms in which our own Church teaches us to pray for it.

Catechism on Chap. III.

1. *Question.*—How do we know that the unity of the Church is an object very near to the heart of its Divine Founder?

   Answer.—Because this was one of the things which He petitioned for on the night before His death, in the prayer which is called the great High-priestly Prayer. The words are "Holy Father, keep through thine own name" (in the original Greek the words are, "*in* thine own name," that is, in the acknowledgment of it) "those whom thou hast given me, that they may be one, as we are" (St. John xvii. 11).

2. *Question.*—What then ought to be the intimacy of the union subsisting between members of the Church?

   Answer.—Their union ought to be as intimate as that subsisting between the Persons of the Blessed Trinity; for our Lord prays that His disciples may be as entirely one as Himself and His Father are.

3. *Catechist.*—But possibly, when He so prayed, He meant by "those whom the Father had given Him,"

only that little flock of disciples who were with Him at the time—in short, the holy Apostles?

Answer.—No; in another part of this prayer He shows that He means others besides the Apostles, and that He wishes all, who are brought to believe on Him, to be one. "Neither pray I for these alone, but for them also which shall believe on me through their word; that they all may be one; as thou, Father, art in me, and I in thee, that they also may be one in us: that the world may believe that thou hast sent me" (St. John xvii. 20, 21).

4. *Question.*—But can our Lord really have meant that, when the Church became very large, so large as to embrace all the most civilized nations upon earth, it was still to be one?

Answer.—Certainly. For He foretold this extraordinary growth of His Church in the Parables of the Mustard-seed and the Draw-net; and yet at the same time He did not speak of more than one tree or more than one net. (See St. Matt. xiii. 31, 32, 47, 48.)

5. *Question.*—What effect did Christ design that the unity of His Church should have upon the world?

Answer.—The same effect as His miracles, which were designed to make men believe in Him as God's great Ambassador to a sinful world. In the verse last quoted He prays "that they also" (all who should believe in Him on the testimony of the Apostles) "may be one in us: *that the world may believe that thou hast sent me.*" And indeed it would be a *moral* miracle, if, with all the tendencies to disunion in the heart of man, people of different races, climates, and manners were all held together in the bond of one society.

6. *Catechist.*—You have traced Christ's plan for His Church; that all Christians, however numerous, should be one; that their union should be as intimate as that of the Persons in the Blessed Trinity; and that this union should be God's great instrument for converting the world to the Faith. From

what we see around us, does this plan seem to have taken effect?

Answer.—No; Christ's grand design seems to have been frustrated by man's sin. The modern Church still has many features which remind us of the Church which Christ founded; it has the Scriptures, and Preaching, and the Sacraments; but unity is a feature which it has lost entirely. The Church is split up into many different Communions, which are so alienated from one another, that the members of one would not partake of the Holy Supper of the Lord at the altar of another Communion.

7. *Question.*—When did the first considerable rupture of the Christian Body take place?

Answer.—In A.D. 1064, when Pope Leo the Ninth, Bishop of Rome, sent legates to Constantinople, who excommunicated Michael Cerularius, Patriarch of Constantinople, and all his adherents. These legates, when the claims which they advanced on behalf of the Pope were indignantly repudiated, laid the act of excommunication on the altar of the great Church of St. Sophia, shook off the dust from their feet, and departed. But the disputes which terminated in this final rupture had been going on for nearly two hundred years; and indeed the political division of the Roman Empire into two parts, under two different Emperors (as early as the year A.D. 395), had prepared the way for the ecclesiastical rupture, which did not take place for upwards of six centuries afterwards.

8. *Question.*—What is the great doctrinal difference between the Eastern and Western Church?

Answer.—The Eastern Church maintains that the Holy Ghost proceeds only from the Father; while the Western Church holds that He proceeds from the Father and the Son.

9. *Question.*—What is the truth on this disputed point?

Answer.—Probably both parties in the original dispute had some amount of truth in their views, but would not acknowledge candidly the truth which there was in the views of their opponents. The Greeks were doubtless right in supposing that there was only One Fountain-head of Deity, from Which issued forth, before Time began, the two other Divine Persons; for this is implied in the doctrine, so constantly inculcated in Holy Scripture, that there is but one God. On the other hand, the Western Church was clearly right in maintaining that the Holy Ghost is sent to us by the risen and ascended Saviour, and in this sense proceeds from Him also; for He Himself says, in St. John xv. 26, "But when the Comforter is come, whom *I will send unto you from the Father*, even the Spirit of truth, which proceedeth from the Father, he shall testify of me." And again, St. John xvi. 7; "It is expedient for you that I go away: for if I go not away, the Comforter will not come unto you; but if I depart, *I will send him unto you.*" But whichever party was in the right in this dispute, there can be no doubt that the addition of the words "and the Son" to the Nicene Creed, without the authority of a General Council, was exceedingly wrong. This insertion was made at the Council of Toledo, by the authority of Pope Leo the First, about the year 447; but it was not received even by the Western Church till some ages afterwards; and Pope Leo III., while he acknowledged the truth of the doctrine, objected at the Council of Aix (A.D. 809) to its being made an article of Faith.

10. *Question.*—What were the ceremonial differences which separated the two Churches?

Answer.—The Eastern Church held that the bread used at the Holy Communion should be leavened; the Western Church that it should be unleavened. Besides this, they differed as to the time of keeping Easter.

11. *Question.*—What was the next considerable schism in the Church?

Answer.—It was that which took place at the Reformation, when the Reformed Communions shook off the yoke of the Papal supremacy.

12. *Question.*—What led them to do this?

Answer.—The grievous corruptions, both in faith and practice, of the Church of the Middle Ages, which were condemned by the Holy Scriptures,—then, for the first time, freely circulated among the people. Had they not shaken off these corruptions, they would have been unfaithful to the guidance of God's written Word.

13. *Question.*—But did the different Reformed Communions unite and form one body?

Answer.—They seem to have made no effort to do so; and indeed the impulse which set on foot the Reformation was rather centrifugal than centripetal—it was a movement away from, and not towards, a centre of unity. For the leading idea of the movement was the making a bold stand for God's Truth; and accordingly all the blessings of the Reformation were on the side of truth, not on the side of unity.

14. *Question.*—But is there not among all good Christians, to whatever Communion they may belong,—whether they belong to the Roman Catholic, or Greek, or English Church, or to any Dissenting body,—a certain unity of spirit, which makes them all one in sentiments and sympathies, however much they differ outwardly?

Answer.—Doubtless there is. All true Christians, of whatever Communion, approach the same Father through the same Mediator, and under the influence of the same Spirit; and as two rays of a circle cannot draw near to the centre without also drawing near to one another, so two souls cannot really approach the same God without having an invisible fellowship with one another.

15. *Question.*—Is not then this invisible unity all the unity which Christ solicited for His Church? Why should we seek for any other kind of unity?

Answer.—Because St. Paul tells us, in Eph. iv. 4,

that there is "one body" as well as "one Spirit." Now, though a spirit is something inward and invisible, a body is something outward and visible, something which may be seen and touched, and the whereabouts of which may be known.

16. *Catechist.*—But some persons seem to be of opinion that, when St. Paul says there is one body and one Spirit, he is only repeating the same truth in two different forms. Can you show that the body of the Church is a distinct thing from the Spirit which animates the Church?

Answer.—Yes; Christ's disciples before the day of Pentecost formed the body of the Church. But this body was not fully animated by the living Spirit till the Holy Ghost came down upon them at Pentecost. Similarly, Adam's body was first formed of the dust of the ground, before the Lord God breathed into his nostrils the breath of life, by which inbreathing he became a living soul (Gen. ii. 7).

17. *Catechist.*—You have said that the Church of Christ ought to be, and was intended by its Founder to be, a united body; but that, in fact, it is rent asunder by many and grievous divisions. Can you suggest anything at all parallel to this in Holy Scripture?

Answer.—Yes; there is something parallel to it in the rupture of the Israelitish monarchy, which took place under King Rehoboam, between the Two Tribes and the Ten.

18. *Question.*—Was this monarchy, of which you speak, a part of God's original design for the government of His people?

Answer.—No; the original design was that God himself should be the King of His people, issuing His directions and commands to them through the judge or the prophet, who might be raised up from time to time as His medium of communication with them.

19. *Question.*—How did it come to pass that this plan failed?

Answer.—Because the people desired to walk by sight rather than by faith, and to have under their eyes a human sovereign surrounded with the emblems of royalty, who might lead them out to battle against their enemies, and the sight of whom might give them confidence, and rally them when they were defeated.

20. *Question.*—How has this preference of an earthly to an invisible Sovereign been repeated in the history of the Christian Church?

Answer.—Our Lord's design for His Church was that He alone should be her Head, ruling her invisibly from His throne in heaven by the influence of His Holy Spirit. (See Eph. iv. 8-17.) His Apostles, and their successors even to the end of the world, were to be His chief ministers upon earth; all having authority of the same kind and degree, all of them receiving from Himself the precepts and doctrines which they were to communicate to His flock, and all of them setting themselves forth merely as ministers by whom men believed, and giving to Him alone all the glory of their success. "We preach not ourselves, but Christ Jesus the Lord," says St. Paul (2 Cor. iv. 5); and see also 1 Cor. iii. 5. But in process of time the authorized pastors began to lord it over God's heritage, and to thrust themselves into the place of their Divine Master. Thus John, surnamed the Faster, Patriarch of Constantinople, adopted the title of Universal Bishop, A.D. 588; against which presumption Pope Gregory the Great made a long and loud protest, but rather, it is to be feared, in a spirit of rivalry and counter-ambition on behalf of his own see, than from any pure desire for the honour of the Chief Shepherd and Bishop of our souls. And since that time the Popes themselves have shown the same unhallowed ambition, which one of them reproved in John the Faster, and have claimed to be Universal Bishops and Vicars of Christ upon earth. And it was this unwarrantable claim which led to the schism at the Reformation. Men could no longer bear the yoke, which the Scriptures showed them was imposed by man in the arrogance of his heart; and they rebelled, and threw it off.

21. *Question.*—Did the earthly monarchy of the Israelites, when it was established, continue undivided?

Answer.—No; God had designed that it should do so, and had annexed all the promises to the throne of David, "the man after His own heart," of whom He said, "I have made a covenant with my chosen, I have sworn unto David my servant, Thy seed will I establish for ever, and build up thy throne to all generations" (Ps. lxxxix. 3, 4). But man's sin disturbed this design also. Solomon's alliance with heathen wives, and his consequent apostasy from the worship of the true God, was punished by the rending away from his son of the Ten Tribes under Jeroboam. And it is remarkable that this punishment was brought about in great measure by the oppressiveness of Solomon's reign. "Thy father," said the people to Rehoboam, "made our yoke grievous: now therefore make thou the grievous service of thy father, and his heavy yoke which he put upon us, lighter, and we will serve thee" (1 Kings xii. 4). This was a result similar to that, of which the history of the Church of Christ has furnished so remarkable an instance—tyranny and oppressive claims leading to a breaking of the yoke on the part of the oppressed.

22. *Question.*—Did the secession of the Ten Tribes receive God's sanction?

Answer.—It did. So much so, that God promised to Jeroboam, the first king of the new dynasty, by the prophet Ahijah, that, if he would only be obedient, "I will be with thee, and build thee a sure house, as I built for David" (1 Kings xi. 38). But Jeroboam not complying with this condition, his house was extirpated by Baasha. And thenceforth the kingdom of the Ten Tribes frequently changed hands, Zimri destroying all the house of Baasha, as Baasha had destroyed all the house of Jeroboam; and Omri supplanting Zimri; and Jehu slaying all the house of Ahab (the son of Omri); and Shallum conspiring against Zachariah (the fourth in descent from Jehu); and Menahem slaying Shallum (after a reign of one month); and Pekah conspiring against Pekahiah (the son of Menahem); and Hoshea conspiring against Pekah. Thus the unhappy kingdom of the Ten Tribes underwent eight changes of dynasty in the course of about two hundred and fifty years, which elapsed between the secession of the Ten Tribes and their transplantation by Shalmaneser into the cities of the Medes. This gives an average of about one change in every thirty-two years.

23. *Question.*—What may we learn on the subject before us from this frequent change of dynasty?

Answer.—That divisions, even when made under the Divine warrant, have a tendency to multiply themselves. Schism naturally begets schism. One departure from the lawful line of succession leads to, and prepares the way for, further departures. The history of the Christian Church furnishes several instances of this. Even where separation has been justifiable, it has always bred fresh separations, and has tended further to disintegrate the one Body of Christ.

24. *Catechist.*—You have mentioned the *verbal* sanction given by God to the kingdom of the Ten Tribes. What *practical* sanction was He pleased to give to it, even at a time when the kingdom was in the worst possible hands?

Answer.—He raised up in their midst Elijah, and his successor Elisha, than whom no prophets were ever mightier in deed, hereby showing that He had by no means forsaken the seceding tribes, but still accounted them to belong to His own true people.

25. *Question.*—What great law of the Divine administration is exemplified, first in the institution of the Israelitish monarchy, and afterwards, not less strikingly, in the establishment and sanction of the schismatical kingdom?

Answer.—That when the first ideal (or, as it might be called, God's original intention) is frustrated by man's sin and perverseness, He introduces a new plan, a "second best thing," and works out His ends by means of it.

26. *Question.*—What was the original design and constitution of the Christian Church, as it came from the hands of its Founder?

Answer.—The original design was that there should be but one Society ("the apostles' fellowship"), which should embrace "all nations"—"One body, and one Spirit, even as ye are called in one hope of your calling; one Lord, one faith, one baptism, one God and Father of all, who is above all, and through all, and in you all" (Eph. iv. 4, 5, 6). And the constitution was, that the ministerial gifts necessary "for the perfecting of the saints" should flow down from the Church's risen Head into this one channel only,—the channel being prolonged by successive ordinations in one line,—a constitution which St. Paul adverts to in immediate connexion with the subject of the Church's unity, as being essential to the maintenance of that unity. "When he ascended up on high, he led captivity captive, and gave gifts unto men. . . . And he gave some, apostles; and some, prophets; and some, evangelists; and some, pastors and teachers; for the perfecting of the saints, for the work of the ministry, for the edifying of the body of Christ" (Eph. iv. 8, 11, 12).

27. *Question.*—How was the original design frustrated?

Answer.—By the great schism of the Greeks and Latins, which rent Christ's seamless vest into two parts.

28. *Question.*—How was the original constitution broken up?

Answer.—By the secessions at the time of the Reformation, which for the most part (though happily not in our own country) broke off from the Apostles' Fellowship, and made a fresh beginning of Christian Ministry, out of the line in which the great Commission had come down.

29. *Question.*—What is our *first* duty under these circumstances?

Answer.—We, as members of the old and true Church, are bound to acknowledge and repent of those sins of the Church, which have given rise to so many divisions, and to such extensive alienation from the Fellowship of the Apostles. The superstitions which disfigured the mediæval Church, its departure in so many points from scriptural and primitive practice, and the ecclesiastical arrogance and ambition which resulted in the formation of the Popedom, should be fully acknowledged and declared. And the abuses and corruptions of our own Communion at the close of the last century,—the carelessness, indolence, and vices of many of the clergy, the dry morality of others among them who led respectable lives, and the bitter opposition offered by them to the doctrines of Grace, ought to be admitted as the real originating cause of that dissent and schism, which has spread itself over all the parishes of our native land.

30. *Question.*—What is our *second* duty in reference to these divisions?

Answer.—To regard them not so much in the light of a sin in the separatists (though this to a certain extent they are), as in that of a visitation upon ourselves of the grievous sins of our forefathers in the Church. And regarding them thus, to avoid to the utmost of our power the particular sins which called them down,—ambition and arrogance in Church-rulers, the unbridled lust of external splendour in ritual among Church-people; controversy about trifles and forms; ministerial unfaithfulness and indolence; the substituting mere morality for the Gospel; and Pharisaism both in doctrine and worship.

31. *Question.*—Would it be possible by these or any other methods within the power of man, to restore perfect unity to the Church, and to mend the rent in the seamless vest of Christ?

Answer.—Probably not. While such a mode of

action, if universally resorted to, would very much mitigate the disorder, and would certainly strike at the root of it, the perfect restoration of unity to the Church, like that of peace to the kingdoms of this world, is probably reserved for the Second Advent of the Prince of Peace, and not to be brought about by any lesser or lower agency.

32. *Question.*—What is our *third* duty in reference to the divisions of Christ's Church?

Answer.—Never to refuse our hearty acknowledgment to the working of the Spirit of God in communities originally schismatical, and wanting a regularly ordained ministry; but to admit, and render thanks to God for, the extensive good which has often been done by the ministers of these Communions, and the brilliant examples of piety which many of the people in such Communions have exhibited.

33. *Question.*—But, if we make these admissions, may we not fear that we shall be driven to the conclusion that these ministries of man's erection are after all regular and legitimate?

Answer.—By no means. God may have but one regular channel for His graces; just as the river Jordan had one only bed. But as "Jordan overflowed all his banks all the time of harvest" (see Josh. iii. 15), so God's Grace may overflow the channel of His own appointment, and inundate and fertilize the country without any channel at all.

34. *Question.*—What is the *last* duty which the subject of this Chapter suggests?

Answer.—That of making the unity of the Church a special subject of prayer.

35. *Question.*—How does the Church of England show her sense of the importance of this duty?

Answer.—By introducing comprehensive petitions for the unity of the Church in the Morning and Evening Offices of each day, as well as in the Office of the Holy Communion.

36. *Catechist.*—Rehearse the petitions to which you refer.

Answer.—In the Morning Prayer (when the Litany is not appointed to be said), and always at Evensong:—

"We pray for the good estate of the Catholick Church; that it may be so guided and governed by thy good Spirit, that all who profess and call themselves Christians may be led into the way of truth, and hold the faith *in unity of spirit, in the bond of peace*, and in righteousness of life."

In the Office of the Holy Communion:—

"Beseeching thee to inspire continually the universal Church with the spirit of truth, *unity, and concord:* And grant, that all they that do confess thy holy Name may *agree in the truth of thy holy Word*, and live *in unity, and godly love.*"

And in the Office for the Queen's Accession there is a most beautiful *Prayer for Unity.* And the Collect for the Festival of St. Simon and St. Jude is a prayer to the same effect.

CHAPTER IV.

THE SURVEY OF ZION'S TOWERS, BULWARKS, AND PALACES.

> "Walk about Zion, and go round about her: tell the towers thereof. Mark ye well her bulwarks, consider her palaces; that ye may tell it to the generation following."—Ps. XLVIII. 12, 13.

The probable date of the forty-eighth Psalm.

THE forty-eighth Psalm probably belongs to the reign of Jehoshaphat, and should be read in connexion with 2 Chronicles xx. We find in that chapter Moab, Ammon, and Edom entering the territories of Judah with an invading army, with the design, no doubt, of aiming a blow at the capital. To this confederacy verse 4 refers:

The confederacy referred to in it.

"Lo, the kings were assembled." Jehoshaphat proclaims a fast, gathers his people, and publicly asks help from the Lord. To this prayer God immediately responds. A token for good upon Judah is shown by the uprising of a Levite in the congregation, who, under the influence of the Spirit of Prophecy, foretells the success of Israel without their striking a blow. Accordingly so it was. The kings mustered in the wilderness of Tekoa, where they caught the first sight of the battlements, domes, and pinnacles of the Holy

City,—the "towers, bulwarks, and palaces" of the text. Israel advanced against them like a crusading army, with the sound of psalms and hymns going up from the forefront of their line. But long before the armies met, a panic seized the confederate kings; they turned their arms against one another, and having made great havoc in their own ranks, fled in trepidation. "They saw it," in the words of the Psalm, "and so they marvelled; they were troubled, and hasted away. Fear took hold upon them there, and pain, as of a woman in travail." When the Jews came up with their enemies, they found not a hand raised to oppose them, but a vast number of corpses, with spoil in such abundance, that they were three days in gathering it. As afterwards in the days of Hezekiah, so now on this earlier occasion, the virgin, the daughter of Zion, had despised the invader and laughed him to scorn; the daughter of Jerusalem had shaken her head at him. There in the distance stood the City of God intact; planted upon her impregnable rock, and proudly rearing her minarets and domes towards heaven. No weapon forged against her should prosper.

Miraculous defeat of the confederacy.

Security of the City of God against hostile invasion.

Such was the original occasion of the Psalm—necessary to be known, as furnishing a clue to the interpretation, but which can never recur. But, like all parts of Scripture, the forty-eighth Psalm has a word for these times, as well as for those in which it was written. Spiritually understood, as we Christians ought to understand the Psalms (for in our mouths they should be "*new* songs"),

Spiritual meaning of the exhortation to 'tell the towers of Zion, and mark well her bulwarks,' etc.

it celebrates the glory, beauty, and stability of the Church, of which the literal Jerusalem was but a figure. And, under this view of it, the passage before us will convey an admonition, too little heeded by some, and magnified by others into the sum and substance of all religion, to consider with devout attention the constitution of the Church, the shelter which she provides for the spiritual life, and her defences.

With this admonition I proceed to comply, and thus to carry on the subject, to which this work is devoted. We shall be able, however, within the limits of the present Chapter, only to go half round the circuit of Zion's walls, reserving for another opportunity the observation of her remaining bulwarks and palaces.

In the natural Creation, the body of man was framed before the breath of life was breathed into it.

In the work of Creation the body of man was first formed, and, that having been done, the spark of life was communicated to the frame. "The Lord God formed man of the dust of the ground" (thus far man was only matter, but it was organized matter, with all the vessels, ducts, and arteries complete, wanting only in sensibility and power of movement), "and breathed into his nostrils the breath of life" (more properly, "lives,"—animal, intellectual, spiritual); "and man became a living soul." Something of

Similarly our Lord framed the structure of His Church before the Holy Spirit descended at Pentecost to animate it.

the same kind is to be observed in Christ's new Creation of His Church. He, as Founder, was to trace the outlines of the structure; and the Holy Ghost at Pentecost was to animate the already prepared organism with the Divine Life. Then St. Peter, according to our Lord's own prophecy,

IV.] *Towers, Bulwarks, and Palaces.*

which formed the subject of our first Chapter, should arise and build.

I propose to show, in the present and succeeding Chapters, how our Lord did actually Himself trace all those outlines,—one or two of the most marked and distinctive in the days of His flesh,—but all of them in the period of Forty Days, which elapsed between His Resurrection and Ascension. This great period had two aspects, both of the highest significance to our Religion; it was partly *evidential*, and partly *constructive*. Partly *evidential*;—"To whom also he showed himself alive after his passion by many infallible proofs, being seen of them *forty days.*" If Christ had been seen after His Resurrection for only one or two days,—if He had not given His Apostles several opportunities of testing the truth of His Resurrection; if He had not allowed Himself to be seen by many pairs of eyes,—on one occasion by as many as five hundred brethren at once;—if time had not been given for appearances to several different persons, at several different places, and under several different circumstances,—in Galilee, in Judea, indoors, out of doors, by day and by night,—room would have been given for reasonable doubt whether the Apostles had not laboured under some illusion of the senses, when they imagined that their risen Lord had come among them and spoken unto them.—But the significance of the great Forty Days was not evidential only; they had another and even a more important aspect: for Christ not only showed Himself alive to them during this period, by many infallible proofs, but

The significance of the great Forty Days—their evidential significance.

their constructive significance.

also spake to them "of the things pertaining to the kingdom of God," or Church. In other words, this was the great *constructive period*, in which Christ, as a wise master builder, traced the plan of the spiritual edifice. And accordingly we find in this period the germs of Church offices, Church institutions, and even Church seasons; I say, their germs or earliest beginnings, by no means their full development. The development of the grand ideas of their Founder was left to the Apostles under the guidance of that Spirit which fell upon them at Pentecost. You see them afterwards developing the Ministry of the Church, when they appoint the Seven Deacons, and devolve upon them their own secular functions; you see them developing the legislative powers of the Church, when they call a Council at Jerusalem, to consider how far the observance of the Jewish ritual was binding upon the Gentiles. —But we are now to look at Church institutions in their earliest rudiments, to see the Sacraments, the Ministry, the Festivals, just budding, like Aaron's rod, in the hand of the Divine Founder. "So is the kingdom of God," said He, "as if a man should cast seed into the ground." He Himself is the man who cast the seed of God's kingdom into the ground of man's heart; and most interesting it will be to trace up all our life as members of the Church, developed as it is now into blossom and fruit, to the seed which fell from His own hand.

The first passage to which I shall refer, because it comes first in the order of thought, is, that

IV.] *Towers, Bulwarks, and Palaces.*

which we find in the eighteenth chapter of St. Matthew's Gospel. St. Matt. xviii. 15-21.

Our Lord is speaking in the foregoing context of His Church; of the duty of hearing the Church; and of the power of excommunication and absolution with which He meant to endow her. Her sentences of excommunication and absolution, He says, shall be ratified in heaven. If the offending brother refuse to listen to the remonstrance of one or two private friends, then (ver. 17) "tell it unto the church: but if he neglect to hear the church, let him be unto thee as an heathen man and a publican. Verily I say unto you, Whatsoever ye shall bind on earth, shall be bound in heaven: and whatsoever ye shall loose on earth, shall be loosed in heaven." Then from the ratification in heaven of sentences of excommunication and absolution, He passes on, by an easy connexion, to another marvellous power which the Church as a body might exercise—that of united or common prayer; (ver. 19), "Again I say unto you, That if two of you shall agree on earth as touching anything that they shall ask, it shall be done for them of my Father which is in heaven." And then, piercing to the very root of the subject, He assigns, as the ground of these wonderful powers which His Church should exercise, His continual presence with her (ver. 20), "For where two or three are gathered together in my name, there am I *in the midst* of them." These words were uttered during our Saviour's lifetime; but after His Resurrection He gave the most forcible commentary upon them by appearing suddenly in The Saviour's promise to be in the midst of the two or three gathered together in His Name, and the context preceding and leading up to it.

Literal fulfilment of the promise during the great Forty Days.

the midst of His disciples, when they were gathered together in a chamber, the doors of which were shut for fear of the Jews. Doubtless they were thinking of Him, and talking of Him; and their separation from the unbelieving world, upon which they had shut the doors, showed that they were His little flock, "gathered together in" His "Name." "Then came Jesus and stood *in the midst*, and saith unto them, Peace be unto you," (according to that foregone word of His, "Where two or three are gathered together in my name, there am I in the midst of them.")

Ordinance of United Prayer.

Now, observe the words narrowly. There is first the institution of a Christian Ordinance, United Prayer. "If two of you shall agree on earth as touching any thing that they shall ask, it shall be done for them." It is on this ground that we meet, Sunday after Sunday, to ask of God "those things which are requisite and necessary, as well for the body as the soul,"—endeavouring to secure agreement on the things to be asked for by a form of prayer, which is in the hands of every worshipper, and with the meaning of which every one may acquaint himself, before he comes to the place of meeting. But the words not only institute the Ordinance of United Prayer, but exhibit the ground also on which the blessing annexed to such prayer rests; "*For* where two or three are gathered together in my name, there am I in the midst of them." The reason why the two or three are heard is, the presence of the Founder in the midst of them, interceding for them. And this presence is covenanted to any gathering

Ground on which the blessing covenanted to that ordinance rests.

together in His Name, however small; for there can be no congregation smaller than two.

We have here, then, the charter, which founds the Christian Society or Church. And it is a charter entirely of a piece with the whole doctrine and example of our Lord. His constant doctrine, His new commandment, was, "that ye love one another." His path through life was eminently social; unlike that of St. John the Baptist, it lay alongside the homes of men. He sat by the hearth of Mary and Martha; He was present at funerals; He was present at weddings; in short, "He went in and out among us." Well, this doctrine, this manner of life, finds itself expressed in the earliest principle of His foundation,—in the charter which establishes the Christian Society, and annexes a special blessing to joint prayer. The most fundamental of all truths respecting the Church is this, that our relations to God and Christ are not those of the individual conscience only,—do not stand clear of our relations to our brethren. The presence of our Founder, with all the rich blessings annexed to it, is to be enjoyed specially in the Communion of Saints.

The promise to 'the two or three' is the charter of the Christian Society.

Christ's example social, while His doctrine was that of mutual love.

Christ then founded a Society, and endowed it, if I may so say, with the assurance of His own presence, and with the promise of an answer to social prayer, however few the number of people joining in it. But was this Society to continue for ever? If so, it must of course be replenished from time to time, because the original members of it would die off in the course of nature. And if it was to be replenished, how was

Question raised as to how the Christian Society was to be extended and replenished.

it to be replenished? what was to be its rule or form of admission? Who was to be considered qualified for admission, and how was he to be grafted into the Society? I trust the reader sees that it is of the very nature of a society that no man can put himself into it; that admission must be from within, according to certain rules made when the society was founded. In some religious societies, there is the rule that a certain annual money payment shall make a man a member; unless he complies with that condition, the society does not own him. In clubs, the admission is usually by election, it being required not only that a candidate for membership shall pay something towards the funds of the club, but that he shall be chosen by a majority of the existing members. Now, what rule did our Blessed Lord make respecting the way in which vacancies in the Church (or Christian Society) were to be filled up? How were people to be induced to wish for membership? How were they to be made members, when they did wish for it? And how were they to be treated and dealt with afterwards, when they had become members?

Self-admission to any society an impossibility.

All these questions our Blessed Lord answers in the last verses of St. Matthew's Gospel, which are among the most important verses in the whole of the New Testament.

St. Matt. xxviii. 16 to end.

(Ver. 16.) "Then the eleven disciples went away into Galilee, into a mountain where Jesus had appointed them." Observe that the scene of the interview was a mountain; for, as you will see presently, it throws light upon the commission

He was about to give. Observe, also, that though the eleven only are *said* to have been present, others may have been there also. This was probably the interview in which Christ appeared to "above five hundred brethren at once," *i.e.* to all His existing disciples; but the Eleven are named as representatives of the whole body, and as such, the persons to whom the commission was to be given. Probably, in the first instance, they caught sight of His figure at the top of the mountain; and then followed what is told us in the 17th verse—"And when they saw Him, they worshipped Him: but some" (*i.e.* some of the five hundred, who were on the skirts of the crowd, perhaps, and could not get glimpses without difficulty) "doubted." "And Jesus came" (He came up closer, so as to be nearer to them) "and spake unto them, saying, All power" (authority) "is given unto me in heaven and in earth"—given unto Me, as the risen and glorified Son of God. God has set Me, according to the word of prophecy, as His King upon His holy hill of Zion. I am His Son, His first-begotten from the dead, and He hath given Me "the heathen for" Mine "inheritance, and the uttermost parts of the earth for" My "possession." And now I am about to proceed under that deed of gift, and to commission you to carry into effect the Father's grant—" Go ye therefore, and teach " (literally, make disciples of) "all nations." "All nations"—the Church, and the Gospel message, by which men were to be brought into it, was to be Catholic or universal—free as the breeze which

Probable reference of St. Paul to this interview of Christ with the Eleven.

Presence of many others at the interview.

The deed of gift referred to in Ps. ii., under which Christ sends His Gospel to the heathen.

careered over the mountain. "The freedom of the open air," says a devout preacher[1] of our own day, "befitted the wideness of the Sacrament of Baptism, just as the privacy of the dying leave-taking beseemed the sacred fellowship of the more advanced and therefore more withdrawn mystery."

"Make disciples of all nations." Thus Christ institutes the preaching of the Gospel in heathen countries,—Missionary Preaching, the heralding of the kingdom of God and of the name of Jesus, among those who never heard of God and Christ. When the preaching has, by God's grace, done its work; when it has created a desire among the benighted people to come into the kingdom of God, and be made disciples of Jesus, then they are to be admitted as disciples. In what follows, He tells us how. "Make disciples by baptizing them into the Name" (one Name, because there is but one God, albeit three Persons—here is the mystery of the Unity in Trinity) "of the Father, and of the Son, and of the Holy Ghost" (here is the mystery of the Trinity in Unity).

But when that is done, and the new converts have been admitted by Baptism to the Christian Society,—what next? Is no provision made for leading them forward in the spiritual life, upon which they have now entered? Nay; for what purpose have they entered into Christ's school, and become disciples of His, but that they may

---

[1] The Rev. Henry Burrows, B.D., Vicar of Christchurch, St. Pancras, one of whose sentences would often make another man's whole sermon.

learn of Him? Hundreds of lessons have to be learned of Him; we shall never have exhausted all the Lord's teaching, even should we live to the age of Methuselah. And therefore it is that in our Baptismal Service, after the administration of the Sacrament, the Sponsors receive this charge from the administrator—"That this infant may know these things the better, ye shall call upon him to *hear Sermons;* and chiefly ye shall provide, that he may learn the Creed, the Lord's Prayer, and the Ten Commandments, in the vulgar tongue, and all other things which a Christian ought to know and believe to his soul's health." This is not a little piece of good advice, given by the compilers of the Service. It is an echo, and a very faithful one, of the great commission under which every Baptism takes place, and which joins closely with Baptism Christian teaching —" Baptizing them in the Name," etc., and, after that is done, "teaching them to observe all things whatsoever I have commanded you." {*Recognition in the Baptismal Service of the necessity of such instruction.*}

In which grave and most significant words our Redeemer institutes two Ordinances of His Church.

1*st*. What we *commonly* call Preaching, the exposition and illustration of Christian Truth to a congregation of baptized believers. It is quite a different thing, and, as you see, is clearly discriminated in the Founder's commission, from the proclamation of the Gospel to the heathen. The two are expressed by totally distinct words. One is μαθητεύσατε, "*Make them disciples;*" the other is διδάσκοντες, "*Teaching them.*" Great con- {*Ordinance of Preaching to Christians instituted.*} {*The different kinds of teaching which are required previously and subsequently to Baptism.*}

fusion of thought springs from classing together under the common name of Preaching the heralding of Christ to those who never heard of Him, and the regular instruction of a Christian congregation. Both were directly instituted by the Lord Himself, and are done to this day under the great commission He issued to the Eleven Apostles; and this being the case, it may be gravely questioned whether the sneers which are launched so generally at preachers and preaching, and the undisguised *ennui* which people confess to suffering when they hear Sermons, are altogether consistent with that profound veneration, which we owe to the Divine Founder of the Church. Preaching, like other means of grace, is very much what the hearer makes it. No man, who has really tried to make it a means of spiritual good to himself, will ever speak of it lightly and disparagingly. The taunts and slights come from itching ears, not from hungry hearts.—But we find in the words before us, "Teaching them to observe all things whatsoever I have commanded you," the institution of another Ordinance. For our Lord must have known perfectly that Infant Baptism was to be the uniform practice of His Church, down to a very late period of her history. He Himself, by blessing young children, and thus showing that they were capable of a special blessing, had solemnly sanctioned the *principle* of Infant Baptism. And therefore "teaching them to observe all things" must certainly embrace, not the instruction of adults only, but the training of children in Christian Truth; in other words, Chris-

Margin notes:
- Popular contempt for preaching condemned by our Lord's institution of it.
- Ordinance of Christian Education.
- How this is to be found in the words, 'Teaching them to observe all things,' etc.

tian Education. Observe that this Education is prescribed as closely connected with, and immediately following upon, Baptism; that, when it is lacking, the Sacrament of Baptism is shorn of its essential accompaniment. The great Founder of the Church having, by the ministry of the priest, taken the infant into His arms and blessed it, thereafter gives it back to those who presented it, with a charge similar to that which Pharaoh's daughter gave to the mother of the infant Moses—"Take this child away, and nurse it for me, and I will give thee thy wages." Yes! nurse it, teach it, train it FOR ME, in My Truth, in My sanctifying Word. And that Christian Education might be more clearly recognised as prescribed by Christ, and as part of the work which His Church and the ministers of His Church were by Him appointed to do, He said to St. Peter, when restoring him after his fall to the Pastoral Office, not only "Feed my sheep," but also "Feed my lambs."

Close and vital connexion of Christian Education with Baptism.

Christ's solemn charge respecting each baptized infant.

How Christian Education is recognised in the restoration of St. Peter to the Pastoral Office.

What shall we say, after this, to a scheme of Education purely secular, from which Bible and Prayer-Book are to be carefully excluded, in which Christ and His Church are to have no part at all? Nay, what shall we say even to a much more apparently plausible scheme, of teaching the Bible to children without any authorized explanation of it? We must say, I fear, that even such a scheme as this last sets at defiance Christ's Ordinance of the Church as a teaching Society; that it labours under the fundamental defect, incidental to so many religious systems, of recognising a Christian

Hence it follows that Education apart from Religion, or even apart from the authority of the Church as a teaching Society, is condemned by Christ's commission to His Church.

Truth, while it discards the idea of an authority specially set and commissioned to teach the Truth; and that therefore those who do recognise the Church of Christ as a Divine Institution cannot be expected to give it sympathy or co-operation. If the Church is merely a society founded by man, and having no Divine Commission to teach and minister, or if she is merely a political engine taken into the service of the State, that of course alters the whole aspect of the question. *Then* no doubt we shall do right to employ Christian Truth in the training of our children, while we banish the Church, with her Creeds, her formularies, and her spiritual pastors.

Thus have we seen Christ instituting, first, the Christian Society, then United Prayer, then Preaching to the heathen, then the Sacrament of Baptism, then the instruction of the baptized (whether adults or children) in Christian Truth. And that the Church was to be perpetually replenished and extended on these principles,— *The Commission to be perpetuated to the successors of the Apostles.* that the great Corporation was to endure in an unbroken line to the Second Advent, handing down the Word and Sacraments to the latest generation, we gather from the latest words of the commission—"Lo, I am with you alway, even unto the end of the world;" to which asseveration, He who is the "Amen, the faithful and true witness," adds His own name, as a sort of seal *Deep significance of the 'Amen' at the close of it.* appended to His charter, "Amen!" as if He would say, "The existence of this Corporation, and My presence with her to the end of time, are matters of which I assure you on the faith of My own name." And His word has stood fast, even when it seemed, from the dark outlook, that it was failing. He has been ever with and in His Church, as He ever will be. Even in the days when she least seemed to realize His grand conceptions of what she ought to be, when superstitions were rife, corruptions flagrant, and a frightful usurpation of His own prerogatives was growing up within her pale, even then He was not absent. For was not the spirit, which should shake off these corruptions and superstitions, even then working within her? And was not that His own Spirit? When a tree sheds its leaves in autumn, and seems to outward eyes a bare pole, it is not really dead; it will bud and blossom next spring. And when the Church seemed stripped of all the comeliness, with which her Founder had decked her, and her spiritual life appeared to be well-nigh extinct, even then there was that within her, by which her youth should be renewed like the eagle's. According as it is written—"As a teil tree, and as an oak, whose substance is in them, when they cast their leaves: so the holy seed shall be the substance thereof."

Christ's Presence with His Church in the darkest periods of her existence, shown by the vigour with which she shook off her corruptions.

And here I should break off for the present, were it not that one word more requires to be said upon the nature and effect of the first Sacrament, which we have seen our Lord instituting.

No one, who has followed the argument hitherto, will fail to understand that Baptism is the form of admission to the Church. But the danger is, if we leave the subject thus, that we should think it to be nothing more. I believe there is a great want of clearness, in the minds even of seriously disposed and thoughtful persons, on this subject. Baptism involves and carries with it, as its necessary consequence, admission to the Church, and, indeed, is the divinely instituted form of admission. Nor does it at all conflict with this view, that, immediately after our public administration of Baptism, when the Sacrament (properly so called) is concluded, the priest is directed to say, while signing the child with the sign of the Cross, "We receive this child into the congregation of Christ's flock." This is the solemn assent, on the part of the Christian Society, to the admission of the child into the Church, which, as it has been received and blessed by Christ, has really taken place already, and only has to be[1] recognised by the congregation. The signing with the Cross is a mere ceremony (though a godly and a primitive one) of man's invention, and might be dispensed with without injuring the effect of the Sacrament. But let no one think that the affusion of water in the Name of the Holy Trinity is a mere cere-

Baptism the divinely instituted form of admission to the Church.

The signing with the sign of the Cross merely an assent to that admission on the part of the Christian Society.

---

[1] "As the thirtieth Canon distinctly says, the signing with the Cross adds nothing to the virtue and perfection of the Baptism, so also we must remember that neither are the accompanying words, 'We receive,' etc., any essential part of the Baptism. They have sometimes been spoken of as if by them the child was 'received into the Church:' but *the act of Baptism is the true reception into the Church, and these words are a ceremonial declaration only of that fact.* In this respect they are analogous to the words used by the Priest in the Marriage Service, after the essential part of the office is completed by the solemn adjuration, 'Those whom God hath joined together, let no man put asunder.' As the

mony. It is a passage from darkness to light, a new supernatural birth into a state of favour, pardon, and acceptance, a translation into the kingdom of God's dear Son, "in whom we have redemption through his blood, even the forgiveness of sins;" according to that word of Christ to Nicodemus, "Except a man be born of water and of the Spirit, he cannot enter into the kingdom of God." Possibly you may have thought that the outward form of Baptism is a matter of little or no moment, and that, should an unbaptized adult have sincere repentance and faith, his forgiveness, and all the other blessings involved in admission to the Church, would be secure, even without Baptism. But surely this view is framed upon our speculations of what God is likely to do, rather than on what He gives us reason to think He will do. What said Ananias to Saul of Tarsus after Saul's sincere conversion? "And now why tarriest thou?" (as much as to say, There is no time to be lost;) "arise, and be baptized, and wash away thy sins, calling on the name of the Lord." "Be baptized, and wash away thy sins." But how?

The outward visible sign of Baptism (where it may be had) shown to be essential to the remission of sins

---

Priest then *pronounces* that the married couple are 'man and wife together,' so here he *pronounces* that the baptized child has become one of the congregation of Christ's flock. This is made still more evident by the rubric and words of the Office for Private Baptism, '... *then shall not he christen the child again, but shall receive him as one of the flock of true Christian people, saying thus,* I certify you ... is now by the laver of Regeneration in Baptism received into the number of the children of God, and heirs of everlasting life.'"—Blunt's Annotated Book of Common Prayer, London, 1866. Note on p. 227. Col. 1.

by Ananias's exhortation to St. Paul.

Is not Saul yet forgiven then, deep as his repentance is, absolutely and unconditionally as he has surrendered his own will to that of Christ, ("Lord, what wilt thou have me to do?") fervently as he has cried to God from the very ground of a humbled heart, as it is said of him, "Behold, he prayeth"? No; his sins are yet upon him; he has yet to wash them away; and it is not obscurely intimated to him by God's messenger that this can only be done in the laver of regeneration; "Arise, and be baptized, and wash away thy sins, calling on the name of the Lord,"—counsel exactly the same as that which was tendered to the anxious inquirers on the day of Pentecost, "Repent, and be baptized every one of you in the name of Jesus Christ for the remission of sins, and ye shall receive the gift of the Holy Ghost." And this effect of Baptism is so fundamental a truth of our religion that it forms one of the Articles of the Faith, as declared at Nicæa: "I acknowledge one Baptism for the remission of sins." If it be objected, as it may be and has been, that the one man of whose forgiveness we have the most absolute assurance,—the penitent malefactor on the cross,—was pardoned and accepted without Baptism, the answer is really very much the same as if it were asked how it comes to pass that Abraham, and Moses, and David were pardoned and accepted without Baptism. Baptism, in the full sense of the term, Baptism with the Holy Ghost, was not formally instituted till after Christ's Resurrection, nor actually practised until the day of Pentecost. "The Holy Ghost was not yet

Saul, though repentant and believing, not forgiven till he was baptized.

Testimony of the Nicene Creed to the necessity of Baptism.

Objection arising from the case of the penitent malefactor answered.

given," when the penitent robber hung upon the cross; and he could not therefore have had a Baptism, which was not in existence. And even had it been in existence, he could have found no opportunity (under his circumstances) of receiving it; and surely we not only may, but must believe that, where there is really no possibility of complying with them, God will dispense even with His own Ordinances. The normal and regular way of salvation, since the effusion of the Holy Ghost on the day of Pentecost, is by "one Baptism for the remission of sins," accompanied of course, in the case of adults, by faith in the recipient. That God never in any instance alters or modifies these terms,—that, in cases widely different from our own, He may not apply the saving merits of Christ by other means than Baptism and faith, so as to extend them even to good heathens, who never had an opportunity of hearing of Jesus,— this it would be presumptuous in a high degree to assert. These were His terms for the three thousand convicted hearers at Pentecost. These were His terms for St. Paul. These are His terms for us; and with these we must comply, as we value our salvation.

Full Christian Baptism not in existence till after the day of Pentecost.

God dispenses with His Ordinances, where they cannot be had.

And here we must stop for the present in that walk about Zion, in the course of which we are setting ourselves, according to the exhortation of Psalm xlviii., to "tell her towers," "mark her bulwarks," and "consider her palaces." But not without a word of reference to our own circumstances. For that branch of the Church, in which we are most interested, and for which we ought to feel (from the great debt which we owe to her) the warmest and tenderest filial affection, the present is a most critical and anxious period. A *reformed* Church, which yet *is* a Church by something more than that courtesy which concedes the name to all professedly Christian communities,—a Church which stands resolutely upon the old foundation of "the apostles and prophets," and which yet has with equal resoluteness cleared her system of all unscriptural corruptions,—is peculiarly exposed to risks, in virtue of her double position. That position of necessity insures for her two classes of foes. She is disliked by those who cannot show the same title-deeds, or pretend to the same spiritual ancestry, with herself. She is equally disliked by those who have no sympathy with the action which she took at the Reformation. There will always be, as there have always been, two parties in her bosom, who represent respectively her connexion with the old Foundation, and her connexion with the Reformation; but not until quite recently has the mutual exasperation of these parties, like the struggle between the infants in Rebecca's womb, imperilled the existence of their common mother. Then, just as this struggle is growing desperate, a cry is raised, by those who are jealous of the Church's political position, for her disestablishment and disendowment—steps which, if carried into effect, would certainly weaken her already feeble powers of coherence, and split her into two or three narrow factions.

Marginalia:
Double aspect of the Church of England,
and the perils and difficulties entailed by it.
Aggravated struggle of the two great parties within the Church.
The cry for Disestablishment and disendowment.

While, further to complicate an already most difficult situation, the general foe of all goodness, and righteousness, and truth,—the foe who began his communications with mankind by the insinuation of a sceptical doubt, "Yea, hath God said?" and proceeded from a sceptical doubt to a flat infidel denial, "Ye shall not surely die,"—now no longer content with assaulting the Church from without, is making encroachments within her camp, and sapping the belief of her children in the supernatural, in Revelation, nay, in the Personality (*i.e.* in the existence) of God. *Scepticism within the Church, undermining the faith of her children.*

In such critical circumstances, what shall we do? One point of holy policy is, that our clergy should endeavour to give our own people a true insight into the preciousness of the spiritual inheritance which in the English Church has fallen to their lot; to lead them to appreciate the advantage of our own position among the Communions of Christendom,—a position at once Scriptural and Catholic. But this is only a small part of what has to be done. The Church must be saved by the love and loyalty of her laity, as much as by the exertions of her ministers. Show your value for Bible and Prayer-Book by studying them more deeply, and comparing them more thoughtfully. The Bible is the text of the Church of England, and the Prayer-Book is her Commentary,—a Commentary (as the late Professor Blunt has most conclusively shown in two Sermons before the University of Cambridge, with which every Churchman should make himself acquainted) which gives us faithfully the sense of the Primi- *The clergy should teach the people to appreciate the advantages of their position as English Churchmen.* *The laity should study more deeply, and compare Bible and Prayer-Book, and seek to understand their mutual relations;*

tive Church on the interpretation of Holy Scripture. And last, not least, cease not to implore Him, "who walketh in the midst of the seven golden candlesticks," that He would not remove our candlestick out of his place, that He would preserve our own beloved Church "from false Apostles," and cause her to be "guided by faithful and true pastors," that He would make her a burning and shining light—burning with love and zeal for His Name, and shining with the quiet ray of a holy and consistent example. Thus meeting the foes leagued against us, we shall not need to be afraid nor dismayed by reason of their great multitude; for the battle will not be our's, but God's. "The city of our solemnities" shall stand unmolested, as if surrounded by a broad and impassable river. "Thine eyes shall see Jerusalem a quiet habitation, a tabernacle that shall not be taken down; not one of the stakes thereof shall ever be removed, neither shall the cords thereof be broken. But there the glorious Lord will be unto us a place of broad rivers and streams; wherein shall go no galley with oars, neither shall gallant ship pass thereby. For the Lord is our judge, the Lord is our lawgiver, the Lord is our king; He will save us."

and all should implore the great Head of the Church to make our candlestick a burning and a shining light.

Catechism on Chap. XV.

1. *Question.*—To what part of Jewish history does Psalm xlviii. refer?

Answer.—Probably to the reign of King Jehoshaphat, when the kings of Moab, Ammon, and Edom invaded the territory of Judah,—a confederacy to which reference is made in verse 4: "Lo, the kings were assembled." (See 2 Chron. xx. 1, 10, 22, 23.)

2. *Question.*—How was this invasion frustrated?

Answer.—Jehoshaphat and all his people asked help of the Lord, and were assured by a prophet that their enemies should be discomfited without their striking a blow; which came to pass on the morrow; for when the singers that went before the Jewish army began to praise God, a panic seized the confederate kings, who turned their arms against one another, and fled in trepidation. To this flight those words of the Psalm refer: "They saw it, and so they marvelled; they were troubled, and hasted away. Fear took hold upon them there, and pain, as of a woman in travail." (Verses 5 and 6.) (See 2 Chron. xx. 5, 6, 14, 17, 21-24.)

3. *Question.*—But to what do verses 12 and 13 refer : "Walk about Zion, and go round about her: tell the towers thereof. Mark ye well her bulwarks, consider her palaces; that ye may tell it to the generation following"?

Answer.—To the fact, that the panic seized the confederate kings, when they first caught sight of the towers, bulwarks, and palaces of the Holy City. So that what was afterwards said of Sennacherib's invasion, might have been said of theirs : "The virgin, the daughter of Zion, hath despised thee, and laughed thee to scorn; the daughter of Jerusalem hath shaken her head at thee." (Isaiah xxxvii. 22.)

4. *Question.*—What is the Christian application of the words—"Walk about Zion, and go round about her," etc. ?

Answer.—Our Zion is the Church of Christ, of which the Holy City was but a figure; and accordingly these words of the Psalm will convey an admonition to survey and study the constitution of the Church, the provision which she makes for the spiritual life, and the defences which God has thrown around her.

5. *Question.*—What then is it proposed to do in the present Chapter?

Answer.—We propose to go round about the walls of the Christian Church, as it were on a tour of observation.

6. *Question.*—What was the order observed by God in the creation of man?

Answer.—His body was first formed of the dust of the ground—a body, as the Psalmist says, "fearfully and wonderfully made" (Psalm cxxxix. 14); and this body having been prepared, the breath of lives was afterwards breathed into it. (See Gen. ii. 7.)

7. *Question.*—Was an order similar to this observed in the creation of the Church?

Answer.—Yes. Christ may be said to have framed the body of the Church, when in the days of His flesh He gathered disciples round Him. He gave this body an organization and a particular structure, when He traced out the institutions and powers of the Church. And the body of the Church having been framed and prepared beforehand, the Holy Ghost descended into it on the day of Pentecost, to animate it with the Divine life.

8. *Question.*—During what period particularly, did our Lord organize His Church, and trace out the various features of it?

Answer.—During the forty days which elapsed between His Resurrection and Ascension.

9. *Question.*—What great objects were answered by this period of forty days?

Answer.—Christ was seen alive for forty days after His Resurrection, for the more confirmation of the Faith. It was God's design to put the fact of His Resurrection beyond all question. It was necessary, therefore, that the risen Saviour should appear on several occasions, to several persons, and under different circumstances; and all this required a considerable space of time.

10. *Question.*—Can you quote any text of Scripture to show that the forty days were designed to afford unquestionable evidence of the Resurrection?

Answer.—Yes. St. Luke, speaking of the Apostles, says, "To whom also he shewed himself alive after his passion by many infallible proofs, being seen of them forty days" (Acts i. 3).

11. *Question.*—What words immediately follow those you have just quoted, and to what other aspect of the forty days do they point?

Answer.—" And speaking of the things pertaining to the kingdom of God." The kingdom of God is the kingdom set up by " the God of heaven " in the days of the fourth or Roman Empire (see Dan. ii. 44); that is, the Christian Church. We are led to suppose, therefore, that during this period our Blessed Lord was engaged in tracing the outline of His Church, in sowing the seeds of Church Offices, Church Institutions, and Church Sacraments, which seeds were to be afterwards unfolded by His Apostles. Christ, like a wise master-builder, was tracing out the foundations of His Church during this period.

12. *Catechist.*—You said that the Apostles in after times unfolded the seeds that Christ had sown. Can you give any instance of their doing so?

Answer.—Yes. Christ instituted the Ministry of His Church, when He breathed upon the Apostles and said, " Receive ye the Holy Ghost," etc. (see St. John xx. 22, 23.) The Apostles developed this institution of the Ministry, when they appointed the seven Deacons to relieve them of the secular part of their work; see Acts vi. 3, 4, 5, 6. So again, Christ gave to His Church the power of binding and loosing (see St. Matt. xviii. 17, 18). The Apostles acted under this power, when they called a council to decide whether or not the Gentile converts should be subject to the ceremonial law, and issued a decree, loosing them from circumcision, and other ceremonial observances, but binding them to abstain from pollutions of idols, and from fornication, and from things strangled, and from blood (Acts xv. 19, 20, 28, 29).

13. *Catechist.*—In observing how Christ traced the foundations of the Church, the first thing which we have to look for is the charter of the Church's foundation. Where do we find it?

Answer.—In the following words, taken from St. Matthew xviii. 19, 20 : " Again I say unto you, That if two of you shall agree on earth as touching any thing that they shall ask, it shall be done for them of my Father which is in heaven. For where two or three are gathered together in my name, there am I in the midst of them."

14. *Question.*—How do you know that these words refer to the Church?

Answer.—Because in the immediately preceding context, to which the word "Again" refers us back, our Lord has been speaking expressly of His Church, and of the powers of excommunication and absolution with which He designed to endow her; see verses 15, 16, 17, 18 : " Moreover if thy brother shall trespass against thee, go and tell him his fault between thee and him alone : if he shall hear thee, thou hast gained thy brother. But if he will not hear thee, then take with thee one or two more, that in the mouth of two or three witnesses every word may be established. And if he shall neglect to hear them, tell it unto the church : but if he neglect to hear the church, let him be unto thee as an heathen man and a publican. Verily I say unto you, Whatsoever ye shall bind on earth shall be bound in heaven : and whatsoever ye shall loose on earth shall be loosed in heaven."

15. *Question.*—What two things do we discover in the verses now under consideration?

Answer.—First, the institution of the Ordinance of United Prayer, ver. 19 : " If two of you shall agree on earth as touching any thing that they shall ask, it shall be done for them of my Father which is in heaven." Secondly, the charter which declares what the Church is,—namely, an assembly of believers gathered together in Christ's Name,—and annexes to such an assembly the promise of His Presence: "For where two or three are gathered together in my name, there am I in the midst of them."

16. *Question.*—How does the Church endeavour to secure the agreement among worshippers, upon which the answer to United Prayer is suspended?

Answer.—By a Form of Common Prayer, with which all may acquaint themselves beforehand, and in the offering of which all may unite with heart and voice.

17. *Catechist.*—You said that the Church is declared by Christ to be an assembly of disciples gathered together in His Name. Does this declaration harmonize with our Lord's teaching and example?

Answer.—Remarkably so. It harmonizes with His teaching; for He constantly enjoined mutual love, and said that it was the badge by which His disciples should be known: "A new commandment I give unto you, That ye love one another; as I have loved you, that ye also love one another. By this shall all men know that ye are my disciples, if ye have love one to another" (St. John xiii. 34, 35). It harmonizes also with His example and manner of life, which was social, and not (like John the Baptist's way of life, or Elijah's) withdrawn from the haunts of men. "The Lord Jesus went in and out among us" (Acts i. 21); He accepted invitations (St. Luke vii. 36); attended weddings (St. John ii. 2); was found in the way of funeral processions (St. Luke vii. 12, 13); and testified of Himself, "I spake openly to the world; I ever taught in the synagogue, and in the temple, whither the Jews always resort; and in secret have I said nothing." (St. John xviii. 20.)

18. *Question.*—What pledge did our Lord give to His Church that He would be mindful of His promise to be in the midst of the two or three gathered together in His Name?

Answer.—After His Resurrection, when the little flock of disciples was gathered together in His Name, having shut the doors upon the unbelieving world, "came Jesus and stood *in the midst*, and saith unto them, Peace be unto you" (St. John xx. 19). And this happened on more than one occasion. (See St. John xx. 26; see also St. Luke xxiv. 13, 14, 15, 36, etc.)

19. *Catechist.*—We have found, in this promise to the two or three gathered together in Christ's Name, the earliest germ of the Christian Church, and of one great Ordinance of it, United Prayer. We must now inquire how new members were to be grafted into this Society thus founded; for, as you pointed out in a previous examination, no one can put himself into a society; he must be admitted into it according to its rules, by those who are members already. Where shall we find the rules of admission into His Church, which Christ laid down?

Answer.—In the five last verses of St. Matthew's Gospel, which run thus: "16. Then the eleven disciples went away into Galilee, into a mountain where Jesus had appointed them. 17. And when they saw him, they worshipped him: but some doubted. 18. And Jesus came and spake unto them, saying, All power is given unto me in heaven and in earth. 19. Go ye therefore, and teach all nations, baptizing them in the name of the Father, and of the Son, and of the Holy Ghost: 20. Teaching them to observe all things whatsoever I have commanded you: and, lo, I am with you alway, even unto the end of the world. Amen."

20. *Question.*—Is there reason to suppose that other disciples besides "the eleven" were present at this interview?

Answer.—Yes. It is generally thought that this was the interview referred to by St. Paul, when he says: "After that, he was seen of above five hundred brethren at once" (1 Cor. xv. 6).

21. *Question.*—Of what words does this supposition

offer an easy explanation, which else might present a little difficulty?

Answer.—Of the words in ver. 17, where it is said that "some doubted." The "some," who "doubted," may have been persons on the outskirts of the crowd, who could not at first command a good view of the Lord.

22. *Question.*—But if it was indeed the case that more than five hundred disciples were present, why does St. Matthew only mention the eleven? (ver. 17.)

Answer.—Because he would have us understand that the words of Christ which he gives us, and which contain the commission to evangelize the world, were spoken only to the eleven, the representatives of the whole body. It was not every one of those five hundred, who was bidden to go forth to the heathen with the Gospel message, and to bring them into the Church.

23. *Question.*—Where is it predicted in the Book of Psalms that the risen Saviour should claim for Himself, as given to Him by God, an authority over the Gentiles?

Answer. In the second Psalm, verses 7 and 8, we read: "I will declare the decree: the Lord hath said unto me, Thou art my Son; this day have I begotten thee. Ask of me, and I shall give thee the heathen for thine inheritance, and the uttermost parts of the earth for thy possession." The "begetting" of the Son means here the raising Him from the dead, as we see from Acts xiii. 32, 33: "And we declare unto you glad tidings, how that the promise which was made unto the fathers, God hath fulfilled the same unto us their children, in that he hath raised up Jesus again; as it is also written in the second psalm, Thou art my Son, this day have I begotten thee;" and also from Rev. i. 5, and Col. i. 18, where Christ is called "the first begotten of the dead," "the firstborn from the dead." Having been thus begotten from the dead, our Lord here claims the heathen for His inheritance, and the uttermost parts of the earth for His possession, by sending His Apostles to bring them to the obedience of faith, and to admit them into His Kingdom, the Church.

24. *Question.*—Why was "a mountain" (ver. 16) an appropriate scene for such a commission as this?

Answer.—Because a mountain is a lofty and exposed place, around which the four winds of Heaven perpetually blow. There was a freedom and universality in this message; "Go ye and teach all the nations," or (as St. Mark has it, chap. xvi. 15) "Go ye into all the world, and preach the gospel to every creature," which made a mountain a very suitable spot for its delivery.

25. *Question.*—What is the marginal translation given in the English Bible of the word "teach," in "Go ye and teach all nations"?

Answer.—*Make disciples*, or, *Christians of all nations.*

26. *Question.*—And how were the Apostles to do this?

Answer.—They were to do it to others in much the same way as their Master had done it to themselves. They had been arrested by the sight of His miracles, and led to pay attention to His words. These words had exerted a great power over them; they listened eagerly, and became deeply interested, and assured that He who spake such words must be an ambassador from God, with a message of hope and grace to men. They were to go forth with similar words, announcing to all mankind the forgiveness of sins through Christ, and exhorting to repentance and faith. And to insure their words being listened to, they were to have the miraculous powers which their Master had, at the outset of their mission.

27. *Question.*—What Ordinance of the Church, then, did our Lord institute, when He bade His Apostles go and make disciples of all nations?

Answer.—Missionary Preaching, the heralding of the

Kingdom of God and the Name of Jesus among the heathen, who have never heard of God or Christ.

28. *Question.*—And when the preaching has done its work, and the heathen have been brought by it to believe in Christ, how are they then formally to be "admitted into the fellowship of Christ's Religion"?

Answer.—This must be done by the Holy Sacrament of Baptism, which our Lord here institutes in these words: " Teach all nations, baptizing them in the name of the Father, and of the Son, and of the Holy Ghost." The more exact translation of which would be, "Make disciples of all the nations [by] baptizing them into the name," etc.

29. *Question.*—Why is the word "name" in the singular number, though the Father, the Son, and the Holy Ghost are all mentioned?

Answer.—To show that there is but One God, although there are three Persons in the Godhead.

30. *Question.*—How does our Lord prescribe that the Baptism of new converts shall be followed up?

Answer.—By Christian teaching. His Apostles were directed not only to baptize the heathen into the Name of the Holy Trinity, but also to teach them to observe all things whatsoever Christ had commanded.

31. *Question.*—What trace of this direction may be found in the Office for " the Ministration of Public Baptism of Infants"?

Answer.—As soon as the Infant has been baptized, and has been declared to be regenerate, and grafted into the body of Christ's Church, and after thanks have been given unto Almighty God for these benefits, the Priest is directed to address the Godfathers and Godmothers thus: " Ye must remember that it is your parts and duties to see that *this Infant* be taught, so soon as *he* shall be able to learn, what a solemn vow, promise, and profession *he hath* made by you. And that *he* may know these things the better, YE SHALL CALL UPON

HIM TO HEAR SERMONS; AND CHIEFLY YE SHALL PROVIDE, THAT HE MAY LEARN THE CREED, THE LORD'S PRAYER, AND THE TEN COMMANDMENTS, IN THE VULGAR TONGUE, AND ALL OTHER THINGS WHICH A CHRISTIAN OUGHT TO KNOW AND BELIEVE TO HIS SOUL'S HEALTH."

32. *Question.*—What two Ordinances does our Lord institute, when He bids His Apostles teach the people they had baptized to observe all things whatsoever He had commanded them?

Answer.—The instruction of Christian congregations in Divine Truth, and the religious education of the young.

33. *Question.*—How does it appear that the instruction of Christians in Divine Truth is a thing of a different character from preaching to the heathen?

Answer.—Because two different words are used to express it. The preaching to the heathen is called (as here) "making disciples of them," "preaching (or heralding) the gospel to them" (St. Mark xvi. 15). The instruction of Christians is called "a teaching them to observe all things whatsoever Christ commanded His disciples." The names being so different, we conclude that there is a difference in the things.

34. *Question.*—If the regular religious instruction of Christians, to which we commonly give the name of Preaching, be an Ordinance appointed by the Lord Himself, can it be right to sneer at preachers, and express great weariness of sermons?

Answer.—Certainly not. To feel God's Ordinances to be irksome must surely indicate a wrong state of mind. This was the sin of those of old, who said; "When will the new moon be gone, that we may sell corn? and the sabbath, that we may set forth wheat?" (Amos viii. 5.) And "The table of the Lord is polluted; and the fruit thereof, even his meat, is contemptible.... Behold, what a weariness is it!" (Mal. i. 12, 13.) And in the New Testament we are warned against a similar state of mind in reference to preaching: "The time will come when they will not endure sound doctrine; but after their own lusts shall they heap to themselves teachers, having itching ears; and they shall turn away their ears from the truth, and shall be turned unto fables " (2 Tim. iv. 3, 4).

35. *Catechist.*—You said that the words "teaching them to observe all things," embraced not only what we call Preaching (that is, the religious instruction of adults), but also the education of children in the principles of Divine Truth. How can you prove this?

Answer.—Our Lord must have foreseen that His Church, under the inspired guidance of His Apostles, would uniformly practise Infant Baptism. He must have known that, after the first establishment of His Church in any country, all the people of that country would receive Baptism as unconscious babes. And therefore, when He prescribes that Christian teaching shall always follow Baptism, He must have had in His thoughts the training of the young in the rudiments of Christian faith and practice.

36. *Question.*—Christ, then, having put Christian Education into very close connexion with Baptism, what sin do those commit who are not careful to follow up the Baptism of children with religious teaching?

Answer.—The sin of those who put asunder what God has joined together (see St. Mark x. 9). And who knows but that the neglect of a child's religious training, the failure to bring him up in the nurture and admonition of the Lord, may be the reason why Holy Baptism never seems to take in him its full effect?

37. *Catechist.*—You have already quoted the charge to see that the child is religiously educated, which is given to the Sponsors in the Baptismal Service. This charge is really given by Christ, who acts and speaks through the ministry of His ordained servants. To what charge given in the Old Testament may you compare it?

Answer.—To that which was given by Pharaoh's

daughter to the mother of Moses: "Take this child away, and nurse it for me, and I will give thee thy wages" (Exod. ii. 9). The baptized child, having been made a member of Christ's kingdom, is given back to its parents, to be by them reared for the glorious inheritance of that kingdom, and for the King thereof, who has just blessed and washed it in the laver of regeneration.

38. *Question.*—From what other passage of the New Testament besides that now before us (St. Matt. xxviii. 20) may we gather that the religious instruction of children is part of the work intrusted by Christ to the Ministers of His Church?

Answer.—From the charge given to St. Peter after the Resurrection to feed Christ's lambs as well as His sheep, St. John xxi. 15: "So when they had dined, Jesus saith to Simon Peter, Simon, son of Jonas, lovest thou me more than these? He saith unto him, Yea, Lord; thou knowest that I love thee. He saith unto him, Feed my lambs."

39. *Question.*—If Christ prescribed that His little ones should be taught all things whatsoever He commanded His disciples, can any plan of Education be right, of which the teaching of the things which He commanded does not form any part?

Answer.—Evidently not. In order that they may rightly and fully understand the things which Christ commanded His disciples, children will need to be taught other things, such as reading, and the rudiments of general knowledge. And they must also be taught to get their living. But these other branches of knowledge are principally valuable for the sake of the great end, which is to make them wise unto salvation, and to enable them to serve God in their calling, whatever it may be. Therefore to teach them nothing but to read, write, and sum, and earn their bread, is to stop short of the great end for which we teach them anything.

40. *Catechist.*—But the New Testament contains all that Christ commanded us. Will it not therefore

be quite enough if, when they can read, they are made to read the Bible, and left very much to themselves to gather the meaning of it?

Answer.—No. Christ commanded that His Ministers should teach the people. And in the words before us He constitutes His Church a teaching Society, and gives her a commission to teach. If we set aside His commission, and say that, because we have the Scriptures, we can do without it, we are in the arrogance of our hearts dispensing with the very aid which He has provided to guide us into all truth, and we cannot expect His blessing on the education of our children. Besides, no one ever did or could gather the true meaning of Holy Scripture without some human instruction. To understand anything of any book, a child must ask frequently to have it explained. The question is, who is to give the explanation?—a minister of Christ's Church, who will give it after the mind of the Church, and under the Church's sanction: or a person who perhaps feels an interest in the Bible as a piece of literature, but has no fixed settled faith in the doctrines which the Church has drawn out of the Bible, and has summed up in her Creeds, and Articles, and Formularies?

41. *Question.*—Will you now reckon up the institutions, of which we have found the earliest traces in these two passages of St. Matthew's Gospel?

Answer.—They are these: the Christian Society, United Prayer, Missionary Preaching, Holy Baptism, Preaching in the Christian Congregation, Religious Education. These things are all really found here, although in their earliest germ, just as the oak is really found in the acorn, and unfolded out of it.

42. *Question.*—What part of the great commission issued by Christ to His Apostles assures us that it was given not to themselves only, but to their successors?

Answer.—The end of it, in which He assures them, "Lo, I am with you alway, even unto the end of the world." Our Lord must have known that the Apostles would not live "unto the end of the world;" and therefore must have addressed Himself, not merely to the eleven men who surrounded Him at the time, but to all who should hereafter succeed them in their office and ministry, even down to the latest generations of mankind.

43. *Question.*—What is the force of the "Amen," with which this solemn assurance concludes?

Answer.—Like a seal affixed to a monarch's charter, it confirms the charter to which it is affixed. Our Lord calls Himself "the Amen, the faithful and true witness," in Rev. iii. 14; and, while on earth, He used to prefix His more solemn and weighty sayings with the words "Verily, verily," which are in the original "Amen, amen"—see St. John viii. 34, 51; x. 1; xiii. 16, 20, 21; xiv. 12; xvi. 20, 23; v. 19, 24, 25, etc. etc. The "Amen," therefore, at the end of this commission is, in a manner, a swearing by Himself, as if He would say: "As I am the Truth, and as my word is true, I will be with you, and with those who succeed you in your office of ministering God's Word and Sacraments, unto the end of Time."

44. *Question.*—But have there not been times, when the Church has seemed so overrun by superstitions and grievous abuses, and Christianity has been so corrupted by the traditions of men, that the one retained hardly a feature of the Society which Christ founded, and the other could hardly be recognised as the Religion which Christ taught? Has Christ's promise of being with His Church to the end of the world failed at such periods?

Answer.—No; His promise can never fail. Hath He said, and shall He not do it? or hath He spoken, and shall He not make it good? Christ is not always absent, when He does not exert His power. He gave no signs of His Presence, when He lay asleep in the ship; yet He was really there, and it needed only the cries of the Apostles to rouse Him, and make Him interpose for their safety. (See St. Mark iv. 35-40.) In like manner He has sometimes suffered His Church to be overwhelmed with errors and corruptions, and threatened even with destruction, that He might induce His true people to cry to Him to save His own ark. Even in the darkest and worst periods of her history, the Church has rallied from her disorders, has shaken off her corruptions, has purged herself, has thrown off her superstitions, and set herself again to her task of witnessing for God in the midst of a crooked and perverse generation. There must have been strength, and a principle of health in her, to make such a recovery possible; and this principle of health and strength has been the covenanted Presence of her Master. Snakes shed their old skins, deer their horns, trees their leaves; but it is only to clothe themselves with new skins, to put forth new horns, to sprout with new leaves. There is life in each of them, which enables them to throw off the old dress, and put on a new. And so, when the Church threw off her corruptions and abuses, and reformed her practice, she did this by the life which was in her. And this life consisted in her Master's Presence with her.

45. *Catechist.*—You have said in the course of this examination, that Baptism is the formal act of admission to the Church (*Question* 28). But is not this admission rather given by the act of signing the person baptized with the sign of the Cross, when the Priest is instructed to say, " We receive this child " (*or*, this person) "into the congregation of Christ's flock "?

Answer.—No; we are clearly taught in St. John iii. 5, that entrance into the kingdom of God (which is the Church) is *by water and the Spirit*. And the same truth is symbolized by the ancient custom of placing the baptismal font at the entrance of the church. The words "We admit this child," etc., mean merely that the Christian Society solemnly assents to the admission, and recognises it as having taken place, by certain words, and by the use of an outward sign.

46. *Question.*—Is Baptism, then, *nothing more* than the formal act of admission to the Church?

Answer.—Yes; much more. It is the passage out of a state of wrath into a state of grace, and carries with it forgiveness of sins, purchased for us by the Blood of Christ, and all other blessings of the Christian Covenant.

47. *Question.*—But would not God certainly forgive the sins of a repentant and believing soul, even without Baptism?

Answer.—There is no reason to think that He would do so *where Baptism can be had;* but, on the contrary, every reason to think He would not.

48. *Question.*—What passage of Holy Scripture are you referring to?

Answer.—To the exhortation given by Ananias to St. Paul after his conversion: " Arise, and be baptized, and wash away thy sins, calling on the name of the Lord " (Acts xxii. 16). St. Paul was at this time deeply penitent, and a true believer, as is shown by his asking, " Lord, what wilt Thou have me to do?" (Acts ix. 6); by his fervent prayers (see Acts ix. 11); and by his immediately afterwards preaching Christ in the synagogues as the Son of God (see Acts ix. 20). Yet his sins were not yet forgiven; for he is bidden to arise, and wash them away in Baptism, the "washing" being an allusion to the outward visible sign in this Sacrament—" water; wherein the person is baptized *In the name of the Father, and of the Son, and of the Holy Ghost.*"

49. *Catechist.*—But surely the malefactor on the cross was saved, and therefore must have been pardoned, without Baptism. Does not this seem to show that repentance and faith can procure pardon by themselves, independently of the Sacrament of Baptism?

Answer.—No; it shows nothing of the kind *under the present circumstances of the Church.* Full Christian Baptism, which was to be " with the Holy Ghost " (St.

Mark i. 8), and which is "birth of water and of the Spirit" (see St. John iii. 5), did not, and could not, exist before the day of Pentecost, when the Holy Ghost came down upon the disciples (see Acts ii. 4). Immediately after that descent of the Holy Ghost, Baptism is declared to be the appointed means for the remission of the sins of those who had been convicted of sin and converted to God. "Repent, and *be baptized every one of you in the name of Jesus Christ for the remission of sins*" (Acts ii. 38). This was said to those who were already "pricked in their heart," and asked the Apostles what they should do, evidently intending to follow the counsel given them (see Acts ii. 37.) To all appearance they were deeply penitent; and yet they are told that they must "be baptized in the name of Jesus Christ *for the remission of sins.*" The penitent malefactor, dying before this Baptism was or could be practised, *could not have had it;* and God does not require from any of us what it is impossible we should have.

50. *Catechist.*—Among the things which God's Word requires us to believe, we may well suppose that some are of greater, some of less importance. What reason is there for thinking that the spiritual effect of Baptism, rightly administered and rightly received, is a fundamental point of Christian Faith, and not a matter of lesser moment?

Answer.—The Nicene Creed, which is a very brief summary of the things to be believed, includes the effect of Holy Baptism among them; "*I acknowledge one Baptism for the remission of sins.*" These words are taken from St. Peter's counsel to his convicted hearers on the day of Pentecost, already quoted; "Repent, and *be baptized* every one of you in the name of Jesus Christ *for the remission of sins*" (Acts ii. 38).

51. *Question.*—What makes the position of the Church of England difficult to maintain under any circumstances?

Answer.—The fact that opposition to her comes

from two different and opposite quarters, from those who dislike the Scriptural purity of her doctrine, as adverse to the superstitions which they would graft upon it, and from those also who make light of (perchance because they themselves have it not) her Apostolical descent.

52. *Catechist.*—State briefly the features of our Church's position.

Answer.—The Church of England is both Scriptural and Apostolic, both pure and primitive, both Catholic and Reformed.

53. *Question.*—In addition to the difficulty inherent in her position, what present dangers threaten the Church from within and without?

Answer.—First, there is the mutual exasperation of the parties, who represent respectively the Catholic and the Reformed element in her constitution. The feud is very likely, if God's mercy prevent not, to rend in sunder the National Church, and to make of it two great religious factions.

54. *Question.*—What renders our present position more critical still?

Answer.—The clamour of the Dissenters for the disestablishment and disendowment of the Church, that is, for bringing the Church down, as regards her temporal advantages, to a level with the sects.

55. *Catechist.*—You say, " as regards her temporal advantages." Do you mean that her spiritual powers could not be affected by such a measure?

Answer.—Certainly not. She would still be the only true Church of Christ in England, and the only Communion which really holds the Lord's commission to preach and administer the Sacraments.

56. *Question.*—But what is the most alarming feature of the present crisis?

Answer.—The thinly-veiled scepticism which is springing up within the Church, and the tendency of which is to deprive Christianity of its supernatural, and indeed of its doctrinal element, and to reduce it to a lofty system of morality, illustrated by a great Example.

57. *Question.*—What steps should be taken by Churchmen in counteraction of these dangers?

Answer.—The clergy should inculcate, more habitually than they do, the advantages of the Church's position, and lead the people to appreciate them. The laity (whose exertions are equally needed with those of the clergy) should thoughtfully study and compare Bible and Prayer-Book, and acquaint themselves with the relation in which they stand to one another, as text and commentary. And all should lift up earnest prayer for our Church to Him " who walketh in the midst of the seven golden candlesticks," that He would not " remove our candlestick out of his place," but would send us faithful and true pastors, to order and guide us according to His will, and would make us a burning and shining light among the Communions of Christendom, giving us repentance for the past, and kindling upon the altar of our hearts the flame of zeal and love in the future.

CHAPTER V.

THE INSTITUTION OF THE MINISTRY, AND ITS RELATION TO THE CHURCH.

"Walk about Zion, and go round about her: tell the towers thereof. Mark ye well her bulwarks, consider her palaces; that ye may tell it to the generation following."—PSALM XLVIII. 12, 13.

The walk about the spiritual Zion resumed.

THE reader will remember that we are endeavouring to comply with this admonition in a spiritual sense. The Church is our Zion, which Christ founded as a shelter, a house, a place of defence for the spiritual life. And we are now going "round about" the Church, to observe the "towers" and "bulwarks" with which He has fortified, and the "palaces" with which He has beautified, her; in other words (dropping the language of figure), we are accompanying our Lord in thought, as He traces the ground-plan of His Church, upon which His Apostles were subsequently to build. We have examined the words by which He formed the Society, and endowed it with His Presence, and those also by which He provided for its extension, and for the instruction of its members, juvenile and adult, in His own life-giving Truth.

CH. V.] *Institution of the Ministry.* 141

In this Chapter we resume our walk round the circuit of the walls of Zion.

Though the word "Church" is of frequent occurrence in the Acts and Epistles (when there *was* a Church), our Lord only uses it on two occasions. But in what He says on these occasions, He opens out a view of the whole subject. One of them is the passage in which, as an acknowledgment of St. Peter's confession, He promises to build His Church "upon this rock." It formed the subject of our first Chapter, and must presently be referred to again. The other is the passage quoted, and partly explained in the last Chapter, in which He directs that the offence of an erring brother (if he will not listen to a private remonstrance) shall be told to the Church, and that the Church (if he neglect to hear it) shall excommunicate him, or deal with him as a heathen man and a publican. "Nobody" (He proceeds—I give the meaning of the words in a free paraphrase) "should think lightly of this censure, for it will be ratified in heaven. The Church hath great power with heaven; for the united prayer of even two or three of you, gathered together in my Name, shall be accepted and answered. And this because I am myself with the Society which I found, however small on any particular occasion its numbers may be."

The word 'Church' only used in the Gospels on two occasions:

in the promise to St. Peter;

and in the direction how to deal with trespassing brother.

We are now about to see Christ's Institution of the Ministry of the Church, and the relation which He designs the Ministry to bear to the Church itself. This relation it is very necessary to understand correctly; and the passage before us throws a great deal of light upon it.

It will be well to have it before us in full. It is found in St. Matt. xviii. 15, *et sequent.* (St. Matt. xviii. 15) "Moreover if thy brother shall trespass against thee, go and tell him his fault between thee and him alone: if he shall hear thee, thou hast gained thy brother. But if he will not hear thee, then take with thee one or two more, that in the mouth of two or three witnesses every word may be established. And if he shall neglect to hear them, tell it unto the church: but if he neglect to hear the church, let him be unto thee as an heathen man and a publican" (in other words, let him be excommunicated,—a practice well known among Jews, and which went among them by the names of being "cast out of the synagogue," and being "delivered unto Satan"). St. Paul echoes this precept of our Lord, for the direction of the Church at Corinth, when he bids them excommunicate one of their members, who had committed incest. "But now I have written unto you not to keep company, if any man that is called a brother" (a Christian brother) "be a fornicator, or covetous, or an idolater, or a railer, or a drunkard, or an extortioner; with such an one no not to eat. For what have I to do to judge them also that are without?" (without the pale of the Church; referring to what he had said just before, that they were not to separate themselves from the *heathen* world; for how should they then be "the light of the world," and "the salt of the earth?" it was not the Apostle's business, or the

Remarkable coincidence between our Lord's directions for excommunication and the record of St. Paul's practice of it.

Church's, to *censure* the heathen, but to *convert* them) "do not ye judge them that are within" (the members of your own body)? "but them that are without God judgeth. Therefore put away from among yourselves that wicked person." In the earlier part of the Chapter we find that the act of excommunication was to be performed "in the name of our Lord Jesus Christ, when ye are *gathered together*, and my spirit, with the power of our Lord Jesus Christ." Observe how exactly this language agrees with that of our Lord, in the context of the passage we are considering. For he traces up the force of excommunication, as also the force of united prayer, to this very simple principle; "For where two or three are *gathered together in my name*" ("*in the name of our Lord Jesus Christ, when ye are gathered together*"), "there am I in the midst of them" (there is "*the power of our Lord Jesus Christ*," to second the sentence). Observe, too (for we must make use of the observation presently) that excommunication is the act of the whole Church, headed by the Apostle; "I have determined, when ye are gathered together, *and my spirit*" (the Apostle could not be present in person, but he would be there in spirit, when the censure was pronounced) ... "to deliver such an one unto Satan." And we find from the Second Epistle that the same parties must concur in relieving a person from this censure. St. Paul there directs the Church to forgive and comfort the offender, who by the sentence of excommunication had been brought to a right mind; and then says; "To whom ye forgive anything, I

The parties which must concur in inflicting, and in relieving from, a sentence of excommunication.

forgive also" (as if the sentence of absolution could not be ratified without his apostolic authority): "for if I forgave anything, to whom I forgave it, for your sakes forgave I it in the person of Christ."

Of excommunication I need say no more than that it is an exercise by the Church of the power, which every society possesses, of expelling such members as bring discredit upon it. If we wish to understand what the moral power and use of excommunication was in the Apostolic Church,—what it might be even now, if united—we may gather some idea of it from the happy result of what is called expulsion in schools and colleges. A youth is doing mischief, leading others into evil, setting an example of indolence and vice, which is infectious to younger boys. In this case the ringleader must be sent away; and one such removal is often sufficient to restore the moral tone of the school. Excommunication is the expulsion by the Church of her own unworthy members, as absolution is their re-instatement in membership on their true repentance. And what makes excommunication so much more serious than expulsion from an ordinary society (what justifies the application to it of such awful names as the being "delivered unto Satan,") is that the Church is a divinely founded Society, the very kingdom of God planted by Christ among the children of men.

But our Lord proceeds thus, after bidding the Church excommunicate the offending brother; "Verily I say unto you, Whatsoever ye shall

The moral power of excommunication exhibited on a small scale, in the expulsion of mischievous members from Schools and Colleges.

bind on earth shall be bound in heaven: and whatsoever ye shall loose on earth shall be loosed in heaven."

The first thing to be observed here is that in the sixteenth Chapter this very power of binding and loosing, which is here lodged with the whole Church ("Whatsoever YE shall bind ... whatsoever YE shall loose"), is given specifically to one only of the Apostles, St. Peter (verse 19), "And I will give unto THEE the keys of the kingdom of heaven" (or Church; the "keys" are doubtless the Word and Sacraments of God, by the use of which St. Peter, first on the day of Pentecost, and afterwards in the house of Cornelius, threw open the doors of the Church, or kingdom of God, for the admission of Jews and Gentiles): "and whatsoever THOU shalt bind on earth shall be bound in heaven: and whatsoever THOU shalt loose on earth shall be loosed in heaven." But what is meant by "binding" and "loosing?" It will be safe to understand by these terms every exercise of Church authority. Partly, excommunication and re-instatement, like that of the incestuous man of Corinth.—The "binding" is also to be understood of those words of censure sometimes spoken by the Apostles, which were attended with a judgment on the offender. St. Peter "bound" Ananias and Sapphira, when he remonstrated with them for their falsehood and sacrilege, and they fell dead at his feet (which last was Heaven's ratification of the binding). St. Paul "bound" Elymas the sorcerer, when he called him the "child of the devil," the "enemy

The power of binding and loosing lodged at one time with the whole Church, at another with a single Apostle.

The meaning of 'binding' and 'loosing.'
1st. Excommunication, and relief from it.

2dly. Censure, followed by temporal judgments, and relief from it.

of all righteousness," and doomed him to be blind for a season, a sentence which immediately came to pass.—But the words have a broader sense than this. The authoritative permission of anything was called by the Jewish doctors "loosing" it (or making it free to people); the authoritative prohibition of it was called "binding" it (or tying it up). So when the first Christian Council at Jerusalem authoritatively declared that the Gentile converts need not circumcise their children, nor observe the Mosaic ritual, this was a "loosing." And when that Council charged them nevertheless to abstain from meats offered to idols, and other abominable things which went on in heathen temples; and when St. Paul, in his First Epistle to the Corinthians, bids Christians not partake of such meats, if a weak brother would be scandalized by their doing so, this was a "binding."—Further still: the authoritative administration of the Sacraments through which, as the appointed channels, mercy and grace are conveyed to man's soul; the authoritative preaching of the Name of Jesus Christ, as that whereby alone we must be saved, and the announcing to men God's offer of pardon and reconciliation through Him, is a "loosing" (a means of releasing the conscience from the guilt of sin). So is every formal absolution, every formal benediction. And, on the contrary, the withholding these means of grace from any one,—the withholding Baptism from a heathen, because he is not yet considered fit for it, or the Lord's Supper from a Christian, because by some grievous sin he has

3bly. Authoritative prohibition and permission.

4thly. The withholding or granting of Sacraments;

Or 5thly. Of any appointed means of grace,

caused a scandal among the congregation, or the rite of burial from one, who had died in a fit of intoxication, or with an avowal of infidelity on his lips,—this would be a "binding," or (in another Scriptural phrase, which is as nearly as possible equivalent) a "retaining of sins." *or even of any rite of the Church.*

And thus we arrive at the passage where this latter phrase occurs, and in which our Blessed Lord institutes the Ministry of His Church, or, in other words, appoints the officers of the Society which He had founded. This great appointment was made on the evening of the first Easter Day. Here is the account of it:—"Then the same day, at evening, being the first day of the week, when the doors were shut where the disciples were assembled for fear of the Jews, came Jesus and stood in the midst" (in exact fulfilment of His foregone assurance, "Where two or three are gathered together in my name, there am I in the midst of them"), "and saith unto them, Peace be unto you. And when he had so said, he shewed unto them his hands and his side. Then were the disciples glad, when they saw the Lord. Then said Jesus to them again" (now here He is speaking to the ten Apostles only, even supposing others to have been present, as is evident from His employing the very verb, from which the word "apostle," which means "a sent one," is derived), "Peace be unto you: as my Father hath sent me" (our Lord is called "the *Apostle* of our profession" in the Epistle to the Hebrews), "even so send I you. And when he had said this, he breathed on them, and saith *Christ's institution of the Ministry on the evening of the Resurrection Day.*

unto them, Receive ye the Holy Ghost: Whosesoever sins ye remit, they are remitted unto them; and whose soever sins ye retain, they are retained." That this passage is connected with the Ordination (or appointment) of Ministers, and that our Church finds in it one of her warrants for Ordination, is clear from the fact that it makes part of the solemn sentence, by which Priest's Orders are still administered among us,—the sentence which accompanies the imposition of hands, and which runs thus; "Receive the Holy Ghost for the Office and Work of a Priest in the Church of God, now committed unto thee by the Imposition of our hands. Whose sins thou dost forgive, they are forgiven; and whose sins thou dost retain, they are retained. And be thou a faithful Dispenser of the Word of God, and of his holy Sacraments; In the Name of the Father, and of the Son, and of the Holy Ghost. Amen."

Without entering into particulars about the meaning of the words "remitting" and "retaining" sins, which might not only lead us much beyond our limits, but involve us in controversy (a thing foreign to the purpose of this work), let us take them in that broad and incontrovertible sense, in which the soundest divines of our Church (Barrow,[1] for instance, and many others) have understood and expounded them, and which the charge that follows them in the sentence of Ordination (to be "faithful in dispensing God's Word and Sacraments") seems to impose upon them. So understood and explained, they mean almost

---

[1] See his treatise *De Potestate Clavium*.

(if not quite) the same as the "binding and loosing," of which we have spoken already. The Ministry of the Gospel is a ministry of reconciliation. The great message of God's Word is, "We pray you in Christ's stead, be *ye reconciled* to God." The one Baptism is "for the *remission of sins*," and subsequently for "*the gift of the Holy Ghost.*" The chalice of the Holy Supper represents and conveys Christ's "blood of the New Testament, which is shed for many *for the remission of sins.*" And in special connexion with the Eucharist, as the great Christian "sacrifice of praise and thanksgiving," we pray that by the merits and death of God's Son Jesus Christ, "and through faith in his blood, we and all thy whole Church may obtain *remission of our sins*, and all other benefits of his passion." Thus the Word and Sacraments of God are the golden conduit-pipes, through which the golden oil of grace, mercy, and peace is poured into man's heart.—Now the Apostles, who represented all ministers to the end of time, in whose ministry all lesser ministries were bound up, as the prismatic colours in the sun, and from whose ministry all lesser ministries are derived, as separate rills from the fulness of a broad and brimming river, were the appointed and ordained administrators of these Ordinances. Where they preached and ministered, there mercy and grace flowed forth to the people through the channel of their ministry. Where they did not preach and minister, there the fountains of mercy and grace were in a manner sealed up. And in this sense, as ministerially the *media*,

[margin: Broad sense of the words, as meaning that the Ministry of the Apostles, and every other Ministry, so far as it is a reproduction of theirs, is the appointed medium through which forgiveness, and all other blessings of the Christian Covenant, flow forth to men.]

through which God's pardoning mercy and restoring grace reached man, "whose soever sins" the Apostles remitted, they were remitted unto them, and "whose soever sins" the Apostles retained, they were retained. And so far forth as any modern and uninspired ministry is a reproduction of the ministry of the Apostles, so far as it is exercised in their spirit, and sets forth their doctrine, as well as proceeds under their commission,—so far, no doubt, the remission and retaining of sins accompanies it also. For that remission and retention is necessarily bound up in the Gospel Ministry.

II. But now we advance to the most delicate and important part of our subject,—the relation which the Ministry of the Church bears to the Church itself. The point is very simple, and may be easily understood by one or two familiar illustrations.

In the passages of the New Testament which we have just reviewed, we observe that the very same power of "binding" and "loosing," which is given first to St. Peter by himself, is given very soon afterwards to the whole body of believers,—to the "two or three gathered together" in Christ's Name. And we observe also that an exactly similar power, that of "remitting and retaining sins," is given also to the Apostles generally, in their character of Apostles, or sent ones.

With whom is the power of binding and loosing really lodged, This raises the question, To whom is the power of binding and loosing, remitting and retaining (*i.e.* as I have explained, carrying on under Christ's commission the great ministry of reconciliation), really given? with whom is it really lodged? Is it with the whole Church (that is, with the whole assembly of baptized believers,) as would seem to be the case from His saying to all His disciples, "Whatsoever YE shall bind on earth shall be bound in heaven?" Or is it with the clergy of the Church only, as would seem to be the case from His giving to His Apostles, when sending them forth in His Name, the power of remitting and retaining sins? In other words, are these powers intrusted to the Society which Christ founded, or only to the officers of the Society?

With the Society or with its officers?

The answer is, (and it is an answer which reconciles the Scriptural notices on the subject, and puts the whole question of the Christian Ministry on its right footing,) that the powers in question are indeed the powers of the whole body, and to be exercised for the benefit of the whole body; but that they are delegated to Christian Ministers as the organs and representatives of the body,—for which reason, though the powers belong essentially to all, it does not follow that all have the right to exercise them.

In all ministerial acts, Christian Ministers act as organs and representatives of the Church, or Society of the faithful.

First, as *organs*.[1] Take an illustration from the

Christian Ministers the organs of the Church.

---

[1] This illustration is borrowed entirely from that very valuable volume, the Bampton Lectures of the present Bishop of Salisbury. The illustration drawn from political representatives is one which I ventured to use in another work, published many years ago. I am greatly pleased to find that the same idea has occurred to Bishop Moberly, and is sanctioned by him.

Illustration from the natural body, the whole of which is endowed with sensation, while at the same time there are special organs, through which sensation is exercised.

natural body. The whole body is endowed with sensation, even down to the extremities. Sensation is not the endowment of a part, but is distributed over the whole. And that sensation is one and the same thing (though the impressions which come to us through the eye, the ear, the touch, are very different in character) may be gathered from the well-known fact that, when a man is deprived of one sense, other senses grow keener. Thus blind people acquire a wonderful delicacy of touch, enabling them (it is said) occasionally to ascertain the colour of a piece of stuff by feeling it. This seems to show that the eye, the ear, the hand, the palate, and so forth, are only avenues of sensation, doors by which sensation goes forth from sensitive creatures, and that, when one door is shut, the sensibility which is spread over the body rallies more strongly at the other doors. Here then is an image of the relation, which the Ministry bears to the Church at large. Christian Ministers are to the Church what the eye, the ear, the palate (and so forth), are to the body,—organs, through which it puts forth its powers and receives impressions. These powers and impressions really belong to the whole body, not exclusively to the Ministry. Life is not the special endowment of the eye, or of the ear, or of the hand; it is the general endowment of the body, which lives in the eye, and the ear, and the hand,—sees in the one, hears in the other, feels in the third. The whole Church of Christ—laity as well as clergy—is endowed with the life of the Holy Ghost, breathed into it continually by its risen Head.

But this does not at all militate against the other truth, that the Ministers of the Church are the organs by which she exerts her powers, by which she utters and expresses herself, and through which also (as through an eye or an ear) she receives that mercy, grace, and peace, which are in the natural world what light and music are in the spiritual.

But Christian Ministers are representatives, as well as organs, of the Church. And this at least is a point which is very easily seized. The priesthood of the Jewish Church was, it will be remembered, a representative priesthood. Originally, the first-born of Israel, the eldest male children of all the families in the nation, were consecrated to God, in commemoration of their having been spared, when the first-born of the Egyptians were destroyed. But afterwards, because such an arrangement might have been inconvenient, the Levites were substituted for the first-born, and made to represent them. "Take the Levites," said the Lord, "instead of all the first-born of the children of Israel." That in the Christian Ministry also there is the same principle of representation, may be gathered from the messages which St. John is instructed to send to the angels of the Seven Churches in Asia. By the angels are meant the bishops who governed those Churches. And a study of the Epistles will show that they are not addressed to the bishops, as individual Christians, but as representatives of the respective Churches over which they presided. In short, it is not so much the bishop who is addressed,

Christian Ministers representatives of the Church.

Representative character of the Jewish priesthood.

The angels (or bishops) of the Seven Asiatic Churches, addressed in the Revelation as representatives of the Churches over which they presided.

as the Church, which is addressed *through* its bishop. I will only quote one passage in proof of what I say; "Unto the angel of the church in Smyrna write. . . . Fear none of those things which *thou* shalt suffer:" (but it does not follow hence that the bishop himself in his own person would suffer, though doubtless he would be a sharer with the rest in the sufferings of Christ; for the verse proceeds), "behold, the devil shall cast *some of you* into prison, that *ye* may be tried; and *ye* shall have tribulation ten days." The "thou" is only addressed as representing the "ye." Every Church is summed up in its bishop, and takes its tone from him.

Representative character of the Christian clergy recognised by the word 'Parson.'

Much is it to be deplored that the English word, which expresses this representative character of the clergy, has been so vulgarized as almost to unfit it for serious use. "Persona" in Latin means a representative, one who plays the part, and sustains the character, of another. Brought into the English tongue, this word became "person," and was applied to the clergy, because in their respective parishes they represent the Church of Christ. You have it in this form in Chaucer;

"There was a poure Persone of a toun;"

(that is, a poor city clergyman). The word still exists, and is applied to the clergy, though the *e* has been changed into *a*,—a change which not only vulgarizes it, but hides its derivation.

The clergy, then, are representatives of the Church. And our political constitution has made us familiar with the office and duties of representatives. Our House of Commons consists of representatives of the people. They are the popular element in the Legislature. They derive all their power, as well as their appointment, from the people. The member for any constituency is sent to Parliament, to act for the constituency in matters of legislation, to speak in their interests, and make their voice heard. He is to be their organ; he has no position independent of them; he has no power but what they (by the votes of the majority) have intrusted to him for the common benefit. But, on the other hand, it is abundantly clear, that once elected and sent to Parliament, he has a right to do many things, which they have no right to do; many things with which they must not presume to meddle. We may say with truth that the members for our county and borough derive all their power from ourselves; but that does not give to any one of us the right to make a speech in the House of Commons, or even to enter the House without permission. This very simple and easy illustration explains (perhaps better than any other could) the true relation between the Christian Ministry and the Church. Every power which we, as Christian Ministers, can be supposed to exercise, even the very highest,—excommunication, absolution, benediction, authoritative declaration and exposition of God's Word, consecration of the elements in the holy Eucharist,—is strictly and essentially a Church power; it was lodged with the Church at first, and we exercise it merely as delegates and representatives of the

[margin: Political representatives describe their power from the people, and yet have prerogatives which the people may not usurp;]

[margin: and so the clergy, who are representatives of the Church.]

whole body of Christ, or (if you please) merely as trustees, who are bound to administer it for the benefit of the party to whom it was bequeathed.

"All the congregation are holy," said rebellious Korah, "every one of them, and the Lord is among them." So far Korah spoke the truth, and had right on his side. All the people of Israel *were* holy, and the Lord *was* among them. All the Christian Church is holy, every member of it; and the Lord is in the midst of the two or three gathered together in His Name, even where there is no Minister and no Ministry. Moreover, every private Christian is a priest, bound to offer up privately on the altar of Christ's Atonement the incense of prayer, the sacrifice of praise, of alms, and of his own body.—But while Korah had one right premiss in his argument, his conclusion was desperately (may I not say damnably?) wrong, and he and all his company bitterly rued their false logic. Though all the congregation were holy, every one of them, God had appointed the seed of Aaron *exclusively* to offer incense before the Lord, and to fulfil the other functions of priesthood. Aaron and his family, in claiming the exclusive right to exercise those functions, had *not* taken too much upon them, nor lifted up themselves above the congregation of the Lord, since they had been expressly called of God to that great Ministry. And, as we all know, miserably did the cavillers against their prerogative perish. And in later days King Uzziah was made an example of the sinfulness of a similar usurpation of sacred functions.

I would not *unduly* press the parallel between the Levitical and the Christian Ministry; but I would insist upon the great principles which underlie it. The individual priesthood of the Christian laity is entirely compatible with the official priesthood of the Christian clergy. All the powers of the priesthood are the Church's powers; but that, while true, is far from warranting any unauthorized member of the Church in exercising them. Many of our laity, animated doubtless by a laudable ambition to do good, mixed up with the desire (natural to all of us) of saying their say on subjects which interest them, are coveting the office of preachers; while others presume (and surely it is a great presumption) to thrust themselves into the office without any call from the Church. Whether or not devout and well-educated laymen might not (after due examination, such as the clergy have to submit to) be licensed by the bishops to preach, with advantage to the Church (as has been the case in former times), it is for the bishops themselves to consider. But with every respect for the large amount of good motive in those who take upon themselves a sacred office without any authorization, I confess that, looking at their action only in the light of Holy Scripture, I cannot help regarding it as (I am using the mildest terms I can find) questionable and hazardous in the highest degree. Were I to undertake such a task without recognition from the Church, the awful words "that he be not as Korah, and as his company," would come chiming in with a jangling disso-

Encroachment upon ministerial functions condemned by this narrative, and by that of Uzziah's leprosy.

nance amidst the echoes of my own voice; and the question whether any man's preaching could be of such importance to the Church, that it must be had at any rate, even in defiance of her own rules, would thoroughly disquiet me in my work. But I desire to judge no man by my own conscience. To his own Master the unauthorized preacher must stand or fall. Suffice it that the author has done his best to give a popular view of the relation subsisting between the Ministry and the Church. It is the reader's part to consider that view, and, if found to be according to the teaching of God's Word, to accept and act upon it.

Catechism on Chap. V.

1. *Question.*—Why is the word "Church" of much rarer occurrence in the Gospels than in the Acts of the Apostles and the Epistles?

    Answer.—Because the Church, though all its foundations were marked out by our Lord Himself, can hardly be said to have been in existence during the period which is described in the Gospels. Hence we hear very little of the Church until after the day of Pentecost, when it was first set up.

2. *Question.*—How often does our Lord use the word "Church"?

    Answer.—Only on two occasions, both of which are recorded in St. Matthew's Gospel. In acknowledgment of St. Peter's confession of Him, our Lord says (St. Matt. xvi. 18): "And I say also unto thee, That thou art Peter, and upon this rock I will build *my church;* and the gates of hell shall not prevail against it." And a little further on in the same Gospel He gives this rule as to the right manner of dealing with an erring brother (chap. xviii. 15, 16, 17): "Moreover, if thy brother shall trespass against thee, go and tell him his fault between thee and him alone: if he shall hear thee, thou hast gained thy brother. But if he will not hear thee, then take with thee one or two more, that in the mouth of two or three witnesses every word may be established. And if he shall neglect to hear them, tell it unto *the church;* but if he neglect to hear *the church*, let him be unto thee as an heathen man and a publican."

3. *Question.*—What is the subject of the present Chapter?

Answer.—The institution of the Christian Ministry, and the relation which it bears to the Church.

4. *Question.*—What passages of Holy Scripture give us instruction on these points?

Answer.—Two principally; the first, that which was last quoted from St. Matthew; the second, that which records the interview of our Lord with His disciples on the evening of the day of His Resurrection (St. John xx. 19-24).

5. *Question.*—In the first of these passages, what do you understand by the words, "Let him be unto thee as an heathen man and a publican"?

Answer.—Let him be excommunicated, and put out of the pale of the Christian Society.

6. *Question.*—Do we find St. Paul echoing this precept of our Lord?

Answer. Yes. He thus writes to the Corinthians with special reference to a member of their Church, who had committed the sin of incest: "Now I have written unto you not to keep company, if any man that is called a brother be a fornicator, or covetous, or an idolater, or a railer, or a drunkard, or an extortioner; with such an one no not to eat. . . . Therefore put away from among yourselves that wicked person" (1 Cor. v. 11, 13).

7. *Question.* What name does he give to this separation of a man from the Christian Society?

Answer.—He calls it "a judgment of them that are within" (a censure, that is, of those who are within the pale of the Church). As for those who are "without" (or beyond) the pale, he says it is not for him to censure them; they are to be left to the judgment of Almighty God. This throws great light upon the admonitory clauses of the Athanasian Creed, and other like censures of the Church. We do not pronounce in them any judgment whatever upon the heathen, not even upon such heathen as have heard, but not closed with, the offers of the Gospel, much less upon those to whom the Gospel has never been made known. "What have I to do to judge them also that are without? . . . them that are without God judgeth" (1 Cor. v. 12, 13).

8. *Question.*—By what other more awful term does the Apostle describe excommunication?

Answer.—He calls it "a delivering unto Satan for the destruction of the flesh." The words are: "For I verily, as absent in body, but present in spirit, have judged already, as though I were present, concerning him that hath so done this deed, in the name of our Lord Jesus Christ, when ye are gathered together, and my spirit, with the power of our Lord Jesus Christ, to deliver such an one unto Satan for the destruction of the flesh, that the spirit may be saved in the day of the Lord Jesus" (1 Cor. v. 3, 4, 5).

9. *Question.*—What observation have you to make on the words, "In the name of our Lord Jesus Christ, when ye are gathered together, and my spirit"?

Answer.—That they coincide remarkably with the words of our Lord in St. Matthew (xviii. 20); "For where two or three are gathered together in my name, there am I in the midst of them," especially when it is remembered that these last words occur in the same paragraph which directs us to regard "as an heathen man and a publican" an offending "brother," who neglects "to hear the Church," and in which the disciples are assured that "whatsoever" they "shall bind on earth shall be bound in heaven;" (see St. Matt. xviii. 17, 18.) Both passages seem to make "the gathering together" of the faithful "in the name of Jesus" to be essential to the infliction of a censure of excommunication.

10. *Question.*—Does the presence of the Apostle seem to have been essential also?

Answer.—Yes; for he says, "When ye are gathered together, and *my spirit.*" He could not be with them in body; but it was necessary that he should be there in spirit, directing the infliction of the censure, as one of Christ's ambassadors. Therefore at the beginning of the Chapter he says: "I verily, as absent in body, but *present in spirit*, have judged already, as though I were present, concerning him that hath so done this deed" (1 Cor. v. 3). And, when the censure was to be taken off, we find the Apostle speaking of his own action in the matter as necessary to be joined with the action of the Church: "So that contrariwise ye ought rather to forgive him, and comfort him, lest perhaps such an one should be swallowed up with overmuch sorrow.... To whom ye forgive any thing, *I forgive* also: for if I forgave any thing, to whom I forgave it, for your sakes *forgave I it in the person of Christ*" (2 Cor. ii. 7, 10).

11. *Question.*—How may we form some notion of the moral power which excommunication had in primitive times, when the Church was a small and united body?

Answer.—By observing the power which the expulsion of one ringleader in evil often exerts in a school or college. An infectious example and an unwholesome influence is gotten rid of, and the moral tone of the school or college is restored.

12. *Question.*—In what words does our Lord assure His

Church that their sentences of excommunication and absolution shall be ratified by God?

Answer.—"Verily I say unto you, Whatsoever ye shall bind on earth shall be bound in heaven: and whatsoever ye shall loose on earth shall be loosed in heaven" (St. Matt. xviii. 18).

13. *Question.*—What is the first observation to be made here?

Answer.—That the same power which is here lodged with the whole Church, had been already given to St. Peter alone. "And I will give unto thee the keys of the kingdom of heaven: and whatsoever *thou* shalt bind on earth shall be bound in heaven: and whatsoever *thou* shalt loose on earth shall be loosed in heaven" (St. Matt. xvi. 19).

14. *Question.*—How are we to understand the terms "binding" and "loosing"?

Answer.—We may understand them generally of every exercise of Church authority, in the way of censure or absolution, of restriction or permission. Thus the delivering the incestuous person unto Satan (1 Cor. v. 5) was a "binding." So also was the censure of St. Peter upon Ananias and Sapphira, which took effect in "the destruction of the flesh" (see Acts v. 3-6, 9, 10), God ratifying "in heaven" the sentence of his Apostle. So also was St. Paul's censure upon Elymas the sorcerer in Acts xiii. 11: "And now, behold, the hand of the Lord is upon thee, and thou shalt be blind, not seeing the sun for a season;" which also was ratified "in heaven;" for we read that, "immediately there fell on him a mist and a darkness; and he went about seeking some to lead him by the hand." And St. Paul's direction to the Corinthians to forgive the incestuous person, upon his true repentance, which was quoted just now (2 Cor. ii. 7, 10), was a "loosing" (or releasing) him from the censure which had been inflicted on him.

15. *Catechist.*—But you said that the terms "binding" and "loosing" were to be understood also of pro-

hibition and permission. Can you give any Scriptural instance of the Church's doing this?

Answer.—Yes. When the first Christian Council (whose proceedings are recorded in Acts xv.) excused the Gentile converts from the obligations of circumcision and the Mosaic ritual, this was a "loosing" (see vers. 10, 19, 28). And when, on the other hand, they still made binding upon these converts abstinence "from meats offered to idols, and from blood, and from things strangled, and from fornication" (vers. 20, 29), this was a "binding" (or restriction). For in the sense of "permission" and "restriction," the Jewish Rabbis were accustomed to use these terms. In like manner, when St. Paul says (Rom. xiv. 14), "I know, and am persuaded by the Lord Jesus, that there is nothing unclean of itself;" and again (1 Cor. viii. 4), "As concerning . . . the eating of those things that are offered in sacrifice unto idols, we know that an idol is nothing in the world;" and again (1 Cor. x. 25), "Whatsoever is sold in the shambles, that eat;" and again (1 Tim. iv. 4), "Every creature of God is good, and nothing to be refused, if it be received with thanksgiving;" he "looses" the meats offered to idols, that is, permits the free use of them, where they can be partaken of with a clear conscience. And where, on the other hand, he says (Rom. xiv. 14), "To him that esteemeth anything to be unclean, to him it is unclean;" and again (ver. 23), "He that doubteth is damned if he eat, because he eateth not of faith;" and again (vers. 13, 20), "Judge this rather, that no man put a stumbling-block or an occasion to fall in his brother's way, . . . for meat destroy not the work of God"—he "binds" Christians in this matter, forbidding them to partake, unless they were fully persuaded of the lawfulness of doing so, and also wherever they might, by so doing, embolden another to act against his own conscience.

16. *Question.*—What further signification may be given to the words "binding" and "loosing"?

Answer.—The authoritative administration of the

Sacraments, through which (as through channels) mercy and grace are conveyed to the soul; the true preaching of Christ, and the relief experienced therein by the sin-burdened conscience; as also every formal absolution or declaration of pardon through His name,—all these are forms of "loosing." While the withholding these means of grace, the refusing Baptism to a candidate considered disqualified for it, or the Lord's Supper to a person of scandalous life, or the Burial Office to one who has died in open sin or avowed infidelity, or the pearl of God's Gospel to a profane man, who would trample it under foot and do a mischief to the preacher,—this would be a "binding" of men's sins upon them,—a "retaining of sins."

17. *Catechist.*—You have now explained the passage of St. Matthew, in which our Lord, directing how offenders are to be dealt with, gives His Church the power of binding and loosing, and directs that he who neglects to hear the Church shall be treated "as a heathen man and a publican." But we do not find here any mention of Christian Ministers. By "the Church" is meant the whole body of the faithful. And so far as this passage goes, we gather from it, that the power of "binding" and "loosing" is lodged with the whole body. Though it is true that, when St. Paul excommunicates, and afterwards restores an offender, by the authority which these words of our Lord give to the Church, *he himself* appears in the matter as acting with authority: "When ye are gathered together, and *my spirit;*" . . . "For your sakes *forgave I* it in the person of Christ." What other words of our Lord fully justify St. Paul in claiming and exercising this authority, in giving directions first for the censure of the offender, and then, when he was brought to a right mind by the censure, for his relief from it?

Answer.—The words which He spake when He met the ten Apostles (St. Thomas being absent) on the evening of the Resurrection Day (St. John xx. 19-24):

" Then the same day at evening, being the first day of the week, when the doors were shut where the disciples were assembled for fear of the Jews, came Jesus and stood in the midst, and saith unto them, Peace be unto you. And when he had so said, he shewed unto them his hands and his side. Then were the disciples glad, when they saw the Lord. Then said Jesus to them again, Peace be unto you: as my Father hath sent me, even so send I you. And when he had said this, he breathed on them, and saith unto them, Receive ye the Holy Ghost. Whose soever sins ye remit, they are remitted unto them; and whose soever sins ye retain, they are retained."

18. *Question.*—Is there anything to connect this passage with that from St. Matthew's Gospel, which gives the power of "binding" and "loosing" to the Church, and which you have just explained?

Answer.—Yes. In the context of the former passage (St. Matt. xviii. 20) our Lord had said, "Where two or three are gathered together in my name, there am I in the midst of them." And here we find His little flock of disciples "gathered together in" His Name, separate from the world, after His Resurrection; and it is said (as if to mark the fulfilment of His promise), that "Jesus came and *stood in the midst.*"

19. *Question.*—How can it be shown that, in the words now before us, our Lord is addressing the Apostles only?

Answer.—Because He begins them thus: "As my Father hath sent me, even so send I you." Now, the word here translated "hath sent" (ἀπέσταλκε) is closely connected with the word "Apostle," which means a messenger, or person sent. Christ was the Father's Apostle, just as St. Peter and St. John were *His* Apostles. He is called so, Heb. iii. 1: "Consider *the Apostle* and High Priest of our profession, Christ Jesus."

20. *Question.*—What warrant have we for connecting this passage of St. John with the rite of Ordination?"

Answer.—Those who compiled the Prayer-Book of the Church of England evidently thought that this passage was the Church's authority for Ordination, because they put these words of our Lord into the mouth of the Bishop, when ordaining Priests. See " The Form and Manner of Ordering of Priests : "—" *When this Prayer is done, the Bishop with the Priests present shall lay their hands severally upon the head of every one that receiveth the Order of Priesthood; the Receivers humbly kneeling upon their knees, and the Bishop saying,* Receive the Holy Ghost for the Office and Work of a Priest in the Church of God, now committed unto thee by the Imposition of our hands. Whose sins thou dost forgive, they are forgiven; and whose sins thou dost retain, they are retained."

21. *Question.*—What is the charge which immediately follows these words in the Ordination Service? and how does it throw light upon the meaning of the words " remitting " and " retaining " sins ?

Answer.—The charge is this: " And be thou a faithful Dispenser of the Word of God, and of His holy Sacraments; In the Name of the Father, and of the Son, and of the Holy Ghost. Amen." This charge seems to show that the " remitting " and " retaining " of sins is to be done by a faithful dispensation of the Word and Sacraments, which are the channels through which God's mercy and grace reach sinful men.

22. *Catechist.*—Show from Scripture that the Word and Sacraments are the channels of God's mercy and grace to man ?

Answer.—" Be it known unto you therefore, men and brethren, that through this man *is preached unto you the forgiveness of sins:* and by him all that believe are justified from all things, from which ye could not be justified by the law of Moses" (Acts xiii. 38, 39). "Thus it behoved . . . that repentance and *remission of sins should be preached in his name* among all nations " (St. Luke xxiv. 46, 47). " And all things are of God, who hath reconciled us to himself by Jesus Christ, and hath given to us *the ministry of reconciliation;* to wit, that God was in Christ, reconciling the world unto himself, not imputing their trespasses unto them; and hath committed unto us *the word of reconciliation.* Now then we are ambassadors for Christ, *as though God did beseech you by us:* we pray you in Christ's stead, *be ye reconciled to God.* For he hath made him to be sin for us, who knew no sin; that we might be made the righteousness of God in him" (2 Cor. v. 18-*end*). "Repent, and *be baptized every one of you* in the name of Jesus Christ *for the remission of sins, and ye shall receive the gift of the Holy Ghost*" (Acts ii. 38). "Arise, and *be baptized, and wash away thy sins,* calling on the name of the Lord" (Acts xxii. 16). "And he took the cup, and gave thanks, and gave it to them, saying, Drink ye all of it; for *this is my blood* of the new testament, *which is shed for many for the remission of sins*" (St. Matt. xxvi. 27, 28). "Whoso eateth my flesh, and drinketh my blood, hath eternal life" (John vi. 54).

23. *Question.*—Will you then paraphrase these words of Christ to His Apostles: " Receive ye the Holy Ghost: whose soever sins ye remit, they are remitted unto them; and whose soever sins ye retain, they are retained"?

Answer.—*Receive* such a measure of the gifts and graces of *the Holy Spirit*, as shall enable you to discharge the office of ambassadors to Me, as I have discharged that of Ambassador to my Father. *Whose soever sins ye,* speaking in my Name and by my Spirit, *pronounce to be remitted, they are remitted.* Whatsoever terms of forgiveness ye, speaking in my Name and by my Spirit, shall lay down, those I will ratify. And *whose soever sins ye,* speaking in my Name and by my Spirit, *condemn and leave without a sentence of absolution, they are condemned and left upon them.* And wherever, by the Ministry of the Sacraments, ye open the sluices of grace and mercy towards man, there grace and mercy shall always flow forth; and wherever ye withhold these holy Ordinances (acting still in my

Name and by my Spirit), there grace and mercy shall be restrained. In brief, I will ratify your preaching, your censures, your absolutions, and all your ministerial acts.

24. *Catechist.*—It is not difficult to understand, that the Ministry of *the Apostles* should receive from their Master such a sanction as this. But can we suppose that the Ministry of uninspired men has a similar sanction? And are we justified in applying the words to modern Ministers?

Answer.—So far forth as modern Ministers preach, warn, censure, absolve, prohibit, permit, according to the principles and rules which the Apostles have laid down in their writings, and by the Spirit which actuated them, so far doubtless their Ministry, both in remitting and retaining sins, will have God's sanction, as that of the Apostles had. And as regards the *Sacramental acts* of a Minister, they will be always effectual, if only "the Sacraments be duly ministered according to Christ's ordinance in all those things that of necessity are requisite to the same" (Art. xix.), and if the parties to whom they are ministered present no obstacle to their effect by impenitence and unbelief. For the grace of Sacraments is as necessary as ever to the being and well-being of the Church; and we have the Lord's own promise that He will be "with" His Ministers "alway, even unto the end of the world." It is Christ's commission which makes Sacraments valid, not the piety or high character of the administrator. No unworthiness of Ministers, therefore, can vitiate them. "The effect of Christ's ordinance" is not "taken away by their wickedness, nor the grace of God's gifts diminished from such as by faith and rightly do receive the Sacraments ministered unto them; which be effectual, because of Christ's institution and promise, although they be ministered by evil men" (Art. xxvi.)

25. *Catechist.*—You have now explained satisfactorily

two difficult passages of Holy Scripture,—one of which speaks of the Church's power of "binding" and "loosing;" the other, of the Apostles' power of "remitting" and "retaining sins." The "loosing" is in all probability the same as the "remitting;" the "binding" the same as the "retaining." But can you account for the fact, that, in one of these passages, a power is given to the "Church," or body of the faithful, which, in the other, seems to be limited to the Apostles, and their representatives?

Answer.—Yes. The power is lodged with the whole body of the faithful; it is the Church's power, the Church's endowment; yet it is delegated to, and can only be wielded by, the Church's officers, who act as her organs and representatives.

26. *Catechist.*—You say that the officers (or Ministers) of the Church are organs of the whole body of the faithful. Expand and explain the image which you use.

Answer.—I can easily do so. The natural body of man is, in every part of it, endowed with sensation. Sensation is the heritage or common property of the entire body. Yet there are certain organs of sensation, through which alone we receive impressions. The organ of the sense of sight, is the eye; of the sense of hearing, the ear; of the sense of smelling, the nose; of the sense of taste, the palate; of the sense of touch, the hand (and indeed every other member). To say that sensation is the property or endowment of the whole body is quite true. But it is also true to say, that the various acts of sensation can only be exercised through the various organs of sense, that we cannot see but through the eye, hear but through the ear, etc. etc. In like manner, the powers of the Church are really the property of the whole body. Laity, as well as clergy, have (or may have) the Holy Spirit, and therefore the powers of binding and loosing, remitting and retaining, which go with that gift, belong originally to all. And yet Ministers are the organs by which these powers are exercised, just as the eye is the organ of sight, and the ear of hearing.

27. *Catechist.*—But I find a flaw in your image. Sight, I admit, is the endowment of the eye; hearing, the endowment of the ear, etc., but you seem to make out that the whole body is endowed with these senses.

Answer.—Nay; I said the whole body is endowed with *sensation.* Sensibility in various forms is the property of all of it. Sensibility in the eye is called sight; in the ear, hearing; in the palate, taste, etc. etc. But that sensibility is really one gift, manifesting itself in various forms, seems to be shown by this, that when one of the avenues of the senses is closed, the other senses seem to become keener. Thus; when a man loses his eyesight, he gains a more delicate sense of touch.

28. *Catechist.*—But you said that Christian Ministers were not only organs, but representatives of the Church. Was this the case with the Ministers of the Old Dispensation also?

Answer.—It was. The first-born males of the children of Israel were properly God's Ministers, sanctified unto Him by His own ordinance from their birth; see Exod. xiii. 2, 15. But afterwards an arrangement was made, by which the tribe of Levi was set apart as a substitute for the first-born, to represent them, and minister to the Lord in their stead; see Numbers viii. 14-19 : " Thus shalt thou separate the Levites from among the children of Israel; and the Levites shall be mine. And after that shall the Levites go in to do the service of the tabernacle of the congregation: and thou shalt cleanse them, and offer them for an offering. For they are wholly given unto me from among the children of Israel; instead of such as open every womb, even instead of the first-born of all the children of Israel, have I taken them unto me. For all the first-born of the children of Israel are mine, both man and beast: on the day that I smote every first-born in the land of Egypt I sanctified them for myself. And I have taken the

Levites for all the first-born of the children of Israel." The same thing is also told us in Numbers iii. 11-14.

29. *Question.*—Can you trace the same principle of representation in the Ministry of the early Apostolic Church?

Answer.—Yes. In the messages which our Lord sends by St. John to the angels or presiding bishops of the Seven Churches of Asia, we find the Churches addressed through their bishops, that is, through their representatives. Each message is a commentary upon the spiritual state of the whole Church, not upon that of the bishop himself. Hence we read (Rev. ii. 10): "Fear none of those things which *thou* shalt suffer: behold, the devil shall cast *some of you* into prison, that *ye* may be tried" (the bishop suffered, when any members of his flock did); and at the end of each message, we have a promise to "him that overcometh," evidently given to the Church generally, as an encouragement to their steadfastness.

30. *Question.*—Does the idea of the representative character of the Clergy still linger in the English language?

Answer.—Yes. It is to be found in the word "parson," which is merely another form of the word "person," and was originally only a vulgar pronunciation, before it became a distinct word. The Latin word "persona," from which our "person" comes, means originally a mask which an actor puts on to personate a character; and the "Dramatis Personæ" of a play are the actors who sustain the various parts, and who are to make such and such speeches, in exhibition of the characters they *personate*. In like manner the "Person of a Parish" is the man who represents it before God, who stands for, and in things pertaining to God acts for, the whole Church in that Parish.

31. *Question.*—What illustration of the office and privileges of representatives may be drawn from our political constitution?

Answer.—We have our Parliamentary representatives in the House of Commons. The powers which they exercise really belong to us, for it is we who delegate those powers to them. They are delegated by us to Parliament, to make the voice of the majority of the constituency heard there. They are our agents, who give to our opinion on political questions its due weight in the government of the country. But it does not follow from the fact of their being our delegates, and wielding powers which are essentially ours, that therefore we may do whatever they have a right to do. We may not invade their privileges. We may not ourselves enter the House of Commons, nor speak there, though they may do so. In like manner, Ministers are only representatives of the Church; and every spiritual power which they exercise belongs originally to the Church, and is only wielded by them as the Church's representatives. It is the Church who through her organs preaches, absolves, excommunicates, blesses, consecrates. But it does not follow that ordinary Christians may intrude upon the functions of the ordained, or take upon them, without a call, to minister the Word and Sacraments, any more than it follows that, because the member of my borough or county represents me, I may do all that he does, or enjoy all his prerogatives.

32. *Question.*—What solemn warning have we in the Old Testament against an invasion of ministerial functions on the part of the laity?

Answer.—The altogether unprecedented punishment of Korah and his company, who were swallowed up by the earth, and went down alive into Hades—the place of departed spirits (Num. xvi. 29-34), as also the leprosy of King Uzziah, which was inflicted upon him in consequence of his presuming to burn incense in the Holy Place: "But when he was strong, his heart was lifted up to his destruction: for he transgressed against the Lord his God, and went into the temple of the Lord to burn incense upon the altar of incense. And Azariah the priest went in after him, and with him fourscore priests of the Lord, that were valiant men: and they withstood Uzziah the king, and said unto him, It appertaineth not unto thee, Uzziah, to burn incense unto the Lord, but to the priests the sons of Aaron, that are consecrated to burn incense: go out of the sanctuary; for thou hast trespassed; neither shall it be for thine honour from the Lord God. Then Uzziah was wroth, and had a censer in his hand to burn incense: and, while he was wroth with the priests, the leprosy even rose up in his forehead before the priests in the house of the Lord, from beside the incense altar. And Azariah the chief priest, and all the priests, looked upon him, and, behold, he was leprous in his forehead, and they thrust him out from thence; yea, himself hasted also to go out, because the Lord had smitten him." (2 Chron. xxvi. 16-21.)

33. *Question.*—What did Korah, Dathan, and Abiram allege as a ground of their rebellion, which was true?

Answer.—They said, " Ye take too much upon you, seeing all the congregation are holy, every one of them, and the Lord is among them" (Num. xvi. 3).

34. *Catechist.*—Show that they were right, when they said that all the congregation was holy.

Answer.—The Lord Himself said as much to Moses: "And Moses went up unto God, and the Lord called unto him out of the mountain, saying, Thus shalt thou say to the house of Jacob, and tell the children of Israel; Ye have seen what I did unto the Egyptians, and how I bare you on eagles' wings, and brought you unto myself. Now therefore, if ye will obey my voice indeed, and keep my covenant, then ye shall be a peculiar treasure unto me above all people: for all the earth is mine: and *ye shall be unto me a kingdom of priests and an holy nation.* These are the words which thou shalt speak unto the children of Israel" (Exod. xix. 3-7).

35. *Catechist.*—Show that the Lord was among the people, as the rebels said.

Answer.—In Exod. xxix. 45, we find God promising

to Moses: "And I will dwell among the children of Israel, and will be their God."

36. *Question.*—Why did not these truths justify the rebels in what they did?

Answer.—Because, though the whole nation was "a kingdom of priests," yet God had appointed a certain tribe and family to be, in things pertaining to God, the representatives of the nation; and no one might trespass upon the functions of this tribe and family without incurring great guilt and signal punishment. Christians are all called priests, laity and clergy alike: "Ye also, as lively stones, are built up a spiritual house, *an holy priesthood*, to offer up spiritual sacrifices, acceptable to God by Jesus Christ. . . . But ye are a chosen generation, *a royal priesthood*, an holy nation, a peculiar people; that ye should show forth the praises of him who hath called you out of darkness into his marvellous light" (1 Pet. ii. 5, 9); and, "Unto him that loved us, and washed us from our sins in his own blood, and hath made us kings and *priests* unto God and his Father; to him be glory and dominion for ever and ever. Amen" (Rev. i. 5, 6). Yet there is among Christians also a representative Ministry; and it does not follow that those who are not called to it may invade the functions of those who are.

37. *Question.*—Is there any ministerial function which the laity might perform, and which has been at various periods and in various Communions performed by them?

Answer.—Yes; they might preach under the licence of the Bishop, issued to them after he had satisfied himself of their competency for that important office. But this would not be ministering without authority. A fragment of the Ministerial Commission would devolve upon the person so licensed. He would have received "authority to preach the Word of God," not indeed as his calling, or the main business of his life, but as opportunity offered, and as his services were sought, in subordination to the regular Ministry.

CHAPTER VI.

THE HOLY EUCHARIST AT ITS SUCCESSIVE STAGES.

"*Being seen of them forty days, and speaking of the things pertaining to the kingdom of God.*"—ACTS I. 3.

THERE was a deep and manifold significance in the period of time (nearly six weeks), which elapsed between our Lord's triumph over death and His triumphant entrance into Heaven. First, so long a tract of time was designed to give "ample room and verge enough" for *evidences* of the Resurrection. Christ was to be seen on all manner of occasions, in divers places, and by divers persons; and this of itself asked time. Then, secondly, the disciples were to be gently and gradually weaned from the support and comfort of His bodily presence; it was not to be abruptly withdrawn from them, but to recede gradually like an ebbing tide, which ever and anon steals up, and kisses that line of sand and sea-weed, where its little foam-flakes are dissolving, and which we thought it had finally abandoned. But, thirdly, we discover a significance in these Forty Days, even more important than the conviction of the world, and the consolation of

Threefold purpose of the great Forty Days, which elapsed between the Resurrection and the Ascension of Christ.

the earliest disciples. Our Lord during those Forty Days traced, as we have seen in the earlier Chapters of this work, the foundations of His Church. "He spake to them," says the Evangelist, "of the things pertaining to the kingdom of God." This was the great seminal period, upon which we find the germs of Church Institutions and Church Ordinances lying, as they were scattered by the hand of Christ Himself. Consider, in order that we may prosecute the argument on a safe basis of fact, how many of these germs we have already found in this period. First, we find constantly the Presence of Christ in His risen body among the three or four disciples gathered together in His Name—the germ this of the Christian Congregation. Secondly, there is the express institution of Missionary Preaching; "Go ye into all the world, and preach the gospel to every creature." Thirdly, the express institution of Christian Baptism; "Go ye and make disciples of all nations, baptizing them into the Name of the Father, and of the Son, and of the Holy Ghost." Fourthly, the express institution of Church Preaching, the regular instruction of Christian people in the truth of Christ; "Teaching them to observe all things whatsoever I have commanded you." Fifthly, the no less clear implication in the same words, that the Church was to conduct Christian Education, since the teaching in question is that which was appointed to follow upon Baptism; and Christ must have known that, when His Church had won for herself a footing in the earth, Infant Baptism would be her universal rule. Sixthly, the

Recapitulation of the several Church Institutions, the germs of which were laid during this period.

direct institution of the Christian Ministry, as an organ and representative of the Church, wielding those powers which had been deposited with the whole body; "Peace be unto you: as my Father hath sent me, even so send I you. And when he had said this, he breathed on them, and saith unto them, Receive ye the Holy Ghost." Seventhly, the power of this Ministry, as representing the Church, both to absolve and censure; "Whose soever sins ye remit, they are remitted unto them; and whose soever sins ye retain, they are retained." The other (and perhaps more attractive) aspect of the Ministry, as a Pastorate appointed for the feeding of the Church with the Word and Sacraments, as also for the guidance and governance of it, was also brought out during this period of Forty Days, by our Lord's threefold charge to the penitent and then re-instated Apostle; "Feed my lambs;" "Feed my sheep;" "Feed my sheep."

Surely all these instances are quite sufficient to establish the position that during His Forty Days' sojourn upon earth our Lord employed Himself in tracing an outline of the various Church Offices and Institutions, which His Apostles, under the influence of His Spirit, sent down upon them at Pentecost, would have to develope.

And if this were indeed so, can we suppose that during this significant period He would omit all reference to the highest and most blessed of all Church Observances—the Supper of the Lord? That Supper, as its nature and peculiar significance demanded, had been of necessity *instituted* previ-

One would expect to find some reference to the Lord's Supper during this period, although it had of necessity, and in conformity with its character, been instituted previously.

ously. A memorial of the dying Lord, by the faithful use of which His followers were to call Him to mind, could have been at no season so appropriately given as on the eve of His death; may we not say, could not have been appropriately given at any other season? By that beautiful and wise arrangement, according to which our Lord connected all His great deeds and discourses with certain circumstances, which in the order of God's Providence emerged under His eyes, the Holy Supper grew out of an occasion—the greatest, most solemn, most tender, most sacred occasion, which ever gave birth to a great Institution. It grew out of the occasion of His partaking of His last meal with His disciples, and was (in one aspect of it, though not the highest, nor the most important for the Church at large) the beautiful utterance and outcome of His exceeding tenderness for those He was leaving behind in a world of sin and sorrow. It was the bequeathing to them of a token of affection, by which, during His bodily absence, He might become present to them, not only to their imaginations by the power of association, but to their hearts and consciences by an invisible, though most real, communion with Him. But as the Supper was to be disentangled from its earliest and personal surroundings, and to become an Ordinance for the Church at large, and for disciples who had never known the Lord in the flesh, it seems the most reasonable of all reasonable expectations that we should find some marked allusion to it during the period of founding the Church, when He was tracing the outline, which

His Apostles were afterwards to fill up, of its various Institutions.

And our expectations are fully met. On the very day of His Resurrection, on the very first occasion of an *in-doors* meeting with two or three of His disciples (for among the various manifestations of that day no such occasion had, as far as we know, yet occurred), He performed an action, which, while it certainly cannot be called a celebration of the Holy Communion (for we read nothing of the species of wine, which bore so prominent a part in the original institution), was yet as certainly an allusion to the Ordinance, and a reminder of it, and an allusion and a reminder full of instruction as to its effects, blessings, and obligation.

And we find that the very day of the Resurrection was not allowed to close without such a reference.

The story is familiar to all. Two of Christ's disciples, plunged into despondency by the disappointment of their hopes respecting Him, and apparently giving up His cause for lost, had gone on the Resurrection Day to Emmaus, which was perhaps their village home. They were neither of them Apostles, but simple disciples, one called Cleopas, the other very probably the Evangelist who narrates the incident. He joined them in a disguise which prevented their recognising Him, asked a share in their conversation and their sorrows, and, when admitted to their confidence, showed them how the events which they deemed so disastrous were really part of Messiah's predicted career, and essential preliminaries of His triumph. Their hearts were in a glow of interest as He unfolded the meaning of the prophecies; so much so, that when they arrived at their desti-

The journey to Emmaus, and the conversation on the road.

nation, they would take no denial but that He must be their guest. "And he went in to tarry with them. And it came to pass, as he sat at meat with them, he took bread, and blessed it, and brake, and gave to them."

Sameness of the phraseology with that in which St. Matthew and St. Mark record the institution of the earlier part of the Eucharist.

The words are almost identical with those by which the two first Evangelists describe the institution of the first part of the Eucharist, and carry our minds irresistibly to that institution. Possibly, however, had no more been said, we might have thought the coincidence of phraseology merely accidental. But more *is* said. The narrator fixes our minds on the action of breaking the bread, as having been attended with an extraordinary effect, which no other part of the interview had produced.

Attention specially called to the action of breaking the Bread.

This was the dropping of the disguise, which hitherto had prevented recognition. "And their eyes were opened, and they knew him." But as soon as they became sensible of His Presence, it was withdrawn. It eluded their grasp; it would not be detained; "he vanished out of their sight." Springing to their feet at once, their doubts removed by sight, and their disconsolateness by the assurance of having held actual communion with Him, they returned to the little company of the Apostles with the glad tidings; "and they told what things were done in the way, and how he was known of them *in breaking of bread*" (ἐν τῇ κλάσει τοῦ ἄρτου);—"the breaking of bread" being the very term used by this St. Luke to denote the Eucharist, and the persistent celebration of it, in the primitive Church. "And

The 'breaking of the Bread' the term used by the Primitive Church to denote the celebration of the Eucharist.

they" (the three thousand souls converted at Pentecost) "continued steadfastly in the apostles' doctrine and fellowship, and in breaking of bread (τῇ κλάσει τοῦ ἄρτου), and in prayers."

"The breaking of the bread"—mark it well. The Church was only just born. It was the day of Pentecost, the day when Christ's risen life had first pervaded the community of the disciples, and knit them together into one communion and fellowship. And yet "the breaking of the bread" is spoken of as a regular Institution, which had burst into full blossom already at this earliest of early periods. It was practised, as St. Luke goes on to inform us, not in public, in the presence of unbelievers, but (as our Lord had set the example) within doors, "from house to house," and it was always an occasion of joy and festal thankfulness —joy and thankfulness, doubtless, arising chiefly from the blessed significance of the rite, now seen under the light of Pentecost, yet not surely without some reference to that earlier burst of joy at Emmaus, when the Lord was made known to two of His disciples "in the breaking of the bread." "And they," the words are, "continuing daily with one accord in the temple, and breaking bread from house to house, did eat their meat" (partook of the entertainments, in the midst of which the Lord's Supper was celebrated) "with gladness and singleness of heart, praising God, and having favour with all the people."

Immediate appearance of the Eucharist on the very birthday of the Church.

Privacy of primitive celebrations.

Let us now study for a short time this Ordinance of the Eucharist, instituted on the eve of our Lord's death, and revived, if I may say so, with new associations on the day of His Resurrection, stamped afresh with His risen authority, consecrated afresh with Easter blessing.

Christ's design of disentangling the Ordinance from its sentimental relation to the Apostles,

1. And first observe (what has been already briefly touched on) how clearly what passed at Emmaus intimates that, in Christ's design, the Ordinance was to be disentangled from what I may venture to call its sentimental relation to the Apostles,—the peculiarly touching and tender associations, with which in their minds it must have been invested, the deep solemnity of the farewell meal, His considerateness in leaving them a memorial of Himself, and so forth. Cleopas and the other

made manifest by what passed at Emmaus.

disciple had not been present at the original Institution,—could not therefore have shared in the associations connected with it. And yet the phraseology used by the Evangelist, and the circumstance of our Lord's fastening the attention of the disciples on the breaking of bread, as the critical point of the interview, by opening their eyes at that point, force upon us (as I have said) the belief that though He is not *celebrating* the Eucharist, He is designedly indicating it, referring to it, and bringing it under the notice of His Church once more. What are we to infer? What but that it was to be an Ordinance for all time, and all believers,—an Ordinance which, though it had local surroundings, and an occasion out of which it grew, was yet to detach itself from these, and soar above them? It was to be much more than a touching and tender greeting of *valediction* to the Apostles (though this it was); it was to be a greeting of *salutation* also by a risen and living Lord to His whole Church, a greeting which had much more in it than a sanctified memory, a greeting which had in it a present power and light. This is the new aspect which the Supper assumed, under the light shed upon it by the Emmaus interview.

2. We shall gain a further insight into the meaning of the holy rite, if we view it in connexion with the words which, in the accounts of all three Evangelists, accompanied the Institution. These I give in St. Luke's version of them, which is somewhat more full than that of the earlier Evangelists: "When the hour was come, he sat down, and the twelve apostles with him. And he said unto them, With desire I have desired to eat this passover with you before I suffer: for I say unto you, *I will not any more eat thereof, until it be fulfilled in the kingdom of God.* And he took the cup, and gave thanks, and said, Take this and divide it among yourselves: for I say unto you, I will not drink of the fruit of the vine, *until the kingdom of God shall come.*" The words evidently imply that when it *should* be fulfilled in the kingdom of God, when the kingdom of God *was* come, our Lord would again eat that Passover with His disciples, and drink with them of the fruit of the vine. They were again to banquet together, only in a new state of things which should supervene hereafter, as He said somewhat more explicitly shortly afterwards; "Ye are they which have continued with me in my temptations. And I appoint unto you a kingdom, as my Father hath

In St. Luke's narrative of the Institution, our Lord holds out hope of again eating and drinking with His disciples, when the kingdom of God should have come.

Words of similar general scope uttered shortly afterwards.

appointed unto me; that *ye may eat and drink at my table in my kingdom.*"

The question which naturally arises upon these passages is, What is the period to which Christ refers, as that at which He shall make His disciples sharers of His Table, and shall Himself eat and drink with them once more? And in answering this question, let us not tie the words up to one fulfilment; for there is a glorious richness and fulness in them, which defies all such limitation. While the meaning of man's words is often poor and thin, God's words have an exhaustless meaning. We must regard these words of our Divine Saviour as having a continuous and progressive fulfilment, reaching down the long perspective of the ages far as the mind's eye can penetrate, till the vista is closed by the Marriage Supper of the Lamb.

Remarkable difference of the two sayings, while their general tenor is the same.

Observe, first, that the two passages just quoted exhibit a general sameness of idea, with however one specific difference of great interest. A common entertainment for Master and disciples is the general idea; but in the former passage it is *He* who is to eat with *them*. "*I* will not any more eat thereof, until" . . . "*I* will not drink of the fruit of the vine, until . . . ;" in the latter it is *they* who are to eat with *Him*; "that *ye* may eat and drink at my table." It is as if in the earlier fulfilments of the words, the disciples should make *for Him* a supper, which He would graciously condescend to share; but in its later or latest fulfilment, *He* would make for *them* a supper, and invite them to partake of it. And such is indeed the course which the fulfilment takes. I find the earliest fulfilment of the words in the Emmaus interview. In a certain sense, though not as yet completely, it had been fulfilled in the kingdom of God, when Christ was risen from the dead. By His Death and Resurrection, the relation between a holy God and guilty sinners had been altered, and the foundations of the New Economy had been securely laid. Christ's work of atonement and merit was finished, and was declared by the resurrection to have been accepted. And now He sits down to meat with them once again, and, while the meat is yet in their mouths, fills them with joy in the discernment of His own Presence —this joy being a drop, if only a drop, of the new wine of the kingdom, the wine which makes glad not the animal but the spiritual part of our nature.

The Emmaus Supper the earliest fulfilment of the promise to eat and drink with them again, after the setting up of the kingdom.

If this Emmaus supper was not an actual Communion (and an actual Communion could not yet take place, any more than an actual Baptism, before the descent of the Holy Ghost), it was a prelude to all the Communions which have ever been, a foreshadowing and an earnest of them all. And the same remark will apply doubtless, more or less, to all the occasions on which our Lord manifested to His disciples in the Body of His Resurrection, ate and drank with them after He rose from the dead. They were all rehearsals of the Communion Feasts, which should take place when the Spirit was given, and when the Institutions of the Church were filled with the risen life of her Master.

This supper not an actual Communion, but a prelude to Communion,

and so also every occasion of eating and drinking with them, after He rose from the dead.

Ten days after the Ascension that great event occurred; a more *complete* fulfilment in the Kingdom of God, a *fuller* and more blessed Advent of the Kingdom, took place, than any of which the world had had experience hitherto; Jesus was exalted and glorified, and His Church, animated and governed by His Spirit, just as the members of the body are animated by the life and governed by the brain, represented Him on earth. And the Lord's Supper, like all other parts of the Church system, received then a glorification and uplifting, as being then first pervaded with the glorified life of Christ. It was now no longer a mere memento and legacy of His dying love, though this earliest character in which it appeared can never be effaced from it. Nor was it a mere banquet of the Risen Saviour with His disciples, a banquet sweetened by the joy of reunion with Him. But it became now the Festival of the New Dispensation, blessed and graced with His Spiritual Presence (a higher and greater thing than even the Presence of His risen natural Body), and in which He communicates Himself to His faithful people in the closest of all unions, they dwelling in Him, as a body in its atmosphere, He in them as a soul in its body. Thus was the Eucharist in a manner raised to a higher platform, and yet without any loss of its early associations. It is still, as of old, Christ eating and drinking with His little flock, presiding at the board, distributing to them the significant and efficacious symbols, not now in the Presence of His natural (or even of His risen) Body, but in the power and plenitude of His Resurrection life. It seems to me that the true view of the Ordinance has been obscured, and a way opened for the entrance of false and unscriptural views, by dropping this very important feature of Christ's personally presiding at the Communion board, as Himself master of the feast, and (through the instrumentality of His Ministers) communicating to each recipient the blessings of the Ordinance. He is also, no doubt, the food partaken of, no less than the master of the feast; but the dropping the thought of Him in the latter character has had no slight mischievous effect in paving the way for the carnal doctrine of Transubstantiation. Revert in thought to the original Institution of the Ordinance, and it is at once seen that what He gave to the Apostles as His Body and Blood cannot have been so in the literal or natural sense.

Yet still its early associations are not dropped; and the dropping of any of them hazards an obscuration of the Ordinance.

But although the Holy Ghost has long since descended, and although since His descent many and various have been the fortunes of the Christian Church, so that we may well suppose her probation to be now drawing to a close, it is not yet *altogether* fulfilled in the kingdom of God, nor, so long as we are yet instructed to pray, "Thy kingdom come," has the kingdom yet arrived *in all its fulness*. "We see not yet all things put under" the Risen Saviour, though doubtless they are in process of subjugation. The Mediatorial Kingdom is still running its course, and cannot be terminated until the counter-agency of sin, to which it has relation, is fully and finally put away. But when all things shall have been sub-

The Church still waits for the final arrival of the kingdom of God.

dued unto Jesus, and the end shall have fully come, then will the Marriage Supper of the Lamb—the solemn eternal ratification of that union between God and man, which was commenced by the Incarnation, and carried on at Pentecost—be celebrated. Then will come the passing in review of the many guests, whom the preached Gospel has gathered from all quarters of the earth, and the thrusting out of all who have not on the wedding-garment,—a spirit of holy joy and thankfulness, a festive spirit suitable to the great occasion. In that Supper, *which the Lord shall make for His people*, and wherein they shall sit down and eat and drink at His table in His kingdom, our Communion Feasts, which have been rehearsals of and preparations for it, shall merge; they shall there find their antitypical fulfilment and highest realization; for this great Supper is our point of hope, closing up for us the Christian's vista of the future. A wonderful coincidence truly; for we cannot but recall that this Lamb of God, who at the end of time will bid His own to the solemnity of a marriage supper, and give them to drink there of the new wine of spiritual joy, is the same who made His first appearance at a marriage in Cana of Galilee, and whose first exertion of miraculous power supplied the guests with wine, when the bridegroom's store was failing.

which will be ushered in by the marriage-supper of the Lamb.

That marriage-supper is the point of sight, for which our Communion Feasts are rehearsals and preparations.

One word, in conclusion, respecting the contrasted character of the two great Institutions of the Church called Sacraments. Baptism (as was pointed out in a previous Chapter) was suitably instituted upon a mountain, round which the free breezes of heaven swept and frolicked. For Baptism is the Sacrament (as has been well remarked) of diffusion, the Sacrament by the instrumentality of which the Church's life is sent forth into the ends of the earth, "to all the nations," "to every creature." But life requires not only to be sent into the extremities of a growing body, but to rally its forces at the heart. There must be a cementing power, as well as a diffusing power, a re-collection of life at its focus, as well as an expansion of it. And this is what the holy Supper is designed to do for the Church. It was suitably instituted in a guest-chamber, where the little flock of disciples was gathered together round their Divine Master, sheltered under His wing, and, as it were, pressed to His heart in a last embrace. It is, as it has well been called, the Sacrament of perpetual re-union,— not only a means of communion with Christ for each individual partaker, but a communion of all the partakers (in and through Christ) with one another. "We being many," says the Apostle, "are one bread and one body: for we are all partakers of that one bread." One loaf (or cake) of bread is broken into fragments, and a fragment is received by, and passes into the frame of, each communicant, as an expressive symbol of our being all spiritually one, through the conveyance and impartation to each of Christ's Body and Blood. Baptism needs for its due performance (as in the case of St. Philip and the Ethiopian) nothing more than an administrator and a recipient. But the conditions of the second Sacrament cannot be

Diffusion of life represented by Baptism.

Concentration of life by the Lord's Supper.

The Lord's Supper the Sacrament of perpetual re-union with Christ, and with His members,

and therefore, as one of its conditions, demands a gathering of two or three in Christ's Name.

satisfied without the joint action of two or three, since the re-union of Christians with one another in and through their common Lord is an essential feature of it, to obliterate which might peril the vitality of the Ordinance. Do we enough consider it in this light, as the Institution which is designed to make the different members of the Body of Christ cohere, designed to be a centre of unity to them, wherever it is celebrated, and to draw them together in closest bonds of spiritual fellowship? And do we, in partaking of it, cultivate a spirit of mutual love, make an effort to throw off our natural selfishness, and intercede for the Christian Brotherhood as well as ourselves?

<small>and should be celebrated in a spirit of mutual love.</small>

But enough for the present. When in our next Chapter we shall have exhibited the powers of the Church in Council, our walk round the walls of Zion will be completed. May we return from the survey with minds enriched, and hearts edified, by a deeper insight into "the things pertaining unto the Kingdom of God."

Catechism on Chap. VI.

1. *Question.*—For what purpose did our Lord spend forty days on earth between His Resurrection and His Ascension?

Answer.—This period of Forty Days had three uses,—a use for the world, a use for His first disciples, and a use for the Church.

2. *Question.*—What was the use of this period for the unbelieving world?

Answer.—To furnish to them satisfactory evidence of Christ's Resurrection. Christ was not to be seen after His Resurrection for a single day or a single week;

but to appear to several different persons (sometimes singly, sometimes when they were together), and on several different occasions, that there might be no room to doubt that He was truly risen.

3. *Question.*—What use had the great Forty Days for the first disciples?

Answer.—During this period they were gradually weaned from the support of Christ's bodily presence, upon which they had long and fondly leant. They saw Him occasionally, but only at intervals; and thus became inured to seeing Him no more in the flesh, and disciplined for seeing Him spiritually by faith.

4. *Question.*—What use had this period for the Church?

Answer.—It was then apparently that our Lord occupied Himself in tracing the foundations of His Church,—in appointing its Ordinances, its Ministers, and its Constitution.

5. *Question.*—How does this appear from the words of St. Luke?

Answer.—He tells us (Acts i. 3) that at the various interviews of our Lord with His Apostles during the Forty Days, He spake to them "of the things pertaining to the Kingdom of God." Now, by the Kingdom of God is meant that Constitution which Christ set up on the Earth, and into which men are called by the Gospel. The same term, "kingdom of heaven" (kingdom "set up" by "the God of heaven," see Daniel ii. 44) is used of the Church in St. Matthew xiii. 47; "The kingdom of heaven is like unto a net, that was cast into the sea and gathered of every kind."

6. *Question.*—How does it appear also from the recorded interviews of our Lord with the Apostles after the Resurrection?

Answer.—In the course of these interviews we find Him instituting Missionary Preaching, Holy Baptism, Preaching to the Christian Congregation, Christian Education, the Pastoral Office, and the Christian

Ministry with its powers of absolution and censure. We may add also that, by frequently appearing during this period to two or three gathered together in His Name, He fulfilled His own promise in St. Matt. xviii. 20, and appointed the Christian Congregation as the trysting-place at which He and His followers should meet. Also by appearing to the Ten on the evening of the Resurrection Day, and again to the Eleven eight days afterwards (which would be, according to the Jewish method of counting, on the seventh day afterwards), He appears to have consecrated the seventh day from His Resurrection, which thenceforth became to Christians the first day of the week, and was called the Lord's Day; see Rev. i. 10. We find from Acts xx. 7, that, "upon the first day of the week," it was the habit of the disciples to come "together to break bread" (that is, to celebrate the Holy Communion); and in 1 Cor. xvi. 2 St. Paul bids his Corinthian converts, "Upon the first day of the week let every one of you lay by him in store, as God hath prospered him," the Sunday being a fit day for almsgiving and "laying up for" themselves "treasures in heaven."

7. *Catechist.*—Sum up then briefly the Institutions of which we find the germs scattered by our Lord during this period.

Answer.—1. The Lord's Day. 2. Public Worship in the Congregation. 3. Preaching to the Heathen. 4. The Sacrament of Baptism. 5. Preaching to the Christian Congregation. 6. Christian Education. 7. Ordination. 8. Absolution and Excommunication. 9. The Pastoral Office. The allusions to all of these things are brief, to some of them faint; but there is not one of them, of which some manifest trace may not be found in the period under consideration.

8. *Question.*—Is it likely, then, that during this period we should find no trace of the Holy Eucharist, which is the highest and most important of all the Ordinances of the Church?

Answer.—Very unlikely; or rather inconceivable.

The Lord's Supper is an Ordinance of such importance, that our Lord made it, and the origin of it, and the method of celebrating it, the subject of a special revelation to the Apostle Paul; see 1 Cor. xi. 23-26. This was not necessary with the other Apostles, since it had been expressly instituted in their presence, and must have been quite fresh in their memories during the great Forty Days. But we should certainly expect that, during a period which was devoted to laying the germs of Church Institutions, and "speaking of the things pertaining to the kingdom of God," there should be some distinct reference to this Ordinance, and to the blessings of it.

9. *Question.*—Where do you find such a reference?

Answer.—In St. Luke's account of the journey of two disciples to Emmaus on the Resurrection Day, in the course of which our Lord joined them, "in another form" (see St. Mark xvi. 12), and took a share in their conversation, and "expounded unto them in all the Scriptures the things concerning himself," and finally "went in to tarry with them." "And it came to pass, as he sat at meat with them, he took bread, and blessed it, and brake, and gave to them. And their eyes were opened, and they knew him; and he vanished out of their sight" (St. Luke xxiv. 30, 31).

10. *Question.*—What leads you to connect this narrative with the Holy Supper?

Answer.—The fact that the words used are almost exactly the same as those which St. Matthew and St. Mark use in describing the Institution of the Lord's Supper:

St. *Matthew* says (xxvi. 26)—	St. *Mark* says (xiv. 22)—	St. *Luke's* words here are (xxiv. 30)—
"As they were eating, Jesus took bread, and blessed it, and brake it, and gave it to the disciples."	"As they did eat, Jesus took bread, and blessed, and brake it, and gave to them."	"As he sat at meat with them, he took bread, and blessed it, and brake, and gave to them."

Also there is the fact, that "the breaking of the bread" was the term applied to the Eucharist by the early disciples. We find it so called in Acts ii. 42, where, if the definite articles used in the original had been preserved by our translators, the words would run thus: "And they continued steadfastly in the doctrine of the Apostles, and in their fellowship, and in the breaking of the bread, and in the prayers." It is to be observed also, that our Lord, in the interview at Emmaus, calls attention to *the breaking of the bread*, by making that action the means of His being recognised by them, so that He may be said to put upon it an especial stress.

11. *Question.*—What does the fact of the Eucharist's having obtained a regular designation in the earliest infancy of the Church, show?

Answer.—That it was already recognised as a great Institution of the Church.

12. *Catechist.*—We may take it for granted, then, that the meal at Emmaus bore a designed reference to the Holy Communion,—was, in short, our Lord's recognition of that holy Sacrament, of its importance and of its effects, during the Forty Days which were spent by Him in tracing the foundations of the Kingdom of God. Under this view of the incident, what is the first lesson respecting the Eucharist which we gather from it?

Answer.—That this holy Sacrament, though it grew out of the occasion of Christ's parting with His Apostles, was to rise above the occasion, and stand out distinct from its original surroundings.

13. *Question.*—How does this appear?

Answer.—Partly from the persons to whom Christ gave the broken bread after the Resurrection; partly from the circumstances under which it was given to them.

14. *Question.*—How does it appear from the persons concerned?

Answer.—Neither of them were Apostles; for it is said that when they returned to Jerusalem, they "*found the eleven gathered together*, and them that were with them" (St. Luke xxiv. 33). Clearly therefore they did not themselves belong to "the eleven." Thus they were not of the number of those who had seen the Holy Supper instituted, and in whose memories every association of it would be fresh and vivid. It was not *from them* that our Lord had parted in this manner; there were no associations of the last evening He had spent upon earth to be wakened in *their* minds; and therefore when He performs *for them* one of the Eucharistic actions, we conclude that He designed the Eucharist to be an Ordinance for the Church generally, not specially for those to whom He first gave it, as a dying token of His Divine Love.

15. *Question.*—How does the same thing appear from the circumstances under which our Lord gave them the broken bread?

Answer.—These circumstances were directly the reverse of those under which the Ordinance had been instituted. Then He was parting from His disciples before His Death. Now He was greeting them again after His Resurrection. We infer that the Holy Supper is designed to be a return of the risen Saviour to His Disciples with an Easter *salutation* on His lips, as well as a token given in remembrance of Himself with words of *valediction*.

16. *Question.*—What prediction of our Lord seems to have received its inchoate fulfilment in the Emmaus meal?

Answer.—That which, according to St. Luke, He uttered *immediately before* the Institution of the Eucharist. "And when the hour was come, he sat down, and the twelve apostles with him. And he said unto them, With desire I have desired to eat this passover with you before I suffer: for I say unto you, I will not any more eat thereof, until it be fulfilled in the kingdom of God. And he took the cup, and gave thanks, and said, Take this, and divide it among yourselves: for I say unto you, I will not drink of the fruit of the vine, until the kingdom of God shall come" (St. Luke xxii. 14-19).

17. *Question.*—What other words of a similar purport did our Lord use (according to the same Evangelist) *after* the Institution of the Eucharist?

Answer.—" Ye are they which have continued with me in my temptations. And I appoint unto you a kingdom, as my Father hath appointed unto me; that ye may eat and drink at my table in my kingdom, and sit on thrones judging the twelve tribes of Israel" (St. Luke xxii. 28-31).

18. *Catechist.*—Yes; the sentiment in this last passage is of the same general character with that in the former. What difference is observable between the two?

Answer.—That in the former passage the Saviour seems to speak of *His* eating and drinking *with the disciples* (compare St. Matt. xxvi. 29, " But I say unto you, I will not drink henceforth of this fruit of the vine, until that day when I drink it new with you in my Father's kingdom"), in the latter, of *their* eating and drinking with *Him;* "that *ye* may eat and drink at *my* table in my kingdom" (St. Luke xxii. 30).

19. *Question.*—What do you infer from this difference in words of the same general character?

Answer.—That the earlier fulfilments of the gracious promise contained in both passages alike would be rather, that the Lord should attend the entertainment *made for Him by the disciples;* whereas its latest fulfilment would be, that they should be *guests of His*, at a festival made for them by Him.

20. *Catechist.*—You said that the earliest fulfilment of these words was to be found in the Emmaus meal. But the words are—" I will not any more eat thereof, *until it be fulfilled in the kingdom of God*" (St. Luke xxii. 16); "I will not drink of the fruit of the vine, until the *kingdom of God shall come*" (ver. 18). In what sense had " the kingdom of God come," in what sense " was it fulfilled in the kingdom of God," when our Lord had risen from the dead?

Answer.—Christ's life of spotless obedience, and His death, by which He made upon the cross " a full, perfect, and sufficient sacrifice, oblation, and satisfaction for the sins of the whole world," were now accomplished; in token of which He exclaimed with His latest breath, " It is finished." And, more than this, God had indicated His acceptance of all that Christ had done and suffered for man by raising up Christ from the dead. Thus far it was already " fulfilled in the kingdom of God ; " although a greater and more glorious fulfilment had still to be brought about.

21. *Question.*—What was this more complete fulfilment to which you refer?

Answer.—The descent of the Holy Spirit at Pentecost, whose first fruits are, " Love, *joy, peace* " (see Gal. v. 22). We are told that " the kingdom of God is righteousness, and *peace, and joy in the Holy Ghost* " (Rom. xiv. 17). When, therefore, the Holy Spirit of peace and joy had descended, there was a more complete fulfilment in the Kingdom of God than hitherto—the Kingdom had more fully come.

22. *Question.*—Will you then briefly show how the Holy Eucharist was raised to a higher character, and stood on a higher level, after than before the Resurrection, and again after than before the day of Pentecost?

Answer.—Before the Resurrection, the Eucharist was merely a memorial of Christ's dying love. After the Resurrection, it became also a greeting of the risen Saviour to His disciples, and a Sacrament of His reunion with them. After the day of Pentecost, it gained yet a new character without losing the old—it became the great channel by which the Saviour's risen Life flowed into and animated His members.

23. *Catechist.*—Yes; these are three distinct views of the Eucharist. Yet what common element is there in all these views?

Answer.—That of Christ Himself presiding at the

Communion Feast: first, in His natural body; secondly, in His risen body; thirdly, in His glorified body, or, in other words, in the fulness of His Resurrection Life.

24. *Question.*—Why is it important to maintain firmly this idea of Christ being Himself not only the Food received, but also the Master of the Banquet (just as in His Sacrifice He is both Priest and Victim)?

Answer.—Because the maintenance of this idea would be a safeguard against erroneous and carnal notions of the Ordinance. If Christ is not only the Heavenly Viand, but also the Distributor thereof, the Viand cannot be in a *carnal* sense His Body and Blood. Christ certainly did not give to His disciples, at the first Institution, the flesh of His hand, or the blood which circulated through it. And so, in His reminder of the Eucharistic action at Emmaus, He was again the giver of the food given.

25. *Question.*—Though the Kingdom of God came more fully at Pentecost than it had hitherto done, has it yet been altogether fulfilled in the Kingdom of God?

Answer.—No; this will not take place until the time of the end, when all things, death not excepted, shall be "put under" Jesus. This period is predicted by the Apostle Paul in 1 Cor. xv. 23-29: "But every man in his own order: Christ the first-fruits; afterward they that are Christ's, at his coming. Then cometh the end, when he shall have delivered up the kingdom to God, even the Father; when he shall have put down all rule, and all authority and power. For he must reign, till he hath put all enemies under his feet. The last enemy that shall be destroyed is death. For he hath put all things under his feet. But when he saith All things are put under him, it is manifest that he is excepted which did put all things under him. And when all things shall be subdued unto him, then shall the Son also himself be subject unto him that put all things under him, that God may be all in all."

26. *Question.*—What will be the eternal Eucharist, which the Lord shall spread for His people, and which shall finally supersede the Eucharists, at which *He* has condescended to be *their* guest?
Answer.—The Marriage Supper of the Lamb.

27. *Question.*—What *foreshadowing and augury* of this final Marriage Supper do we find in our Lord's earthly career?
Answer.—We read that He made His first public appearance at a marriage in Cana of Galilee, where He exerted His miraculous power to furnish the guests with a large store of wine. See St. John ii. 1-12.

28. *Question.*—What *prophecy* of the final Marriage Supper do we find in our Lord's teaching?
Answer.—The Parable of the king who made a marriage for his son, and, after rejecting those whom he had first invited, gathered together a great multitude out of the highways, "both bad and good," and among them "a man which had not on a wedding garment." This man, having no excuse to offer for appearing in ordinary attire, was by the king's order bound hand and foot, and taken away, and cast into outer darkness; see St. Matt. xxii. 1-15.

29. *Catechist.*—Exhibit briefly the meaning of this Parable.
Answer.—God, by His servants the prophets, bade the Jews to the "feast of fat things," which he had prepared in the Gospel of Christ,—to the solemnization of His Son's marriage with our nature by the Incarnation, and with the individual partakers of our nature by His spiritual union to His Church. The Jews slighting this feast and neglecting to come, while some of them persecuted and slew God's messengers who invited them to it, the invitation was sent to the Gentiles, who accepted it in numbers. The altars of the

Church, at which the Lord had ordained a rehearsal and foretaste to be made of the great Marriage Supper, which should be at the end of time, were "furnished with guests," "bad and good," faithful and unbelieving, sincere and hypocritical. But these guests shall not all be admitted to the eternal Marriage Supper. There shall be a sifting of the guests (as there ought to be a sifting of the conscience previously to the Eucharistic Supper), and a rejection of those who have not on the wedding garment,—who are not clothed with a spirit of holy joy, in harmony with the great Festival.

30. *Question.*—What *prophetic vision* of the eternal Marriage Supper is found in the Scriptures of the New Testament?

Answer.—The following, which was vouchsafed to St. John the Divine: "And I heard as it were the voice of a great multitude, and as the voice of many waters, and as the voice of mighty thunderings, saying, Alleluia: for the Lord God omnipotent reigneth. Let us be glad and rejoice, and give honour to him: for the marriage of the Lamb is come, and his wife hath made herself ready. And to her was granted that she should be arrayed in fine linen, clean and white: for the fine linen is the righteousness of saints. And he saith unto me, Write, Blessed are they which are called unto the marriage supper of the Lamb. And he saith unto me, These are the true sayings of God" (Rev. xix. 6-10).

31. *Question.*—What contrast may be observed between the character of the two Sacraments?

Answer.—A similar contrast to that which may be observed in the places where they were respectively instituted. Baptism was instituted on a mountain, round which the free breezes of heaven careered. The Holy Supper was instituted in the chamber of a dwelling-house, and was celebrated by the early Christians (before they had churches) "from house to house;" see Acts ii. 46, "breaking bread from house to house." The first is a Sacrament of diffusion; "Go ye therefore, and *teach all nations*, baptizing them;" "Go ye into *all the world*, and preach the Gospel to *every creature*" (St. Matt. xxviii. 19; St. Mark xvi. 15). The second is a Sacrament of re-union; "*Say ye to the goodman of the house, The Master saith, Where is the guest chamber, where I shall eat the passover with my disciples?*" (St. Mark xiv. 14.)

32. *Question.*—What practical lesson respecting the Supper of the Lord do we learn from hence?

Answer.—That it is designed to be a bond of spiritual fellowship between Christians, as well as between the Lord and the individual soul; or rather of fellowship between individual souls in and through the one Lord and Saviour.

33. *Question.*—In what words does St. Paul teach this lesson?

Answer.—"We being many are one bread" (one cake), "and one body: for we are all partakers of that one bread" (1 Cor. x. 17); that is to say, a fragment of one cake or loaf passes into the living frame of each communicant, and is assimilated thereby: even so the Saviour's flesh and blood, received in the Ordinance by faith, pass into the immortal spirit of each communicant, and assimilate all to Christ, and blend all together in the unity of the Spirit.

34. *Question.*—What spirit, then, should be cultivated in receiving the Lord's Supper, if we wish to give full effect to the significance of the Ordinance?

Answer.—A spirit of mutual love, such as shows itself by Christian sympathy, intercessory prayer, and efforts to help one another.

35. *Question.*—How does the Communion Office of the Church of England recognise the doctrine that the re-union of Christians with one another is an essential feature of the Holy Communion?

Answer.—By the second and third Rubrics at the close of the Office:—

"¶ *And there shall be no celebration of the Lord's*

Supper, except there be a convenient number to communicate with the Priest, according to his discretion.

"¶ *And if there be not above twenty persons in the Parish of discretion to receive the Communion; yet there shall be no Communion, except four (or three at the least) communicate with the Priest.*"

And even in the Communion of the Sick, there must be *two* communicants at the least, besides the sick person and the Priest. (See the Rubric at the commencement of the Office.)

CHAPTER VII.

ON THE POWERS OF THE CHURCH IN COUNCIL.

"It seemed good to the Holy Ghost, and to us."
ACTS xv. 28.

WE have seen more than once, in the course of this work, that the great Forty Days which intervened between the Resurrection and the Ascension of Christ, were the seminal period of the Church's history, during which our Lord occupied Himself in tracing her foundations. We now come down to a later period of New Testament history, and pass from the Gospels to the Acts of the Apostles, there to observe the actual exercise of the powers, and the actual assertion of the prerogatives, which Christ had given to His little flock. *A later period of New Testament history brought under review in the present chapter.*

The decree of the first Christian Council ever held runs in this solemn formula; "It seemed good to the Holy Ghost, and to us." But who are the persons who dare to couple their *placet* with the *placet* of the Holy Ghost, and to affirm their own sentence as the sentence of the Divine Spirit? We turn to the preamble of the decree to find who they were: "The apostles and elders and brethren,"—in other words, the bishops, clergy, *The authority claimed for the decree of the first Christian Council.*

and laity of the then Christian Church in council assembled,—" send greeting unto the brethren which are of the Gentiles in Antioch and Syria and Cilicia."

The natural means by which the conclusion had been arrived at.

How had these men arrived at the conclusion, for which they venture (apparently without hesitation) to claim so awful a sanction? They had arrived at it by mutual conference, upon which no doubt God's blessing and guidance had been previously asked, though that circumstance is not mentioned in the narrative. "There had been much disputing" (verse 7); that is, a general discussion in the first instance; after which the assembly had listened to speeches from the great leaders of the Christian movement, St. Peter, St. Paul, and St. Barnabas. St. James, who probably presided over the assembly as bishop of the diocese in which it was held, summed up the argument, and proposed a sentence or decree as the result of that summary. This decree meeting the approbation of the assembly, it was determined to forward it by letter to the parties, for whose guidance it was drawn up.

The decree founded on principles previously admitted.

But was the decree merely arbitrary, or was it founded on principles, the truth of which was previously admitted? Most clearly the latter. In St. Peter's speech he recites what God had done, and had directed him to do, in reference to the admission of Cornelius, and lays down that dealing of God's as the ground of proceedings in the present instance. Observe this narrowly. He does not say "I, Cephas, a pillar of the Church, —nay the rock-man ($\Pi\acute{\epsilon}\tau\rho o\varsigma$) on which the

Church is built,—I, in the exercise of my independent judgment, prompted and guided by the Holy Ghost, whose illapse I experienced at Pentecost, declare it to be the will of God that these Gentile Christians shall not have the heavy burden of the Ceremonial Law laid upon them." His professing successor might have spoken so; but the remarkable point in St. Peter's judgment is not its independence, but its professed dependence upon what God had said and done :—" God made choice among us, that the Gentiles by my mouth should hear the word of the gospel, and believe. And God, which knoweth the hearts, bare them witness, giving them the Holy Ghost, even as he did unto us; and put no difference between us and them, purifying their hearts by faith."— St. James founds his opinion upon the same dealing of God, and in further illustration of this dealing quotes a passage from the book of the prophet Amos, predicting apparently that admission of the Gentiles to full religious privileges, which had been inaugurated by the baptism of Cornelius, and arguing thence that the minds of the Gentile converts were not to be needlessly disturbed. So that the question, though settled by Apostles, was settled by a reference to the foregone sayings and doings of the Almighty, of which they do not for a moment claim independence.

St. Peter builds his argument on God's previous dealings with himself and with the Gentiles;

St. James on the same dealings, of which he finds a prediction in the book of the prophet Amos.

But was not the decision, after all, a result arrived at by the mere exercise of the human faculties? Had "the apostles and elders and brethren" any right to claim for it the sanction of

The sanction of the Holy Ghost claimed for a decision so arrived at,

the Holy Spirit, as they most distinctly do in the text? Most assuredly they had such a right; and had they claimed anything less than this, they would have failed to recognise their true position and prerogative.

In the first place, the Founder of the Church had distinctly given them an assurance of His own presence, when they were gathered together in His name. It is true that this promise had been made specifically in reference to united *prayer* :—
"If two of you shall agree upon earth as touching *any thing that they shall ask*," etc. But God's promises (like His commandments) are exceeding broad; and it would refer also to the united deliberations of the disciples, before entering upon which they would doubtless seek for Divine guidance, according to, and on the ground of, that word;—"When he, the Spirit of truth, is come, he will guide you into all truth." And we are to remember that, at the time of which we are now speaking, the Spirit of truth *had* come. Not only had the framework of the Church been constructed, it had also been animated and organized—fully pervaded with the Saviour's risen Life. This grand event, which took place at Pentecost, is thus rehearsed by the Apostle Paul :—"When he ascended up on high, he led captivity captive, and gave gifts unto men . . . And he gave some, apostles; and some, prophets; and some, evangelists; and some, pastors and teachers; for the perfecting of the saints, for the work of the ministry, for the edifying of the body of Christ: till we all come in the unity of the faith, and of

[margin: on the ground of the Lord's own promises of guidance by the Spirit of truth,]

[margin: which Spirit had been given at Pentecost,]

[margin: and had flowed down upon the Church through various channels of Ministry.]

the knowledge of the Son of God, unto a perfect man, unto the measure of the stature of the fulness of Christ."

These then are the grounds on which a decree of the assembled Church claims for itself the ratification of the Holy Ghost. The decree was the voice of the Holy Ghost, speaking in the body of Christ. By this Spirit the Church was to be continually guided; and by the governance of this Spirit she was to shape her course, as difficulties arose, and heresies and contradictions crossed her path. The heresies and contradictions were to be legislated for, as time brought them to the birth. There was an unerring standard of reference, whereby to adjudicate upon them, in the Word of God. And there was in the Church an indwelling light and wisdom, enabling her to discriminate between good and evil, truth and falsehood, by the application of that criterion. This is the true theory of Church Government. There was no pre-ordained scheme for dealing with the emergencies, which the progress of Society, or the dispensations of Providence might throw up to the surface. Our Lord legislated for no such emergencies. The Apostles legislated for no such emergencies. Our Lord did not say to his Apostles; "You will have the Judaizers to deal with ere long, who will propose to entangle the Gentile converts in the yoke of bondage; I give you a hint beforehand how to handle that controversy, when time brings it to the birth." Why should He give them hints beforehand, like a departing friend, who after his decease is

Being endowed with the Spirit, as well as with the Word of God, the Church might be left to legislate for herself in such emergencies as might arise;

nor did our Lord give to his apostles,

to live with us only in memory and in the associations of the past? He was to live with them —ay, and with their successors, "even to the end of the world"—by the power and presence of His Spirit flowing down into and inundating all the Church's Ministry—a better presence, He distinctly tells them, and a stronger power than His presence and power in the flesh had ever been. What need that He should direct them in all things beforehand, when He could say to them that far more helpful word; "Lo, I am with you alway, even unto the end of the world;" "Where two or three are gathered together in my name, there am I in the midst of them"?—And as their Master dealt with the Apostles, so the Apostles dealt with the inheritors of their Ministry. They have warned us indeed, in general terms, of dangers which should beset the faith and patience of Christians in the last days, and of the awful revelation of a certain mysterious personage called "the Man of Sin," in order that, when these contradictions and heresies appeared, Christians, remembering them to have been all foretold, might be nothing staggered by them; but as for any definite directions how to act on the occurrence of definite emergencies, such as the rise of the Arian, or Macedonian, or Pelagian heresy, the Apostles left no such instructions behind them. What need was there to do so? Their successors in the Faith, as well as themselves, would share in the sacred gift of Pentecost, which indeed was nothing less than the gift of the perpetual presence of Christ, through His Representative, the

nor His Apostles to their successors, any definite directions as to the method of meeting such emergencies.

Comforter. Was not that presence competent to guide the Church of the latter days, as it had guided themselves, into all truth? More especially as there was an external guidance available for the Church in the written Word of God. If hundreds of cases might arise which the Apostles never foresaw, none could arise which did not admit of a solution by reference to the principles laid down in their writings. The New Testament, like all other parts of Scripture, is a seed; it contains within it in germ, though by no means explicitly, the decision of every controversy which has ever vexed and harassed the Church.

The Apostles bequeathed to the Church their inspired writings, in which are laid down the principles on which every controversy must be decided.

But here a difficulty may arise in the mind of a reader who is following the argument. We will give expression to it in this shape:—"It is an axiom of good government that there must be one head. Now, in the government of the Church of Christ you virtually say that there are two co-ordinate authorities. One is, as you have told us, the Church herself, organized under her rulers, deriving her Ministries from the Lord Jesus Himself through His Apostles, and thus having His presence and power transmitted to the latest ages of her history. Well and good. But you tell us also of another authority, which you imply must check and control the agency of the Church, this authority being the sacred volume of the Holy Scriptures, written by inspiration of God, and emanating from God Himself. You have then a living corporation, inhabited by the Holy Spirit. And you have also a book, animated in every part

Objection raised against two co-ordinate authorities in the government of the Church.

(for this is the meaning of the word *inspired*) by the breath of that Spirit? May there not be a danger of collision between the two authorities? How if the Church shall approve what the Scripture condemns, or censure in cases where the Scripture does not say 'Anathema,' or fail to condemn, where the Scripture is very strong and explicit in disapproval? Is there not great hazard in this divided allegiance? Would it not be simpler, and less confusing to plain people, to go by the Church exclusively, as the Romanist professes to do, or by the Bible exclusively, as the ultra-Protestant professes to do?"

Complexity of the finer organizations in Nature.

Simpler, certainly, in the sense of giving us only one thing to attend to; but the finest and highest organizations in Nature are not simple, but complex; and the higher they are, the more complex the structure becomes. A zoophyte has only one organ to serve him for stomach, liver, and lungs; but in the body of a man, which stands at the head of animal life, the stomach, liver, and lungs are distinct, and each member has its own function, upon which others must not (and in the condition of health do not) trespass. Who shall wonder, then, if in the administration of the Christian Society there are two authorities which have distinct and independent functions,—the living corporation of the Church of Christ, organized under its Ministers, and the inspired Word of God, quickened in every part by the breath of His Spirit? I say that the functions of these two authorities are independent; and the idea ought to present no difficulty to those acquainted, as

Englishmen are, with constitutional checks. The Church's power, as defined by our twentieth Article, is in part legislative, and in part only judicial. "The Church hath power to decree Rites or Ceremonies,"—that is, new ones, if she judge it to be expedient. This is her legislative power. The earliest exercise of this power, or perhaps I should say the principle of it, may be traced in the Chapter on which we are founding our remarks. The matter laid before "the apostles and elders and brethren" was a ceremonial one, inasmuch as it had reference to the Jewish ceremonial law. The question was, whether the Gentile converts were bound to the observance of the ceremonial law. And after much discussion and deliberation it was determined that they were under no such obligation, and that the only restrictions which they need observe were such as were necessary in order to break off all connexion with the worship of idols; "that ye abstain from meats offered to idols, and from blood, and from things strangled, and from fornication" (a moral offence being here classed with ceremonial ones, not as if the two things were put on a level, but because one and all were abominations sanctioned and patronized by heathen worship). A decree to this effect was issued by the Council, and circulated by St. Paul and his colleague in their missionary tour. And three most beneficial effects of the decree are mentioned,—"consolation" (flowing from the relief experienced by harassed consciences, when a moot point was set at rest), establishment of the churches in the faith, and

The Church's legislative power: how far it extends.

In the decree of the Council of Jerusalem we find an exercise of it.

their numerical increase. Nor can it be doubted that the Church, in its several branches, has at present a power of legislating in matters merely ritual. Our branch of the Church exercised such power, when she determined to retain the sign of the Cross in Baptism, a ceremony most impressive and edifying, though by no means part of the Sacrament, nor at all affecting its validity. And she might move further in the same direction, as far as her spiritual constitution and prerogatives are concerned. She might add, for example, new Offices to the Book of Common Prayer, as an Office of Thanksgiving on occasion of the Harvest, or an Office at the Induction of a new Minister, or an Office to be used over a Criminal lying under Sentence of Death. But even here the Church's power is guarded by a constitutional check. "Yet it is not lawful," proceeds the Article, "for the Church to ordain anything that is contrary to God's Word written." If, for example, into an Office of Harvest Thanksgiving it were proposed to insert some words of adoration to the holy Angels, as being very possibly the ministers of natural blessings to mankind, this would be a flagrant stretch of the Church's prerogative, since St. Paul condemns the worshipping of angels, and, when St. John fell down to worship before the feet of an angel, the being to whom the homage was offered replied: "See thou do it not: for I am thy fellow-servant." —The second part of the Church's function is judicial only. She "hath authority in Controversies of Faith,"—not authority to *make* a single Article of Faith, but authority in a doctrinal controversy to pronounce what is the true doctrine, ruling her decisions by a reference to the Holy Scripture, and to the interpretation put upon it by the Church, when as yet Christendom was undivided. You may see the germ of this power also in the record of the Council in the Acts. For the decision that compliance with the ceremonial law was not necessary to salvation was, in a certain point of view, a doctrinal judgment; and we cannot help observing the great anxiety of the Apostles to frame their decision upon God's previous sayings and doings,—upon His works and Word,—part of which every speaker at the meeting sets himself to interpret. They speak as those who can make no ruling out of their own minds, and are simply bent upon expounding and applying the mind of God. Let it therefore be clearly understood that the Articles of Faith are to be sought *only* in Holy Scripture. As in this country the Imperial Parliament is the alone source of Law, so the alone source of Christian doctrine is the volume of Holy Scripture. But as, when laws have been made by Parliaments, judges are found necessary, not to make new ones, but to expound, declare, and administer the old, so in matters of Christian doctrine, while the Bible is the sole statute-book, the Church is the sole judge. And there can be no question that, in order to a healthy and vigorous administration of that great body politic, the Church, there must be a judge, and a judge in continual action, as well as a statute-book. It is not enough to have good laws; they must be applied,

just as a judge expounds and declares, though he does not make, the Law.

and administered, and justice done in pursuance of them, unless the country is to go to rack and ruin.

The Church has also a power of organising herself, which is not noticed in Art. xx., but exhibited in Acts vi.

Our twentieth Article, which we have been thus far following, says nothing respecting one department of the Church's powers, which yet is brought out with sufficient distinctness in the Acts of the Apostles,—*the authority to organize.* And at a time when new organizations are so much wanted to meet the new needs, which emerge with the progress of Society, when the Church system has been forced to give itself a great measure of elasticity (lest by its too great stiffness it should split), and to find room for Sisterhoods, Deaconesses, and Lay-Readers, it is quite necessary that the great Scriptural authority for such movements,—the authority which is required, and which (we think) is sufficient, to sanction them, should be held before our eyes. The Apostles then, not long after the Ascension, took a most important step in organizing the community over which they were called upon to preside, for which (as far as we are told) they had no direct instructions from Christ. They created a subordinate order of Ministers, to whose shoulders they transferred the responsibility and burden of administering Church charities, reserving to themselves the more spiritual functions of the Ministry. "Christ may have said nothing about this new order of Ministers" (says Canon Norris, a learned and devout writer of our own day, whom it is a pleasure to quote); "but Christ had said plainly that His Church was to go on growing and expanding like the branches of the mustard-tree, ever assimilating new elements; and that for these new elements the old forms might not suffice; new wine must not be put into old bottles.

The new organization was in conformity with principles laid down by Christ; and with what had been done in the Old Testament Church.

> 'The old order changeth, yielding place to new,
> And God fulfils Himself in many ways,
> Lest one good custom should corrupt the world.'"

This shows us how the Apostles, in the appointment of the seven subordinate Ministers, may have had in view, if not the literal instructions of Christ, yet at all events the great principles laid down by their Master; and I cannot help thinking that as Jews, whose minds were thoroughly imbued with, and thrown into the mould of, the Old Testament, they had their eyes also upon the way in which Moses was twice relieved of an excessive burden of work and responsibility, first, at the advice of Jethro, by the appointment of subordinate magistrates to hear the lesser cases, and secondly, by the qualification of the seventy elders to bear the burden of the people with him. But, however this may be, it is very important to remark that this step in Church Organization was not taken without consulting, and procuring the entire concurrence of, the assembled Church. "Then the twelve," we read, "called *the multitude of the disciples* unto them," and explained the need of a division of labour in order to efficiency of administration. "And *the saying pleased the whole multitude.*" The new legislation was the act of the whole Church, to which collectively the promise of the Spirit had been made.—We hold that the points of this narrative, which we here

Points of the narrative which should be borne in mind in proposed new organisations for Church help.

exhibit summarily, are extremely important to be borne in mind in any movement made for fresh Church Organizations; and we commend them to the reader's notice and consideration. *First,* Growing Church work demands new forms of Church help. *Secondly,* Relief is given to the overtasked, on the principle of division of labour. *Thirdly,* The arrangement made has manifest reference to the principles inculcated by Christ, and to Church administration under the Old Economy. *Fourthly,* The concurrence of the Church is sought and obtained, before any step is taken. *Fifthly,* The rulers of the Church are called upon to give their authoritative sanction and blessing to the new Organization.

But it may be asked,—it is daily being asked, by some invidiously, by others with a sincere desire for a satisfactory answer,—" If the above be the true theory of Church Government, where is *your* judge of heresy, where is *your* power to decree rites and ceremonies, or even your authority for new organizations, in the Church of England?" If the Church has indeed authority (I borrow the language of the latest and best commentator on the Thirty-nine Articles) not to make truth, but "to declare truth, to maintain truth, to discern truth from error, to judge, when controversies arise, whether one party is heretical or not, and to reject from communion such as are in grievous falsehood or error,"—where is the body in our own Communion which has any such power as this, or which even claims such power?

Alas! it must be confessed that while the Church still lives among us (and with a vigorous life) in her Ministries, her legislative and judicial functions are, for the present, in abeyance. We sorely need greater elasticity in our Church Services, more power of adapting the old framework of the Prayer-Book (a framework which has often proved the greatest of safeguards, but which is somewhat stiff and antiquated) to the devotional exigencies of the present day. We have now Harvest Services, Choral Festivals, religious Brotherhoods and Sisterhoods, organizations of women's work, and many other agencies which we had not half a century ago. Our present Offices and Prayers are admirably suited to the occasions for which they were compiled; but these new agencies cannot all run in the old groove; we want some expansion of our existing devotional forms, to suit them to current needs. In the absence of any such authorized expansion, the new spirit which is fermenting in the Church will carve out new channels for itself, and we shall have Services according to fancy, not according to rubrics, —the new wine will burst the old bottles. What we want is just what is tersely expressed in the Article, an exercise of "the Church's power to decree rites or ceremonies."—And again, the progress of thought on religious subjects, which can no more be stayed in its course than the sun can, if it has been productive of some good, has also been attended with serious dangers to the faith in Christ, has given rise to heresies and wanton contradictions of the popular creed, which

The legislative and judicial powers of the Church are, in our own Communion, in abeyance.

Need of new Services, to meet new forms of religious activity.

cause doubt in some minds, and extreme perplexity in others. Here, then, is just the emergency, in which we want the adjudication of a properly constituted Church tribunal. But we have it not. We have it not at all in practice, and very insufficiently in theory. The Convocations of the Northern and Southern Provinces might, no doubt, frame new Services, or make any modifications and adaptations of the Book of Common Prayer which might be thought desirable; but so long as the union between Church and State subsists (an union fraught with great blessings to both), the Acts of Convocation must have the sanction of Acts of Parliament, before they could have any legal force, and the difficulty of procuring such Acts in these days, when so many Members of Parliament are hostile or indifferent to the Church, would be so great that it might reasonably be called insuperable. The same obstacle would present itself to any approval by Parliament of a synodical censure passed by Convocation on heretical writings. It is true that such writings may be, and are occasionally, pronounced inconsistent with the formularies of the Church of England, by the Judicial Committee of Privy Council, and their authors punished by suspension or deprivation; but the Judicial Committee is not a Church court; it represents (and professes to represent) not the Church, but the State; nor (to do them justice) can anything be more emphatic than their disavowal of any claim to be a court of heresy. They announce that they do not try the writing submitted to them by the standard of the Holy Scriptures and primitive antiquity, which in an orthodox Church Council would be the only criteria. Their business, they say, and doubtless truly, is simply to say whether a limited context extracted from certain suspicious documents, is so entirely contradictory to another limited context, extracted from the Articles or Formularies of the Church, that the writers must be deprived of the means of gaining a livelihood from the exercise of their Ministry.—Such, then, is our sore point in the Church of England,— the abeyance in which the legislative and judicial functions of the Church are at present held amongst us. We may hope that the acknowledgment of the sore point is the first step to a remedy; and I must add my strong conviction that the principle, upon which the remedy should proceed, ought to be, to acknowledge practically that the State and the Church must not interfere in any measure with one another's functions; that as, on the one hand, the Church must not claim to inflict temporal penalties, so, on the other, the State must not presume to pronounce judgment either of acquittal or censure in charges spiritual. *But if it must be admitted that the Church of England has its defects.*

Meanwhile, let us couple this admission against ourselves with the reflection that all other Communions have their sore points also. The Lord predicted that there should be tares among the wheat in the harvest-field of His Church; and the tares may be taken to represent not only wicked people in the community, but defects and vicious debilitating principles in the system of *so have all other Communions.*

each Communion. Every individual has his faults; and every Church has its flaws. This is my answer to those persons who have consulted me as to whether the failure of our Communion in censuring what they regard as heresy, does not oblige them to migrate to some other Communion, where the living voice of the Church may be heard. My answer is; "Granted that the dear old Mother Church has her faults, where will you go that you will not find faults more fatal and more fundamental? If you can show me a Christian community *upon the whole* more Scriptural in its doctrine, and more primitive and apostolic in its discipline, I will not only allow you to migrate thither, but will gladly strike my own tent and march out in your company. But to take a leap in a matter so momentous to our best interests, without looking well before us, to see what will be our exact condition when we alight, would be, to my mind, an act no less sinful than foolish. Whither do we think of going, or whither, at least, that we shall be certain to better ourselves? To Rome? What! To a communion which can indeed boast an ecclesiastical authority, but an authority which sets at defiance, nay, tramples under foot, the great statute-book of God's realm, and the Magna Charta of our spiritual liberties; an authority which mutilates Sacraments, and deprives the laity of the consecrated symbol of the Blood of Christ; an authority which, in defiance of God's law, 'Thou shalt not bow down to graven images, nor worship them,' practically says, 'Thou shalt bow down;' an autho-

Marginalia:
The question is, Where can we find the fewest defects?
The shortcomings of the Roman Communion.

rity which has had the intolerable impudence to frame a new dogma in the nineteenth century, and to make the immaculate conception, not of our Lord, but of His mother, an Article of Faith?" No! without denying for a moment that there have been many eminent saints in the Church of Rome (an instance that God's grace in the heart can neutralize any amount of speculative error), we still maintain that speculative error (especially on points which lie so near to the core of true religion as those on which our controversy with Rome turns) is most dangerous, and likely to prove even fatal to those who, not from early associations, but from pique and petulant impatience with their own position, embrace it deliberately, after having known a purer faith.— Where, then, shall we go, if a migration to Rome be utterly out of the question? To some sect of Christians, among whom Holy Scripture is duly honoured and made the standard of appeal, but among whom also the living voice of the Church is heard, ordaining rites, judging heresies, censuring offenders? But not to speak of the sacrifice of the Book of Common Prayer, which we should thus have to make, and which, painfully as it would jar upon all our devotional instincts, might not yet be thought to involve a fundamental principle, what apostolic authority has such a sect? Without daring to deny to Presbyterian and other communities a Ministry and Sacraments (on the ground that God's grace is so abounding as often to overflow the regular channels of His own appointment), we yet should

The shortcomings of the Christian sects.

be loath indeed to exchange a regular for an irregular channel. There is always the possibility and the hope, which we may charitably cherish, that long centuries of irregular usage may more or less have sanctioned that usage in the sight of God (as long inheritance of a Crown must be held to give a title, even though long ages back it was gained by usurpation); but whoever he was in the history of the Church, who first of all sought to confer or receive Orders out of the apostolic line, "illi robur et æs triplex circa pectus erat,"—he had a superhuman hardihood, to face out so boldly the story of Korah and his company; and the great blot on the escutcheon of Wesley—an escutcheon otherwise of eminent sanctity and wide-spread usefulness—is, that in his latter days (when we may believe that his faculties were somewhat on the wane) he took upon him to communicate a power which he had never received, and to consecrate a bishop.

Long usage may possibly sanction irregularities in the sight of God.

But must we confine the recommendations of our own Church to the negative praise of its having fewer faults than its rivals? Surely not so. We believe, in the first place, that the sore point itself is in process of being remedied; that recent events have made thinking people feel that we must have an ecclesiastical legislature, and a properly constituted ecclesiastical tribunal. The desired consummation may be long in coming, but it will patiently work itself out, when the subject has been thoroughly ventilated, prejudices overcome, and convictions sufficiently matured. Meanwhile, if the legisla-

We may reasonably hope that our defects are in process of being remedied;

ture and judicature of the Church be somewhat in abeyance, in that other department of action, her Ministries, our Church shows greater vitality than ever. Never, probably, has any period of English history witnessed a greater activity among the clergy. Not very often has greater learning or ability been displayed by the champions of religion, in defending Truth against those who have assailed her. Never has there been a time, when more schemes were originated for promoting the temporal and spiritual welfare of the masses, and even for the evangelization of the heathen. These and the like signs ought surely to be accepted by candid persons as an evidence that while our system, like all others, has its defects, the living presence of our Lord is still with our beloved Church. If so, we are safe, and should be happy and thankful where we are. All is well, if the Lord be in the boat, whatever waves of controversy may surge and swell around her. And by seeking to know the power of His presence in our own hearts, and by staunch fidelity to our principles as Christians and Churchmen, we may perchance be allowed to be His honoured instruments to set in order some of the things which are wanting, and to give to our own Communion such symmetry and beauty, that we may be able to challenge admiration for her, and to commend her to posterity, in the words of the Psalmist:—

"Walk about Zion, and go round about her: tell the towers thereof. Mark ye well her bulwarks, consider her palaces; that ye may tell it to the generation following."

and certainly the Ministries of our Church show greater vitality than ever.

and religious activity is everywhere abroad within her pale.

All is well, if our Lord be with us.

Catechism on Chap. VII.

1. *Catechist.*—In your former examinations you have pointed out how our Lord occupied Himself in the period which elapsed between His Resurrection and Ascension, in laying the foundations of His Church. What further light may we expect that the book of the Acts of the Apostles will throw upon the subject?

Answer.—It may be expected to show how the prerogatives and powers bestowed by Christ upon His Church were actually asserted and exerted.

2. *Question.*—In what style does the decree of the first Christian Council run?

Answer.—In this style; "It seemed good to the Holy Ghost, and to us" (see Acts xv. 28).

3. *Question.*—By whom was the decree issued?

Answer.—By "the apostles and elders and brethren" (see ver. 23).

4. *Question.*—How had the members of the Council arrived at their conclusion?

Answer.—By a discussion in which St. Peter and St. Paul (with his associate, St. Barnabas) had taken prominent parts; and which was summed up by St. James, who presided at the meeting, and, having heard what was said, suggested a measure, which was carried.

5. *Question.*—By what principle were the members of the Council guided to the conclusion at which they arrived?

Answer.—By considering what God had recently done, and what He had formerly said.

6. *Question.*—What had God recently done, to which appeal was made by St. Peter?

Answer.—He had indicated, by several unmistakable signs, His will that the Gentiles should be admitted to the Church; and had shown them to be proper subjects for Baptism, by sending down His Holy Spirit upon them, just as He had done at Pentecost upon Jewish believers (see Acts x. 11, 12, 15, 17, 19, 44).

7. *Question.*—What does St. Peter argue from this circumstance?

Answer.—That the Gentiles were not to be brought under the yoke of the Ceremonial Law (see Acts xv. 10), God having bestowed His grace upon them without any such requirement.

8. *Question.*—What is there very worthy of observation in this argument of St. Peter's?

Answer.—The fact that it is an argument. Though our Lord had said to him, " Thou art Peter, and upon this rock I will build my Church " (St. Matt. xvi. 18); and though he certainly was a great pillar of the Church, and is spoken of as such by St. Paul (see Gal. ii. 9); yet he does not settle the question before the Council on his own authority. On the contrary, he reasons on God's past dealings with him, and so arrives at the conclusion as to what ought to be done in the matter.

9. *Question.*—What melancholy contrast to St. Peter's modest conduct on this occasion is exhibited in Christendom nowadays?

Answer.—The pretension of the Pope (or Bishop of Rome) to decide all questions of faith on his own authority, and even without reference to a General Council, contrasts strangely with the conduct of St. Peter, whose successor the Pope claims to be. So that he almost lays himself open to the stricture, " If thou wert St. Peter's successor, thou wouldest do the works of St. Peter."

10. *Catechist.*—But you said that appeal was made at the Council, not only to God's recent dealings, but to His ancient sayings. How was this?

Answer.—St. James, in summing up the question, and recommending a measure for the adoption of the Council, quoted a passage from the book of Amos, to show that the admission of the Gentiles into the Church

P

(*as* Gentiles, and without any preliminary discipline from the Ceremonial Law) was designed by God long ages before it was brought about. So that in dispensing the Gentiles from any observance of that Law, they would have Holy Scripture, as well as God's dealings with themselves, for what they were doing (Acts xv. 15-19).

11. *Question.*—But if the conclusion was arrived at by argument from God's Word and dealings, and thus by the exercise of the human faculties, was it not presumptuous in "the apostles and elders and brethren" to ascribe it to the Holy Ghost, as they do when they say; "It seemed good to the Holy Ghost, and to us"?

Answer.—No; because they had promises from the great Head of the Church of His presence with them, and His guidance of their minds, to doubt which would have been sinful in them.

12. *Question.*—What promises do you more especially refer to?

Answer.—The promise of Christ's presence to the two or three gathered together in His Name, which is found in St. Matt. xviii. 20. Now His presence with them would be a presence by the Holy Ghost, according to that word of His own; "I will pray the Father, and he shall give you *another Comforter*, that he may abide with you for ever, even *the Spirit of truth.* . . . *I will not leave you comfortless: I will come to you*" (St. John xiv. 16-19). And then again there is the more special promise of the guidance of their minds by the Holy Spirit; "Howbeit when he, the Spirit of truth, is come, *he will guide you into all truth*" (St. John xvi. 13), and, "The Comforter, which is the Holy Ghost, whom the Father will send in my name, *he shall teach you all things*" (St. John xiv. 26). And the Evangelist who records these promises makes no doubt of their fulfilment. Writing to Christians, he speaks of them as divinely taught and guided. "*Ye have an unction from the Holy One, and ye know all things* . . . the anointing which ye have received of him abideth in you, and *ye need not that any man teach you:* but as *the same anointing teacheth you of all things*, and is truth, and is no lie, and even as it hath taught you, ye shall abide in him" (1 John ii. 20, 27). This is quite as peremptory an assertion of the guidance of Christians by the Holy Spirit, as the style in which the decree of the first Council runs; "It seemed good to the Holy Ghost, and to us."

13. *Catechist.*—To complete your proof of the Council's not having spoken presumptuously, you have only now to show that the Spirit of truth had already come at the time they professed to be guided by it.

Answer.—That is easily done. The first Council is ascribed to the year A.D. 51 or 52. But the great day of Pentecost, which was marked by the descent of the Holy Ghost on the Church, when the Lord Jesus, "being by the right hand of God exalted, and having received of the Father the promise of the Holy Ghost," shed forth the "cloven tongues like as of fire," and the "other tongues" (see Acts ii. 33, 34), fell in the year A.D. 33, nearly twenty years previously. St. Paul speaks of the pouring out of the Holy Ghost as standing in close connexion with, and as the immediate consequence of, the Ascension of Christ: "Wherefore he saith, *When he ascended up on high*, he led captivity captive, and *gave gifts unto men* . . . He that descended is the same also *that ascended up far above all heavens, that he might fill all things.* And he gave some, apostles; and some, prophets, etc. etc. (see Eph. iv. 8, 10, 11).

14. *Question.*—What sort of government must that of the Church be, if Christ is ever present with her, "even unto the end of world," by His Holy Spirit?

Answer.—A government which legislates as (and not before) the occasion for legislation arises. Thus, for example, when officers were found necessary to relieve the Apostles of some of the secular business which devolved upon them, such officers were appointed and ordained (see Acts vi. 1-7). And some time afterwards, when a grave question had arisen touching the obligation of Gentiles to observe the Ceremonial Law, a Council was called together to decide it. The Church, under the guidance of the Holy Spirit, spoke and acted as the occasion for utterance and action arose.

15. *Catechist.*—This mode of government might be very safe and proper, so long as those inspired rulers of the Church, the Apostles, were alive. But after their removal by death, could the Church be trusted to legislate for herself as emergencies arose?

Answer.—Yes: because Christ's presence is assured to His Church, not merely till the death of the Apostles, but "even unto the end of the world" (see St. Matt. xxviii. 20). And the gift of the Holy Ghost was for the whole Church, not for the Apostles only. Thus St. John clearly recognises the gift as being in the possession of the believers to whom he addresses his first epistle (see 1 John ii. 20, 27, which I have recently quoted, and from which it would appear that they could dispense with all human teaching and guidance). Nor do we ever find that the Apostles give to the Church any definite instructions how to act under the particular heresies and contradictions which should from time to time arise, though they frequently warn us of the appearance of such heresies, in order that we may be prepared for them when they arise, and not be staggered or have our faith shaken by them. Witness what St. Paul says in taking leave of the Ephesian presbyters; "For I know this, that after my departing shall grievous wolves enter in among you, not sparing the flock. Also of your own selves shall men arise, speaking perverse things, to draw away disciples after them. Therefore watch," etc. (Acts xx. 29-32); and what St. Jude says respecting the general testimony of the Apostles as to the future; " But, beloved, remember ye the words which were spoken before of the apostles of our Lord Jesus Christ; how that they told you there should be mockers in the last time, who should walk after their own ungodly lusts," etc. (Jude 17, 18). But this warning of future perils, that the Church might take comfort under trial by knowing it to have been foreseen and foreordained, is quite a different thing from definite instructions as to how to act in future difficulties, which we never find in the Apostles' writings.

16. *Question.*—Do you mean then to imply that, when the Apostles were removed, the Church was to be left *entirely* to the guidance of the Holy Spirit, acting upon the natural faculties with which God had endowed her?

Answer.—By no means. God has taken care to furnish the Church with a standard of appeal as to the principles which should guide her, and has only left her to adjust her decisions of particular questions to those principles. We have seen that the Apostles in Council referred to the Old Testament, as furnishing the principles by which they should be guided (see Acts xv. 15-18). And when the Apostles themselves were removed by death, they and their inspired contemporaries and associates left behind them those writings which go under the name of the New Testament. Thus it appears that the guidance under which the Church is placed in all the difficulties and oppositions, which time and the course of Divine Providence bring to the birth, is twofold; *first*, the guidance of the Spirit of truth, enlightening her judgment; *secondly*, the guidance of Holy Scripture, which, without explicitly giving the solution of all questions which may arise, announces the principles on which all questions must be solved.

17. *Catechist.*—But may not objections reasonably be raised to this twofold guidance? Is it not probable that people will be perplexed between the two authorities? And may not God be expected to give to souls desirous of arriving at the Truth such

easy straightforward guidance, as that it shall be impossible to miss the right road, or to be perplexed as to the direction in which it lies?

Answer.—On the contrary, if God designs to try a man's character, and to exercise his spiritual instincts in the discovery of religious truth, it is not likely that He will make the truth so plain, as that it shall be impossible to miss it.

18. *Catechist.*—You answer rightly. It is a very important principle of God's dealings with us that He makes the discovery of His truth a trial of character to us, while at the same time He gives us important helps towards the discovery. Can you give me an illustration of this mode of dealing with us?

Answer.—Yes. If a father wished to exercise the mind of his child by making him find the way to a certain place, he would not get a sign-post put up at every turn where two or three roads met; this would make it impossible for the child to miss the road; but he would place a map and a compass in the child's hand, and point out to him on the map the place from which he is to start, and that which he is to reach. When the child comes to a place where several roads meet, he will have to look at the map, and see the direction which he ought to take; and then the compass will tell him which of the roads leads in that direction.

19. *Question.*—What are the two helps with which God has furnished us for arriving at the Truth, and which will certainly, if faithfully used, conduct us to the end?

Answer.—The Holy Scriptures and the Church, the first of which may be called our spiritual chart, and the second our spiritual compass.

20. *Catechist.*—Yes. The guidance, therefore, which God gives us, is complex and not simple; we have two things to consult and not one. Does the analogy of Nature teach us that complex structures are of a higher order than simple?

Answer.—It does. The lowest forms of animal life are those in which one organ serves for every natural function. As we rise higher in the scale, a different organ is developed for each function, until we reach the body of man, which, as it is the highest, so it is also the most highly complicated animal structure.

21. *Catechist.*—But surely, if the authority of the Church has such an important position in the scheme of Human Salvation as you ascribe to it, it must be clearly defined. There must be no doubt as to what the Church's province is,—as to what she may and may not do. Can you then define her powers?

Answer. They are chiefly two; legislative and judicial.

22. *Question.*—How far does the Church's legislative power extend?

Answer.—She " hath power to decree Rites or Ceremonies."

23. *Question.*—What was the earliest exercise of this power?

Answer. The decree of the Council of Jerusalem, which declared the observance of the Jewish Ceremonial Law not to be binding upon the Gentiles, while, at the same time, it laid certain ceremonial restrictions upon them.

24. *Question.*—With what beneficial effects was this exercise of the Church's legislative power attended?

Answer.—1*st*, consolation. See Acts xv. 30, 31: " So when they were dismissed, they came to Antioch; and when they had gathered the multitude together, they delivered the epistle : which when they had read, they rejoiced for *the consolation.*" 2*d*, establishment in the faith ; and 3d, increase in numbers. See Acts xvi. 4, 5 : " And as they went through the cities, they delivered them the decrees for to keep, that were ordained of the apostles and elders which were at Jerusalem. And so were the churches *established in the faith*, and *increased in number* daily."

25. *Catechist.*—Give an instance in which the Reformed Church of England has exercised the "power to decree Rites or Ceremonies."

Answer.—She exercised this power when she determined to retain the sign of the Cross in Baptism, which is an edifying ceremony, though it adds nothing to the spiritual effect of the Sacrament.

26. *Question.*—What steps might our Church lawfully take in the same direction at present?

Answer.—She might add new Services to the Book of Common Prayer; such as, a Service for a Harvest Thanksgiving, or a Service for the Induction of a new Minister.

27. *Question.*—Is the power of the Church "to decree Rites or Ceremonies" limited by any constitutional check?

Answer.—Most assuredly. "It is not lawful for the Church," says our Twentieth Article, "to ordain any thing that is contrary to God's Word written."

28. *Question.*—By way of illustration, can you suppose a case in which the Church might ordain something contrary to God's Word written?

Answer.—Let us suppose that, in a Harvest Thanksgiving Service, it was proposed to insert some such words as these: "O ye holy angels of heaven, by whose ministrations God sends us dew, and rain, and sunshine, we offer unto you praise and adoration for the conveyance of these blessings."

29. *Question.*—To what parts of "God's Word written" would such an ascription of praise be contrary?

Answer.—To Rev. xxii. 8, 9: "And when I had heard and seen, I fell down to worship before the feet of the angel which shewed me these things. Then saith he unto me, See thou do it not: for I am thy fellow-servant, and of thy brethren the prophets, and of them which keep the sayings of this book: worship God." (And see also Rev. xix. 10.) And to Col. ii. 18, 19: "Let no man beguile you of your reward in a voluntary humility and worshipping of angels, intruding into those things which he hath not seen, vainly puffed up by his fleshly mind, and not holding the Head."

30. *Question.*—Will you define the Church's judicial power?

Answer.—She "hath authority in Controversies of Faith," that is, power, in a doctrinal controversy, to declare, by a reference to Holy Scripture, and to the way in which it was understood by the primitive Church, what the true Faith is.

31. *Question.*—Did "the apostles and elders" who met in Council at Jerusalem, refer to God's Word to sanction their decision?

Answer.—Yes; I have already shown that they did so in the earlier part of this examination. See especially my answer to Question 10.

32. *Catechist.*—The Church, then, can only declare, not make, an Article of Faith. And she can declare it only out of Holy Scripture, which is the alone source of Doctrine. Can you compare this function of the Church to the function of any order of men among ourselves?

Answer.—Yes; to the function of judges. It is not the province of a judge to make the law—that is done by the Imperial Parliament. The judge's business is merely to expound the law, and declare what it is. Similarly, Holy Scripture is God's statute-book; and the Church's province is to expound and declare the doctrines and precepts found in that statute-book.

33. *Question.*—What other power, besides the legislative and judicial, has the Church, which is not distinctly recognised in the Twentieth Article?

Answer.—The power of organizing herself to meet the varying emergencies, to which the progress of Society and the march of God's Providence may give rise.

34. *Question.*—Why is the present a time when the Scriptural warrant for such action on the part of the Church should be well considered?

Answer.—Because the Church in our own country, pressed by many needs, is daily putting forth new organizations to meet them; such as Sisterhoods, Deaconess Institutions, Lay Readerships, and the like.

35. *Question.*—Where is the Scriptural warrant for such organizations to be found?

Answer.—In Acts vi., where we read (ver. 1) that "when the number of the disciples was multiplied, there arose a murmuring of the Grecians against the Hebrews, because their widows were neglected in the daily ministration." To meet this exigency, the Apostles suggested to "the multitude of the disciples" the appointment of "seven men of honest report, full of the Holy Ghost and wisdom," upon whom the duty of distributing the funds of the Church (see Acts iv. 35) might be devolved. These officers were accordingly elected by the Church, and "set before the apostles," who ordained them with prayer and laying on of hands (Acts vi. 5, 6).

36. *Question.*—In what part of His teaching had our Lord laid down the principle of such an arrangement?

Answer.—He had said (St. Luke v. 37, 38), "No man putteth new wine into old bottles; else the new wine will burst the bottles, and be spilled, and the bottles shall perish. But new wine must be put into new bottles, and both are preserved." That is, when a new spirit is fermenting in the Church, old forms will not suffice; but new ones must be devised to retain it. This was said, in the first instance, of fasting, which is a discipline suited for certain circumstances of the Church, but unsuited to the period of the Bridegroom's presence, when a new and strange joy filled the hearts of the disciples. But it will apply generally to all such old forms as, having been once useful and necessary, are found too narrow for the Church in new developments of life and activity.

37. *Question.*—What Old Testament precedent may the Apostles have had in view, in shifting part of the burden of Church administration to the shoulders of subordinate ministers?

Answer.—The precedent of what Moses did, by the advice of Jethro, his father-in-law: "Moses chose able men out of all Israel, and made them heads over the people .... and they judged the people at all seasons: the hard causes they brought unto Moses, but every small matter they judged themselves" (Ex. xviii. 25, 26). And again we read in Num. xi. 14, etc., that when Moses complained that he was not able to bear all the people alone, God gave him this command; "Gather unto me seventy men of the elders of Israel, whom thou knowest to be the elders of the people, and officers over them .... and I will take of the spirit which is upon thee, and will put it upon them; and they shall bear the burden of the people with thee, that thou bear it not thyself alone" (Num. xi. 16, 17).

38. *Question.*—What are the principles by which we should be guided in new Church organizations?

Answer.—1. Church help should grow with Church work; 2. This help will frequently take the form of division of labour; 3. The Church (that is, the body of the disciples) should concur in the new arrangement; 4. The rulers of the Church should give their sanction and blessing.

39. *Catechist.*—You have now pointed out that the powers of the Church are threefold: legislative, judicial, and economical. What makes it especially desirable at the present time that the Church should exert her legislative and economical powers?

Answer.—The fact that the course of Providence and the progress of Society are bringing about a new state of things, which requires new organizations to meet it. If these organizations are not authoritatively sanctioned by the Church, they will exist without sanction, and therefore without control; and thus existing, they will soon become extravagant. The framework of our Book of Common Prayer, excellent in itself, and admirably adapted to the time at which it was put forth, requires expansion to meet the devotional exigencies of the present day. And this expansion should be given to it by the action of the Church herself, not by the fancies of individuals or of parties. But if the Church does not act, individuals and parties will take action of themselves, and the result will be a general condition of ecclesiastical lawlessness.

40. *Question.*—And what circumstances of our own Communion make it especially desirable that the Church should exert her judicial powers?

Answer.—The scepticism and denial of the Faith, which the progress of religious thought is bringing with it in its train, and which call for the censure of some properly constituted Church tribunal.

41. *Question.*—But does not the Convocation of the Provinces of Canterbury and York, which is the Church of England by representation, possess the required power to decree Rites or Ceremonies, to declare what is true doctrine and to censure what is false, and also to sanction new religious organizations?

Answer.—Doubtless the Convocation has rightfully this power, but its hands are tied, so that it is unable to exert it.

42. *Question.*—What is the impediment in the way of the action of Convocation, to which you refer?

Answer.—The connexion of the Church with the State (a connexion fraught with great blessings to both), which makes it necessary to obtain an Act of Parliament before an Act of Convocation could have any legal or obligatory force.

43. *Catechist.*—This circumstance may indeed make it difficult, or even impossible, to procure a legal and authoritative sanction to any new Liturgical office or Church organization. But surely the judicial power of the Church is not wholly in abeyance amongst us, so long as erroneous writings may be censured as contrary to the doctrine of the English Church, and their writers, if Ministers of the Church, punished by suspension or deprivation. And this is done occasionally by the Judicial Committee of Privy Council.

Answer.—The Judicial Committee is not a Church Court, and cannot speak in the name of the Church. It represents the authority of the Crown, not that of the Spiritualty.

44. *Question.*—In what respect are the proceedings of the Judicial Committee, in trying the writings submitted to it, altogether different from those of a Church Court?

Answer.—The standard of reference in a Church Court would be the Holy Scriptures and Primitive Antiquity, whereas the Committee of Council never applies these tests.

45. *Question.*—What then is their standard of reference?

Answer.—The Articles and Formularies of the Church of England. Their professed business is only to ascertain whether the passages in the writings of the accused, which are quoted in the indictment, are so contrary to those Articles and Formularies, that the writers must be suspended or deprived. Nor is even this question of conformity or nonconformity with the Articles and Formularies handled by them as a spiritual or ecclesiastical offence. The only punishment they inflict is one of deprivation of temporalities.

46. *Catechist.*—Yes; and temporal penalties are properly inflicted by a temporal Court. And the Committee of Council, by inflicting such penalties, declares itself to be such a Court. The offending party is

censured, not for religious error, but for a breach of contract with the State in teaching what he had entered into an engagement with the State not to teach. But if this be the case, what is still wanting to the Church of England, notwithstanding the occasional action of the Committee of Council?

Answer.—A rightly constituted Church Court, which may, in the name of the Spiritualty, pronounce upon and censure religious error.

47. *Question.*—Should these defects of the Church of England, in respect of the present exercise of the Church's judicial and legislative powers, move her children to forsake her Communion?

Answer. Certainly not, unless they can find a Communion more free from defects elsewhere.

48. *Catechist.*—But surely Communions may be found, in which the defects you have mentioned either do not exist at all, or are not so apparent. In the Roman Church, for example, there is a wonderful elasticity, which enables it to adapt itself to fresh emergencies, and also a strong discipline, in virtue of which penance, censure, and excommunication are administered freely.

Answer.—Yes; but defects of discipline, organization, and elasticity are by no means the worst which can disfigure a Church. How much more vital is the defect of ordaining something contrary to Holy Scripture, as the Roman Church does when she forbids the cup to all but the celebrant, sanctions the adoration of images, pronounces that the Blessed Virgin was conceived without sin, and ascribes infallibility to the Bishop of Rome.

49. *Catechist.*—But there are Protestant Communities, which are entirely free from these abominations of Rome, and yet exercise a more or less effective discipline upon their members, and have a living synodical government. Why not give in your adhesion to one of these?

Answer.—Because I cannot see in them the "Apostles' fellowship," even if upon the whole they maintain, with tolerable fidelity, the "Apostles' doctrine." They all broke off (with more or less excuse) from the Old Church, and discarded the Ministerial Succession, and so cannot be said to be built upon the foundation of the Apostles and Prophets.

50. *Catechist.*—But this rupture took place a long time ago. May we not hope that the usage of many generations has more or less sanctioned the irregularity?

Answer.—Surely we may. We may hope and believe everything for those who had no participation in the sin of the original schism. Yet surely, as we find ourselves elsewhere and in a regularly constituted Catholic Church, unquestionably built upon the foundation of the Apostles and Prophets, it were madness to throw away the advantage of our position, and join a community whose spiritual claims are (to say the least) dubious.

51. *Catechist.*—You have admitted, in the course of this examination, the existence of some serious defects in the English Church. Can you adduce any grounds of consolation and thankfulness, which ought to cheer her true children, and encourage them in their allegiance to her?

Answer.—Yes. There is consolation to be found in patient hope, and in certain cheering symptoms in the present state of things.

52. *Question.*—What is the consolatory hope to which you refer?

Answer.—That what is wanting to the full vigour and efficiency of our Church system will be in due time supplied. Thinking and devout people are so struck with these defects, that even now things seem working towards a remedy.

53. *Question.*—What cheering symptoms are there in the present state of things?

Answer.—The unusual activity manifested by the Church in her Ministries; the zeal both of Clergy and Laity, which shows itself in many new forms of Church work; the energy and ability with which the Truth is maintained against error, and with which efforts are made to bring the masses under the influence of true religion.

54. *Question.*—What do all these things seem to prove?

Answer.—That the Lord is still with our Church, and will eventually exert His power for her salvation from the dangers which threaten her. And if this be so, we are safe, however much the waves of controversy, which surge and swell around the Church's bark, may disquiet and terrify us. "Therefore will we not fear, though the earth be moved: and though the hills be carried into the midst of the sea. Though the waters thereof rage and swell: and though the mountains shake at the tempest of the same. God is in the midst of her, therefore shall she not be removed: God shall help her and that right early." (Ps. xlvi. P.B.V. vv. 2, 3, 5.)

CHAPTER VIII.

THE CHURCH PRESENTING, EXHIBITING, AND DEFENDING THE TRUTH.

"The house of God, which is the Church of the living God, the pillar and ground of the truth. And, without controversy, great is the mystery of godliness: God was manifest in the flesh, justified in the Spirit, seen of angels, preached unto the Gentiles, believed on in the world, received up into glory."—1 TIMOTHY III. 15, 16.

THE subject on which we are at present engaged cannot be treated satisfactorily, without pointing out the relations which subsist between the Church of God and the Truth of God—relations often grievously misconceived, and not very easily apprehended except by candid and well-balanced minds. These relations are exhibited to us in the passage which stands at the head of this Chapter; and we cannot better secure ourselves against error on this important subject, than by studying the designation which is here given of the Church as "the pillar and ground of the truth." This plan will have another advantage, as falling in with the orderly treatment of the subject. In the Gospels we have seen our Lord first predicting the

Relations of the Church to the Truth, exhibited in St Paul's designation of the Church.

Church, and then, subsequently to His Resurrection, tracing the outlines of the Institution. In the Acts we have seen the actual building of it by the ministry of the Apostle Peter, and the actual exercise of its powers in Council. We now come further down in the Canon of the New Testament, to consider a brief but pregnant description of the Church given us in the Epistles of St. Paul. Thus we shall be gathering up instruction on our subject from each great division of the New Testament.

Desirableness of consulting the Epistles as well as the Gospels and the Acts, on the subject under consideration.

"The Church of the *living* God." The Apostle had just called the Church the *House* of God. And it is probable that, in using the term "living," he had in his thoughts the great temple at Ephesus (of which city Timothy was Bishop), which was the house of a dead god, containing, as it did, the "image" of the many-breasted Diana, "which fell down from Jupiter," in the midst of which there was no breath at all, could neither see, nor hear, nor eat, nor sm "The pillar and ground" (more properly, the pedestal or basement) "of the truth." There is very probably a twofold allusion—one, as before, to the temples of heathen gods, which had grand columns supporting their pediments, and pedestals or bases at the foot of the columns. Pillars are the stay of a building. When Samson pushed down the two middle pillars on which Dagon's house stood, the house fell and became a heap of ruins. If such is the allusion, the Church is here exhibited *as supporting and upholding God's Truth.* But the Apostle being a Jew, and his mind imbued

Possible allusion, in the term 'Church of the living God,' to the idol in the Ephesian temple.

Support of the Truth, one notion pictured by the word 'pillar.'

with Old Testament imagery, it is probable that the words have another reference, which yields a different idea. He may have mentally compared the Church to "the pillar of fire and of the cloud," which God took not away from before the people in their journeying through the wilderness. If such is the reference, the Church is here exhibited under a distinct aspect, not as maintaining Truth, but *as guiding into it and illustrating it.* For the pillar was both a guiding column, and an illuminating column. "And the Lord," we read, "went before them by day in a pillar of cloud, *to lead them the way;* and by night in a pillar of fire, *to give them light.*" We will consider the phrase "pillar and pedestal of the truth" as conveying both these ideas,—maintenance and support of truth, in the first place, guidance into truth, and illustration of it, in the second. The latter aspect of the Church's functions will be considered in the Chapter.

Guidance and illumination a second notion.

The first function which the Church has to fulfil towards the Truth is that of upholding and supporting it. And this the Church does in three ways: by way of presentation and recommendation; by way of exhibition; and by way of defence.

Three different modes in which the Church upholds the Truth.

1st, *By way of presentation and recommendation.* To the Jews of old, descended lineally from Abraham, and sealed with the seal of God's Covenant in Circumcision, "were committed the oracles of God," the books of the Old Testament. And similarly to the Christian Church, descended in a right line from the

By presentation and recommendation.

The Jewish Church intrusted with the Old Testament.

the Christian Church with the New.

Apostles by successive incorporations into the Society which they (under Christ) founded, and brought into the pale of God's Covenant by the Sacrament of Baptism, is committed that still more sacred and precious deposit, the volume of the New Testament. The Church, Jewish or Christian, is the custodian of the Holy Scriptures, and her office is to put those Scriptures into the hands of her children, as soon as they are able to understand them. We observe here an analogy between the history of the world[1] and that of the individual soul. The Church was before the Bible in the history of the world. Abel, Noah, Abraham, and Jacob belonged to the people of God, and lived in the faith of God's promise before there was any written Scripture at all; for,

The Church the appointed keeper of Holy Writ.

Analogy between the history of the world and that of the individual, in that the Church was before the Bible in the world's history.

The spoken Word must exist before the Church, though the Church existed before the written Word.

[1] It is important to observe that this analogy only holds good of the Bible (or *written* Truth), not of those *unwritten* words of God which were handed down orally. *In the history of the individual*, the Church must always be before the Word. The young child of one of the twelve Patriarchs must have received *from its mother* the great promise of the Seed of the woman, and the promises made to Abraham. The young child born of Christian Parents shortly after the day of Pentecost, must have received *from its mother* the brief summary of doctrine, which represented the belief of the first disciples. Thus, *in the order of the child's experience*, the mother was before the unwritten Word. But IN THE HISTORY OF THE WORLD, THE UNWRITTEN WORD OF GOD MUST OF COURSE BE BEFORE THE CHURCH. For what is a Church (in the wider sense of the word) but a group of believers in God's Word? And before the Word is spoken, how can there be believers in it? "Faith cometh by hearing, and hearing by the word of God." Therefore the Word of God must be *before* faith. It is only of the Bible, or written volume of God's oracles, assuredly *not* of God's spoken Word, that we assert it to have been brought into existence later than the Church.

so far as we know, Moses was the earliest Scriptural writer. And in the same way, there was a Christian Church,—ay, and Christian martyrs, and Christian ministers, and Christian teaching,— before a line of the New Testament was written, much more before it was published and thoroughly circulated. And just so it is in the history of the individual. He necessarily becomes acquainted with the Church before he becomes acquainted with the Bible,—it is the natural order of things. Some one must put the Bible in our hands, tell us what it professes to be, and invite us to read it. This is done, in the first instance, by our parents, who are for us the earliest Ministers of the Church, and very often Ministers whose instruction is more effective than any we meet with in after life. The mother teaches her child to kneel down at her knees, and puts words of prayer in his mouth, and tells him about God and Jesus. And what is this but the very same thing which, on a scale adapted to the enlarged capacities of the adult, is done by Ministers of the Church as part of their ministry? Is not this a very fair summary of our office as Ministers, to announce to people the glorious message of the Gospel, and by that means bring them to their knees in right earnest? And if it should suggest itself to any, that mothers, whatever be the obligations under which they are laid by natural affection, are not officially ministers of the Church, let it be remembered that sponsors *are* officially charged to see that each child admitted to Church-membership is brought up in a knowledge of the rudiments of

and that to the individual it is the Church who presents the Bible.

Christian parents are the Church's earliest agents.

Sponsors are bound officially (and not by mere natural affection) to see that each child receives instruction in the Truth.

the Faith, and to lead a godly and a Christian life; so that in *theory*, at all events, the Divine Society of the Church lays hold of the youngest children, and makes provision for their having the Truth taught them, as soon as consciousness begins to dawn. Nay, long before consciousness begins to dawn, the Divine Society lays holds of them, consecrating them in Baptism to the service of its Founder, and thus making them the subjects of a great Church ministry, and of an operation of Divine grace, before they can possibly know that there is a Bible. If, then, God's written Word is deposited with the Church, and she is solemnly bound to place this written Word in the hands of her children and commend it to them, and in their youth to train them in the rudiments of it, most appropriately is she called "the pillar and ground of the truth;"—it is her witness to the written Truth which leads, in the first instance, to our receiving it.

It is the business of the Church to place Holy Scripture in the hands of her children, and call their attention to it.

Again; the Church maintains and upholds the truth *by way of exhibition*. She embodies it in her system of worship, and thus makes it visible to the eye. "O foolish Galatians," writes St. Paul, "who hath bewitched you, that ye should not obey the truth, before whose eyes Jesus Christ hath been evidently set forth, crucified among you." We are so much under the dominion of sense, and the things we see make so far more lively an impression on us than the things we only hear, that God has provided, by the Ministry of His Church, for the exhibition to the eye of the greater Gospel truths. He has not only sent us a

The Church maintains the Truth by exhibition of it.

The principle of our nature on which this exhibition is made to the eye.

VIII.] *exhibiting, defending the Truth.* 247

message, but ordained Sacraments which embody the chief features of the message. Thus Baptism represents our need of spiritual cleansing by the Blood and Grace of Christ (a fundamental truth of our Religion); our death unto sin in Christ, our burial with Christ, our resurrection with Him unto newness of life (the body of the baptized, in the primitive form of administration, being plunged beneath the water, and, after a moment of suspended animation, lifted out of it again); and in short our new creation in Christ, brought about (as the first creation was), by "the Spirit of God moving upon the face of the waters." The Holy Communion represents the bruising of Christ's Body, and the shedding of His precious Blood for us, and the necessity of feeding upon this Body and Blood by faith, in order to the maintenance of that spiritual life, which is communicated in Baptism. See how many vital truths are by these two Sacraments compendiously exhibited to the eye,—our natural defilement and need of cleansing; the purifying efficacy of Christ's Blood and Spirit; Christ's vicarious suffering, death, burial, resurrection; our participation in His sufferings, and in His acceptance, by faith; the need of constant sustenance for the spiritual life; that sustenance only to be had by feeding spiritually on His Body and Blood, etc. I say the Sacraments *represent* these truths; not, *did once represent them*. In order to a perpetual representation you must have a present and living Church, in which, or "among" the members of which, the representation shall be

[marginal notes: Truths represented in Baptism, and in the Lord's Supper. The representation a living and effectual one, making a conveyance of the grace represented.]

made. If Christ had founded no Church, or if the Church He founded had been designed to pass away with the early believers who were the first members of it, the accounts of the Institution of Baptism and the Lord's Supper might be regarded as curious pieces of ancient sacred history, having little more than a literary and antiquarian interest for us. But the living Church proclaims aloud; "Here are Baptism and the Lord's Supper alive at present, their natural force nothing abated since the Lord instituted them. Here they are under your eyes; and the union with Christ in His death, which both of them teach and convey, is as necessary for you, and as freely offered to you, as it was necessary for and offered to the earliest believers." And so with other and lower rites; for the whole system of the Church's worship has more or less of a sacramental character. Her ordinary offices express the truth that He is "in the midst of the two or three gathered together in His Name" (the human presence in the congregation being the symbol of His); Confirmation exhibits God's fatherly hand extended over the baptized, and their need of His strengthening Grace; Absolution is a visible testimony to the great truth that the forgiveness of sins through Christ's Blood travels in the Church's train down the stream of time, like the smitten rock which followed Israel in the wilderness. And all of these are living powers in the Church, disentangled indeed from the miraculous element, which attended them at their first appearance, but still efficacious in the spiritual world, and

The symbolism of Public Worship, Confirmation, and Absolution.

conveying what they represent to every prepared and faithful heart. If you desire to learn the Truth, it might be ascertained from a careful analysis of these rites, which embody and represent it. You might ask of the Lord's Supper, for example, "What meaneth this service? what is its history? how did it take its rise? what truth is it designed to convey?" And if this last question were fully and faithfully answered, you would gather from the answer the whole doctrine of the Gospel, which is all comprehended briefly in this one Ordinance. *Possibility of arriving at the Truth by an analysis of the rites embodying it.*

Lastly, the Church upholds the Truth *in the way of vindication and defence*. The early Creeds or Confessions of Faith were very simple and very brief. But as new heresies and forms of error developed themselves, the Church, having been solemnly intrusted with the guardianship of the Faith, was compelled to make new definitions, thereby considerably enlarging the bulk of her Creeds. If any one should think these definitions dry, hard, wanting in interest at best, and in some instances repulsive, surely he may be reminded usefully of their defensive character. A man thrown on the defensive is not perhaps in the most pleasing attitude in which he can be placed, nor are his words and actions at that moment attractive. A city must have a girdle of fortifications, lest it should fall an easy prey to an invader,—it must have its arsenal, in which are ranged side by side guns and pikes, and in whose vaults are stored up combustible and explosive materials. Fortifications are in many respects an *The Church maintains the Truth by vindicating and defending it.* *New heresies necessitated the expansion of early Creeds.* *Usefulness and necessity of fortifications, however little attractive they may be.*

inconvenience; they are certainly not as picturesque or as agreeable as parks and pleasure-grounds, nor are piled arms as pleasant to look upon as beautiful waving trees, white with blossom, or laden with fruit;—any one can make such comments as these, but it is somewhat weak to make them, if we want the fortifications and arms for defence. *If we want them, they must be had.* Doubtless it would be far more delightful to live without controversy, and never to be under the necessity of protesting against error; but how if error will raise its head, will insinuate itself into the minds of the weak and wavering, and rob Christ of the souls which are His purchase? Is the Church, which is set by God in the earth to be "the pillar and ground of the truth," to make no remonstrance, no protest, while this is going on under her eyes? Is the pillar of the truth to give way, when what it was designed to uphold is attacked? So thought not our forefathers in the Faith in earlier and purer times. As heresies showed their head, the Church condemned them, and added the definition of the Faith so necessitated to her existing formularies. And I cannot help observing that these definitions have far more than a defensive value,—that they tend wonderfully to clear the minds of believers on the subjects of which they treat. Let me give one instance before passing on. Many persons think of Christ as a demi-god, half God and half man,—almost as of a man apotheosized and raised to the skies, as having been the greatest benefactor of the human race. All this is heathenish, false, and

[margin: The Church would betray her trust, if she protested not against heresies.]

[margin: Clearness of mind on subjects of Faith, the gain which believers derive from the Church's definitions.]

unscriptural. Christ is perfect God, and also at the same time perfect man, but without any confusion or mixture of the two natures. The two natures remain in their distinctness, though united indissolubly in the single Person of the Son of God, just as mind and body are perfectly distinct, though united indissolubly in one man. It was not our Lord's Godhead which suffered, or died, or wept, or agonized. On the other hand, it was not our Lord's manhood which said on the edge of the grave, "Lazarus, come forth;" or from the seat of the Cross; "Verily I say unto thee, To-day shalt thou be with me in paradise;" nor is it His manhood of which it is written; "The Word was in the beginning with God. All things were made by him; and without him was not anything made that was made." Christ is wholly and distinctly man, and wholly and distinctly God. There is not a sympathy of our nature, nor an attribute of God's nature, which He lacks; for which reason He is both infinitely tender and infinitely strong.—Now, I ask whether this definition of the Faith is not a little helpful in clearing the mind on the subject with which it professes to deal? And if it be helpful and valuable, I then ask further from what source the definition was obtained? Whence do these words come?—"Perfect God and perfect Man." . . . "He is not two, but one Christ, . . . One altogether; not by confusion of Substance: but by unity of Person. For as the reasonable soul and flesh is one man" (as mind is one thing, and body a distinct thing, though both go to make up one

The definition of the two natures and one Person in Christ, an instance of this.

Helpfulness of that definition.

Its source, the Athanasian Creed.

man), "so God and Man is one Christ." They come from an elaborate Confession of Faith, drawn up probably by a French Bishop in the earlier half of the fifth century, and expressing the general sense of the Western Church in his time,—never, indeed, received by the whole of Christendom, as the Nicene Creed is, but received by our own National Church, and declared by her to be provable " by most certain warrants of Holy Scripture."

I have spoken of Christian Creeds in their defensive aspect, and have explained that the reason why they grew in bulk was that the Church was thrown from time to time on the defensive against heretics, and obliged to fortify herself by new definitions. But let it be remembered that the Creeds were not defensive at the outset of their history; in their germ and nucleus they did not partake of this character. The Church always had a Faith and a Truth to guard, though there was a time when she had no Scripture. Adam, and Abel, and Enoch, and Abraham had a Faith, and were possessed of a Truth, long ages before the Law was written. They had God's promise of the Seed of the woman, handed down by oral tradition; that was their Faith and their Truth. They looked for a city which had foundations, whose builder and maker is God; that was their hope. And similarly St. Stephen had a New Testament Faith, and a New Testament Truth, and died in the full sunshine of New Testament hope, though not a line of the New Testament was written in his days. And what does St. Paul mean by the Truth, when he calls the

Creeds, in their origin, were not defensive.
Before there was a Scripture, there was a Truth.
What the Truth was in Patriarchal times.
Earliest shape in which the Truth appeared in New Testament times.

Church its pillar and ground? I have applied his words without hesitation to the Gospel, as contained in the volume of the New Testament, because to *us*, who live since it has been written, this volume *is* God's Truth, and because the Holy Spirit, who inspired St. Paul, wrote, no doubt, in the foresight of the New Testament, and adapted his language to the circumstances and needs of the modern, as well as of the ancient, Church. But as the volume of the New Testament was certainly not compiled, and a large part of it not written, when St. Paul addressed his first letter to Timothy, he clearly could not have been thinking of the New Testament, when he spoke of the Truth. No; he meant the Gospel Revelation, the few salient features of which were embodied even at that early date in a Creed or Confession of Faith, which the Apostle calls elsewhere "a form of sound words." This Truth or Revelation was, as he here calls it, a "mystery of godliness." The persons he wrote for knew well what "mysteries of ungodliness" were; for there were several such mysteries, which formed a part of the old Pagan religions. Mysteries were certain sacred rites, in which (as they say is the case in Freemasonry) a traditional secret was divulged to the initiated, and made the nucleus and centre of a form of worship. Some of the rites connected with this worship were horribly impure and cruel; the heathen mysteries were "mysteries of *ungodliness*." But God's Revelation in Christ, the magnificent secret into which the Church indoctrinates mankind, the secret of redeeming love

What St. Paul means by 'the Truth' in the passage under consideration.

Why he calls 'the Truth' 'the mystery of godliness.'

Contrast between 'the mystery of godliness' and heathen mysteries.

and grace, the secret of the Atonement and its allied truths, which also is the centre and nucleus of the Church's whole system of worship, is a "mystery of godliness;" that is, a secret which, really imbibed by the inner man, produces the fruit of godliness. And the Apostle proceeds to give "the mystery" in the express terms in which the Church had received it. "God was manifest in the flesh, justified in the spirit, seen of angels, preached unto the Gentiles, believed on in the world, received up into glory,"—this is obviously a fragment of some early Confession of Faith, some dogmatic statement of the Truth, with which Timothy was familiar, and which was recited in meetings of the Church, and handed down as a "form of sound words." "The truth" in this instance (hear it all ye who, while you profess a love for the Holy Scriptures, freely evince a dislike of dogmatic statements), "the truth" in the present instance, which St. Paul dignifies by calling it the "great" (or magnificent) "mystery of godliness," was nothing more nor less than a Creed.[1]

The mystery of godliness a fragment of an early Creed.

Metrical character of this doctrinal summary, and the light thrown on its meaning by a metrical arrangement of it.

[1] In all probability it is also a Hymn; for it is manifestly metrical in its construction, the first and second lines corresponding to one another, as also the fourth and fifth. In all probability, therefore, the sixth corresponds with the third.

1. Ὅς ἐφανερώθη ἐν σαρκὶ,
2. Ἐδικαιώθη ἐν πνεύματι,
3. Ὤφθη ἀγγέλοις,
4. Ἐκηρύχθη ἐν ἔθνεσιν,
5. Ἐπιστεύθη ἐν κόσμῳ,
6.   Ἀνελήφθη ἐν δόξῃ.

I cannot but think that this arrangement throws light upon the meaning of ver. 3. The correspondence of vers. 1 and

And what a precious Creed, with its statements of the incarnation, the justification of Christ (involving also our justification in Him), by the solemn testimony which, on various occasions, the Spirit made to Him, the angelic acknowledgment and adoration of Christ, the universal mission of the Gospel to every creature, the reception of the Gospel in the world by simple faith, and His ascension into heaven! I would rather regard it as a song of triumph put by God into our mouths, than as the bastions of a fortification, which girdles round the city of God. If we regard the Creeds (and surely we may do so) as being brief summaries of God's glorious Revelation to man, jubilation and not controversy becomes their leading feature. When we regard the Athanasian Creed as *the Hymn* " Quicunque vult "—a joyous exposition of the truths which go to make up our faith,—what a different aspect does it assume! Its defiant tones, if they still exist, are drowned in its tones of Christian exultation—" it is not the voice of them that

Comprehensiveness of this short doctrinal summary.

A triumph song rather than a fortification.

Jubilant aspect of the Christian Creeds may well

drown in our minds, when we use them, their polemical associations.

2, as also of vers. 4 and 5, is marked. "God was manifested in the flesh" (amidst all the weaknesses and humiliations which "flesh" involves), yet "justified in the Spirit" (at His Baptism, by His miracles, by His Resurrection, and by the Spirit's testimony to Him after Pentecost). He was "preached unto the Gentiles," and (as the marvellous result of such preaching) "believed on in the world." Now, may we not suppose from Psalm xxiv. (part of which seems to be the utterance of Angels, escorting Christ back to Heaven), that at the Ascension there was some general act of homage paid to our Lord by the Angels;—"Seen of Angels," and then (after He had received the tribute of their homage) "received up into glory," "angels and authorities and powers being made subject unto Him"?

shout for mastery . . . but the noise of them that sing do I hear." The recital of a Creed is in fact, under this view, the highest of all acts of praise. And in order to give effect and expression to this view, the Creeds should beyond all question be sung. Three out of our four Creed Rubrics prescribe that they shall be "sung or said," as if singing here were to have the preference over saying. Oh that it might be so throughout every parish in the land! and oh that the heart of every one who sings might rejoice secretly in hope of the glory of God, being justified (as we can only be justified) by the faith which we then profess, and in the exercise of that faith having "peace with God through our Lord Jesus Christ, by whom we have now received the atonement!"

Creeds are better sung than said.

Catechism on Chap. VIII.

1. *Question.*—What subject was touched upon in your last examination, which requires to be more clearly and exactly defined?

Answer.—The relations which subsist between the Church of God and the Truth of God.

2. *Question.*—From what passage of Holy Scripture is it proposed to gather these relations?

Answer.—From St. Paul's definition of the Church as "the pillar and ground of the truth" (1 Tim. iii. 15).

3. *Question.*—Is there any incidental advantage in taking the passage which we are to study for information on this great subject from *the Epistles?*

Answer.—Yes; because thus we embrace, in the consideration of our subject, another great division of the New Testament. In *the Gospels* we have seen our Lord predicting the Church during His life, and, after His Resurrection, tracing the foundations of it. In *the Acts* we have seen the Church's superstructure rising under the ministry of St. Peter, and her legislative and judicial powers put forth in the first Council. We turn now to *the Epistles* for an exact definition of the relation in which the Church stands to God's Truth.

4. *Question.*—To what does the Apostle probably allude, when, after calling the Church "the *house* of God," he then adds that it is "the Church of the *living* God?"

Answer.—As he is writing to Timothy, who was Bishop of Ephesus, it is very probable that he is alluding to the celebrated temple of Diana at Ephesus, of which mention is made in Acts xix. 27, and which, containing as it did "the image which fell down from Jupiter" (see Acts xix. 35), a many-breasted idol placed upright on a rude block, was the house of a *dead* God, in which there was no breath at all.

5. *Question.*—In the expression "pillar and ground of the truth," what is the exact meaning of the word "ground"?

Answer.—It means the pedestal (or base) of a column.

6. *Question.*—What is the first idea which we obtain from the words "the pillar and ground of the truth?"

Answer.—That of *support.* The Church supports the truth as a pillar supports a pediment or roof, and as a pedestal supports a pillar.

7. *Question.*—Where in Bible history do you read of pillars acting as a support to the building?

Answer.—In Judges xvi., where we are told of "two middle pillars upon which the house" (of Dagon) "stood, and on which it was borne up;" of which pillars when Samson "took hold," and "bowed himself with all his might," "the house fell upon the lords, and upon all the people that were therein." (See ver. 29, 30.)

8. *Question.* But is it probable that the Apostle, in calling the Church "the pillar and ground of the truth," is referring to some particular pillar, of which we read in the history of the Old Testament?

Answer.—Yes. He may have mentally compared the Church to "the pillar of fire and of the cloud," which the Lord "took not away from before the people" in their journeying through the wilderness.

9. *Question.*—If this was the allusion in his mind, what two ideas does this pillar of fire and of the cloud give? It did not support anything, as the pillar of a building does. What useful offices then did it perform?

Answer.—That of *guiding* the people by day, and *illuminating* them by night. For we read in Exod. xiii. 21, "And the Lord went before them by day in a pillar of a cloud *to lead them the way;* and by night in a pillar of fire *to give them light;* to go by day and night."

10. *Catechist.*—We will postpone to another occasion the consideration of these two ideas, drawn from "the pillar of fire and of the cloud," and confine ourselves to the idea of the Church's supporting (or maintaining) the Truth. Tell me in what way she does this?

Answer.—Chiefly in three ways. 1*st.* By presenting and recommending the Truth. 2*dly.* By exhibiting (or representing) it. 3*dly.* By defending it.

11. *Question.*—What do you mean by the Church's presenting and recommending the truth?

Answer.—I mean that as soon as we are of age to understand the Scriptures of truth, it is the business of the Church of our country, from which in our infancy we received Baptism, to put these Scriptures into our hands, and earnestly to commend them to our perusal and consideration.

12. *Question.*—Does our Twentieth Article (*Of the authority of the Church*), to which you referred in your last examination, notice this presentation and recommendation of Holy Scripture as one of the Church's functions?

Answer.—Yes. It speaks of the Church as being "a witness and a keeper of holy Writ." Holy Writ is a treasure committed to her custody (or "keeping"), that she may hand it down to the successive generations of her children; and when she does this, she testifies (or bears "witness") to these books that they contain "the true sayings of God," "given by inspiration of God," and written by "holy men of God," who "spake as they were moved by the Holy Ghost." (See 2 Tim. iii. 16, and 2 Pet. i. 21.) Thus our first acquaintance with Holy Scripture and with its claims is brought about by the Church.

13. *Question.*—Can you show from Holy Scripture itself that the Church is the appointed witness and keeper of the oracles of God?

Answer.—This is expressly stated of the books of the Old Testament by St. Paul (Rom. iii. 1, 2). "What advantage then hath the Jew? or what profit is there of circumcision? Much every way; chiefly, because that *unto them were committed the oracles of God.*" We may reasonably argue from analogy that the books of the New Testament are committed to the Christian Church, just as those of the Old were to the Jewish; though indeed this is implied in those passages where the faith is spoken of as a deposit, which is to be kept by those to whom it is handed down, and with whom it is lodged, as for example; "O Timothy, keep that which is committed to thy trust" (1 Tim. vi. 20); "Hold fast the form of sound words which thou hast heard of me, in faith and love which is in Christ Jesus. That good thing which was committed unto thee keep by the Holy Ghost which dwelleth in us" (2 Tim. i. 13, 14); "The things that thou hast heard of me among many witnesses, the same commit thou to faithful men, who shall be able to teach others also" (2 Tim.

ii. 2). And the same thing is taught in the passage before us, in which "the truth," of which the Church is said to be "the pillar and ground," is evidently the same thing with "the mystery of godliness," that is, with the leading Articles of the Christian Faith.

14. *Question.*—In what shape, as a matter of fact, does our first introduction to God's Truth come to us?

Answer.—It comes to us through the teaching of a mother, who makes us read the Bible and explains it, and teaches us about God and Jesus, and puts into our mouth words of prayer. This is the first commencement of the religious instruction, which we obtain from the Church of our country.

15. *Catechist.*—But this does not satisfy me. A Christian mother, who feels that the truths of the Bible are of the utmost interest and importance, will doubtless teach them to her children out of natural affection. But there is nothing *official* in this teaching. Nor do I see that a mother can strictly be called a minister, or even an agent, of the Church, though she may (of her own free will) act as one. I think you should show that provision is actually made by the Church for the sufficient religious instruction of every baptized child, independently of those ties of natural affection, which bind parents to teach their children the truths necessary to salvation.

Answer.—That I can easily do. The Church takes such care for the religious instruction of her children that she appoints three agents for every child, called Godfathers and Godmothers, to whom she gives this charge. "You must remember that it is your parts and duties to see that this infant be taught, so soon as *he* shall be able to learn, what a solemn vow, promise, and profession *he* hath here made by you. And that *he* may know these things the better, ye shall call upon *him* to hear sermons; and chiefly ye shall provide that *he* may learn the Creed, the Lord's Prayer, and the

Ten Commandments in the vulgar tongue, and all other things which a Christian ought to know and believe to his soul's health." If the Church were to give this charge to the parents, and make *them* her agents for the religious instruction of the child, this would not recognise with sufficient distinctness the great difference between the family of nature, to which the child belongs by its natural birth, and that of grace, into which it is introduced by Holy Baptism.

17. *Catechist.*—It follows from what you have said that each one of us becomes acquainted with the Church before he becomes acquainted with the Scripture. Of course this is so. The first thing we become conscious of is the persons around and about us, and we cannot reach any truth without their instruction. The child cannot get at the Scriptures without a mother's teaching. Can you point out anything in the world's history similar to this fact in the history of the individual?

Answer.—Yes. There was an Old Testament Church in the world before there was an Old Testament, and there was a New Testament Church in the world before a line of the New Testament was written.

18. *Catechist.*—Prove this to me.

Answer.—Moses was the writer of the earliest books in the Bible; but there was a Church (or family of God) before Moses. Abel belonged to it, and Noah, and Abraham, and Jacob. And even if it should not be thought strictly correct to speak of Abel and Noah as members of *a Church*, if it should be maintained that there was no Church till God gave to Abraham and his seed the Sacrament of Circumcision, or none until the children of Israel were led through the Red Sea, which was a type of baptism (see 1 Cor. x. 1, 2), the same truth will hold good. Abraham lived long before Moses, and Moses could scarcely have written even the Book of Genesis,—certainly could not have written that of Exodus,—before the passage of the Red Sea took place. And as regards the *New* Testament, St.

Matthew's Gospel, supposed to be its earliest book in point of date, is attributed by learned men to the year A.D. 38. Now the day of Pentecost, when the Christian Church was fully set up, fell in the year A.D. 33. There must have been then an interval of five years, during which the Christian Church did not possess a line of New Testament Scripture. St. Stephen fell asleep in Jesus without the privilege of having read a single verse of the New Testament.

19. *Catechist.*—I understand you to be speaking only of the Old and New Testament *in the form in which we have them;* in short, only of the *written* Word of God. There must surely have been a *spoken* Word of God before there could be anything for faith to lay hold of, and therefore before, in any sense whatsoever, there could be a *Church.*

Answer.—Undoubtedly there was such a spoken Word. The first promise to fallen man (which was dropped in the course of the sentence upon the serpent) contains in itself the germ of the Gospel, for it spoke of a Virgin-born Champion of the human race ("the seed of the woman"), of His passion and death in the lower nature he assumed ("thou shalt bruise his heel"), and of the triumph He should achieve over the devil ("it shall bruise thy head"). See Gen. ii. 15. Our first parents no doubt laid hold of this first promise by faith, and doing so became of the number of God's true people, and may be called (in the broadest sense in which the words can be used) members of the Church. This promise, which constituted their only Bible, they handed on to their posterity. And all similar promises were handed on in a similar way, by oral tradition when there was no writing, or when writing could not be rapidly and widely circulated. Doubtless as soon as any form of writing was invented, it would be adopted (however rude it might be), to preserve the record of these oracles of God. And Moses may have had some such older written records before him when he composed the Pentateuch.—So that, although the

Church existed before the Bible, it did not exist before the Word of God.

20. *Question.*—What is the second way in which the Church supports the Truth?
Answer.—By exhibiting (or representing) it.

21. *Question.*—How does the Church exhibit the Truth?
Answer.—By means of the holy Sacraments.

22. *Question.*—How does this method of presenting the Truth differ from that which we have just considered?
Answer.—The mode of presenting the Truth, which we have just considered, consisted in either handing down by tradition the unwritten words of God (before there was any Scripture), or, since Scripture has been written and published, in placing it in the hands of the children of the Church, and giving an explanation of it. This is done by means of words, either spoken to the ear or read; but, unlike the *Word* of God, His *Sacraments* preach the Gospel to *the eye.*

23. *Question.*—What principle of our nature may we suppose Almighty God to have had in view when ordaining the Sacraments of the Church?
Answer.—The principle that we are affected in a more lively manner by what passes under our eyes, than by what we only hear of.

24. *Question.*—What does the Sacrament of Baptism represent?
Answer.—Several vital truths of the utmost importance; such as the necessity of spiritual cleansing by the blood and grace of Christ, the burial of the Christian with Christ (by the plunging of the baptized person under the water, which is the primitive and correct form of administering the Sacrament), his resurrection with Christ unto newness of life (by the lifting of the person into the air after immersion), and the new creation of our human nature in and through Christ, which new creation takes its rise out of water, and is

brought about by the Holy Ghost,—reminding us of the first creation, respecting which it is written that it, too, had a similar origin, for "the Spirit of God moved upon the face of the waters." (See Gen. i. 2.)

25. *Question.*—What does the Sacrament of the Lord's Supper represent?

Answer.—The bruising of Christ's body, and the shedding of His precious blood for the sins of the whole world, and the necessity of feeding upon this body and blood by faith in order to the maintenance of that spiritual life, which is communicated in Baptism.

26. *Question.*—In what passage of his Epistles does St. Paul probably allude to this representation of Christ's death in the Lord's Supper?

Answer.—In Gal. iii. 1, where he says, "O foolish Galatians, who hath bewitched you, that ye should not obey the truth, *before whose eyes Jesus Christ hath been evidently set forth, crucified among you.*"

27. *Question.*—But why must we here suppose any allusion to Sacraments? Why may not the Apostle mean that he had preached Christ crucified to them in so lively and effective a manner, that it seemed to bring back the whole awful scene of the Crucifixion, and make it present to them as if it had been enacted among them?

Answer.—This probably *is* part of his meaning; but had he meant nothing else but this, he would rather have said, "crucified *for* you" than "*among* you." And then it should also be borne in mind that the allusion to witchery (or fascination) in the earlier part of the verse lends probability to the idea that he has the Lord's Supper in his thoughts. For fascination was anciently supposed to be exercised through the eye; so that the meaning may very possibly be, "Who hath laid upon you *the spell of an evil eye*, and thereby distracted you from that touching and hallowing spectacle of a crucified Saviour, which, in the holy Supper, has been so often *presented before your eyes?*"

28. *Catechist.*—Yes; it is certainly remarkable that

the Apostle should speak of Christ having been crucified "*among*" the Galatian Christians, and "before" their "eyes." It seems to hint at something which made the power and efficacy of His death present to them, although it had been transacted in a past time, and in a country remote from theirs. And this must be the ordinance of the Lord's Supper, in which Christ's death is not indeed repeated—for He "offered one sacrifice for sins *for ever*" (Heb. x. 12); "we are sanctified through the offering of the body of Jesus Christ *once for all*" (Heb. x. 10); and we are expressly told that he does not "offer himself *often*, as the high priest entereth into the holy place every year with blood of others" (Heb. ix. 25),—but powerfully and efficaciously exhibited before God and man, so as to become the spiritual food and sustenance of believers in every successive age of the Church. So that Christ's death, though an event which took place more than eighteen centuries ago, lives in the Church of to-day with a present power and efficacy.—But the two Sacraments are only *the centre* of the Church's system of worship. May the same thing which you have said of them (namely, that they exhibit and represent the Truth) be said also in a lesser degree of all parts of the system?

Answer.—Yes; every part of the system of worship represents, and, as being a *living* ordinance, efficaciously represents, some part of the Truth. Thus, for example, Absolution represents the great doctrine of "forgiveness of sins," brought home to the heart and conscience of the individual; Confirmation represents our need of the strengthening influences of the Holy Ghost, in order to a successful warfare with our spiritual foes; while Public Worship generally represents the truth that "where two or three are gathered together in" Christ's "name, there" is He "in the midst of them."

29. *Catechist.*—Show that these several ordinances are

not merely representations, but powerful and efficacious representations.

Answer.—Where Absolution is sought with a true penitent heart and lively faith, it is really granted to him who seeks it, and peace is ministered to his conscience thereby. When young persons present themselves for Confirmation with real and single devotedness of heart, bent upon wholly consecrating themselves to God, and looking up to him for strength to put their vows in practice, the Holy Ghost is really "given through laying on of hands" (see Acts viii. 18, and xix. 6); and whenever two or three Christians meet seriously and devoutly (and not as a mere formality) in the Name of Christ, and humbly claim His promise to united prayer, He is as certainly in the midst of them, though not as visibly, as He was in the midst of the disciples on the evening of the first Easter Day, when the little flock was gathered together with closed doors "for fear of the Jews." (See St. John xx. 19.)

30. *Catechist.*—What you have said under this head of your examination amounts to this, that the Ordinances of the Church, and especially the Sacraments, are an expression and embodiment of the Truth. How then might we arrive at the Truth from them?

Answer.—By studying them profoundly, and inquiring of each of them, "What meaneth this service?" "How did this institution take its rise?" "What truths of religion is it meant to express?" The single Ordinance of the Lord's Supper, studied thus, would be found to be a Gospel in itself.

31. *Catechist.*—You said that the third way in which the Church supports the Truth is *by defending it.* How does she do this?

Answer.—By means of her Creeds and Confessions of Faith.

32. *Question.*—What is the character of all the earliest Creeds?

Answer.—They are very brief and simple.

33. *Question.*—What made it necessary for the Church to enlarge the bulk of her Creeds by adding new articles to them?

Answer.—The rise of false doctrines, against which it was the Church's duty to protest, in order to warn her children back from vital error. Each new heresy gave rise to some fresh definition of the Faith, which was added on to the old Creed, and in time caused it not only to assume larger proportions, but to have the appearance of subtlety, fine distinctions being introduced, of which nothing was ever heard until it was found that they were needed.

34. *Catechist.*—Many persons call these distinctions and definitions uncouth and ugly, and find fault with the Church for having made them. How will you answer their objections?

Answer.—By pointing out that fortifications too are uncouth and ugly, shut out the view of the country, and remind us unpleasantly of war; but still that they may be absolutely necessary for the security of a city. In like manner Creeds and Confessions may wear a dogmatic and repulsive aspect in one view of them, and yet be necessary as a security for the members of the Church, when an attempt is made by heretics to corrupt and deprave the Faith.

35. *Catechist.*—Yes; Creeds must of necessity carry about on them the marks of controversy, seeing that controversy gave rise to them. And controversy is always a harassing and disturbing thing. What makes it necessary?

Answer.—The fact that false doctrines will constantly be broached, and that, when they are broached, it would be a breach of trust in the Church not to condemn them, she being the "pillar and ground of the truth."

36. *Question.*—Are we warned in Holy Scripture that the future of the Church will be marked by the rise of heresies and soul-destroying errors?

Answer.—We are. The New Testament is full of such warnings. St. Paul, in taking leave of the Ephesian elders at Miletus, warned them to this effect, "For I know this, that after my departing shall grievous wolves enter in among you, not sparing the flock. Also of your own selves shall men arise, speaking perverse things, to draw away disciples after them. Therefore watch" (Acts xx. 29, 30, 31). And St. Peter, speaking generally to all Christians, says (2 Pet. ii. 1, 2), "But there were false prophets also among the people, even as there shall be false teachers among you, who privily shall bring in damnable heresies, even denying the Lord that bought them, and bring upon themselves swift destruction. And many shall follow their pernicious ways; by reason of whom the way of truth shall be evil spoken of." And so again St. Paul to Timothy (1 Tim. iv. 1), "Now the Spirit speaketh expressly that in the latter times some shall depart from the faith, giving heed to seducing spirits, and doctrines of devils." The key-note of all these warnings had been already struck by our Lord Himself in His Sermon on the Mount (St. Matt. vii. 15), "Beware of false prophets, which come to you in sheep's clothing, but inwardly they are ravening wolves;" and in His Prophecy on the Mount (St. Matt. xxiv. 11), "And many false prophets shall rise, and shall deceive many." And St. Paul shows that there is *a necessity* for the rise of heresies in the Church, in order that the faith of the faithful may be approved by trial. "For there must be also heresies among you, that they which are approved may be made manifest among you" (1 Cor. xi. 19).

37. *Catechist.*—You have pointed out that the Church's Creeds and Confessions are defensive in their character. Can you mention another and more attractive purpose which they subserve?

Answer.—Yes; they are elucidatory. These subtle definitions, made originally against heresy, serve to clear the mind on the high subjects of which they treat.

38. *Question.*—Will you give an instance of what you mean?

Answer.—Many persons entertain confused and erroneous notions about our Blessed Lord, drawn rather from heathen mythology than from the Holy Scriptures. They think of Him as a demigod, half god and half man, whereas He is "perfect God and perfect Man," having all the attributes of both, and at one time speaking and acting in one of these natures, at another in another. And yet He is not two Persons, but one Person, the eternal Son of God "manifest in the flesh." We have an image of all this in ourselves. Each one of us has a rational, and also an animal, nature. We are not half rational and half animal, but wholly rational and wholly animal. The two natures are quite distinct; one of them never fulfils the functions of the other; they never trespass on each other's spheres. I calculate a problem in my mind. I hunger in my body. The body never calculates; the mind never hungers; and yet, though the rational and animal natures are so distinct, certain it is that they both exist in the same person. A. B. is not two men, because he has both a body and a mind.

39. *Catechist.*—Yes; that illustration is very happy. Where did you borrow it from?

Answer.—It comes from the Athanasian Creed, an elaborate Confession of Faith, of whose origin little is known with any certainty, but which has certainly existed in the Church for a thousand years, and has been received by all Western Christendom, and even by some parts of Eastern. Its language on the doctrine of Christ's single personality, but twofold nature, is as follows:—

" Who although he be God and Man: yet he is not two, but one Christ;

" One; not by conversion of the Godhead into flesh: but by taking of the Manhood into God;

" One altogether; not by confusion of Substance: but by unity of Person.

"*For as the reasonable soul and flesh is one man:* so God and Man is one Christ."

40. *Catechist.*—You have spoken of creeds as defensive in their character. And that the later developments of them were so, there can be no question. But were quite the earliest Confessions of Faith defensive?

Answer.—No. They were simple statements of the Faith held by the Church, brief summaries of saving truth, in meditating upon which, Christians might always find peace and joy and edification, and in the confession of which they gloried, even when they suffered for it.

41. *Question.*—Do we meet with any of these brief doctrinal summaries in Holy Scripture?

Answer.—Yes; one of them is found in the passage which is under consideration at present (1 Tim. iii. 16). It seems to have been a Confession of Faith constructed in parallel clauses, and with a sort of rhythmical cadence, to assist the memory.

> "God was manifest in the flesh,
> Justified in the Spirit,
> Seen of angels,
> Preached unto the Gentiles,
> Believed on in the world,
> Received up into glory."

42. *Question.*—What does the Apostle mean by calling this Confession of Faith a "mystery"?

Answer.—He calls it so in allusion to "the mysteries" of heathen worship. These mysteries were sacred rites, in which a certain secret was divulged to those who were initiated. In like manner, those who were initiated by Baptism into the religion of Christ, had a certain "form of sound words" intrusted to them, containing the secret of redeeming love and grace, and lodged in their memories as a sort of watchword, by the use of which they might be recognised.

43. *Catechist.*—Quote some passages of St. Paul's

Epistles in which he speaks of the doctrines of the Gospel as a secret or "mystery" divulged by preaching.

Answer.—" Now to him that is of power to stablish you according to *my gospel, and the preaching of Jesus Christ,* according to *the revelation of the mystery, which was kept secret since the world began, but now is made manifest,* and by the scriptures of the prophets made known to all nations for the obedience of faith" (Rom. xvi. 25, 26). " By revelation he made known unto me the mystery, . . . *which in other ages was not made known unto the sons of men, as it is now revealed unto his holy apostles and prophets by the Spirit;* that the Gentiles should be fellow-heirs, and of the same body, and partakers of his promise in Christ by the gospel" (Eph. iii. 3, 5, 6). " The Church, whereof I am made a minister, according to the dispensation of God which is given to me for you, to fulfil" (or, fully to preach) " the word of God; even *the mystery which hath been hid from ages and from generations, but now is made manifest to his saints:* to whom God would make known what is the riches of the glory of this mystery among the Gentiles; which is Christ in you, the hope of glory: whom we preach " (Col. i. 24-29).

44. *Question.*—But why does he call this Confession of Faith a " mystery of *godliness*"?

Answer.—By way of contrast with the heathen mysteries, some of the rites connected with which were impure and cruel. *They* were mysteries of *ungodliness.* But the grand secret of God's redeeming love and grace in Christ, which was communicated to the baptized, and by them embraced as their Profession of Faith, was productive only of godliness. It engendered love to God and man, and, by its testimony respecting the efficacy of Christ's blood, purged "the conscience from dead works to serve the living God." (See Heb. ix. 14.)

45. *Question.*—What are the doctrines enumerated in this short Confession of Faith?

Answer.—*First*, the Incarnation of a Person in the Godhead, that is, His appearance in human nature; *secondly*, the justification of Him as man (and therefore the justification of all who are united to Him) by such events as the descent of the Spirit upon Him, the voice from heaven at His Baptism, His resurrection from the dead, and the testimony borne to Him in men's hearts by the Holy Ghost; *thirdly*, the manifestation of Him to the angels (which possibly took place at his Ascension), and their compliance with the exhortation, "Let all the angels of God worship him" (Heb. i. 6); *fourthly*, the preaching of the gospel to every creature under heaven (see Col. i. 23, and Rom. xvi. 26); *fifthly*, its acceptance in all the world, and the consequent gathering of a Catholic (or Universal) Church, "of all nations, and kindreds, and people, and tongues" (see Rev. vii. 9); and *sixthly*, the Ascension of Christ into heaven, and His session at the right hand of God, "till his enemies be made his footstool" (see Acts ii. 34, 35). Stated in the language of the Apostles' Creed, these doctrines are—"I believe . . . in Jesus Christ, [God's] only Son, our Lord, Who was conceived by the Holy Ghost, Born of the Virgin Mary. . . . The third day he rose again from the dead, He ascended into heaven, And sitteth on the right hand of God the Father Almighty. . . . I believe in the Holy Ghost; The holy Catholic Church; The Forgiveness of sins."

46. *Question.*—What spirit will these great doctrines, if heartily embraced, stir within us?

Answer.—A spirit of joy and praise, in the thought of all the glorious things which God hath done for our souls.

47. *Question.*—And how ought this spirit of joy and praise to express itself in our method of reciting the Christian Creeds?

Answer.—By song, which is the natural vehicle of praise.

48. *Question.*—Are the Creeds in the Book of Common Prayer appointed to be sung?

Answer.—Not necessarily. An option is given either to "sing" or "say" them. But as in "The Order for Morning Prayer," and in "The Order of the Administration of the Holy Communion," "singing" is named before "saying" ("*Then shall be sung or said the Apostles' Creed;*" "*Upon these Feasts . . . shall be sung or said at Morning Prayer . . . the Creed of Saint* Athanasius;" "*The Gospel ended, shall be sung or said the Creed following;*") we conclude that "singing" is the method of recitation to which the Church gives the preference.

49. *Question.*—In what new and attractive aspect would the compliance with this order for singing them present the Creeds?

Answer.—In the aspect of hymns of praise. Their controversial character would be for the moment dropped by the mind, and we should regard them as "triumph-songs of heaven," cheering onward, as with martial music, the soldiers of Christ, who "manfully fight under his banner against sin, the world, and the devil." "For the joy of the Lord is our strength." (See Neh. viii. 10.)

CHAPTER IX.

THE CHURCH GUIDING INTO AND ILLUSTRATING THE TRUTH.

> "And the Lord will create upon every dwelling-place of Mount Zion, and upon her assemblies, a cloud and smoke by day, and the shining of a flaming fire by night."—ISAIAH IV. 5.

THE reader will remember that we are now considering the relations of the Church of God to the Truth of God, as those relations are sketched for us by the Apostle Paul, where he calls the Church "the pillar and ground of the truth." The notion gained generally from the expression "pillar and pedestal" is that of maintenance and support; and it was pointed out in the last Chapter in what senses the Church may be said to maintain and support the Truth. But we saw that there might have been another and more specific allusion in the mind of the Apostle, when he termed the Church "the pillar of the truth." He might refer to "the pillar of fire and of the cloud"—at once a guiding and an illuminating pillar—which went before Israel in their march through the wilderness. Now the restoration to the people of this "pillar of fire and of the cloud," after Jerusalem had been

Possible reference of the words 'pillar of the truth' to the pillar of fire and of the cloud.

"purged" "by the spirit of judgment and by the spirit of burning," seems to be foretold in the passage of Isaiah which stands at the head of this Chapter. This prophecy, like all other Scriptural prophecies, is no doubt rich in meaning, and the fulfilment may be expected to repeat itself several times, and in several shapes, before it becomes full-orbed. But we can hardly be mistaken in thinking that one fulfilment of it will be found in the Christian Church, which is the spiritual or true Zion. And if so, "the cloud and smoke by day," and "the shining of a flaming fire by night," which the Lord will create upon the assemblies of Mount Zion, may very properly be taken to express the guiding and illuminating functions of the Church, in reference to the true sense of Holy Scripture, of which we are now to speak.

Restoration of the pillar of fire and of the cloud predicted by Isaiah.

The guiding and illuminating functions of the Church a partial fulfilment of this prediction.

"Guidance and illumination as to the true sense of Holy Scripture." Perhaps there are some who honestly think that we need no such guidance or illumination, beyond what is supplied by our natural faculties, and a moderate amount of general education. Instead of saying with the Ethiopian nobleman, "How can I understand what I read, except some man should guide me?" these people ask, not at all from self-conceit or sinful presumption, but because the exigencies of a theory seem to demand it of them, and because their Protestantism seems to them imperilled by any other view of the subject; "Why cannot I interpret Scripture aright for myself by the exercise of my own faculties, and dispense altogether with human interpretation? Is not Scripture its own

Objection raised that, in order to understand Holy Scripture, we want no guidance save that of average education and intelligence.

sufficient interpreter?" Now, if any principle is a sound one, it must admit of being tested by a crucial experiment, and will hold good, if tried in an extreme case. If, then, you are sincerely and earnestly convinced of the soundness of this principle, that the Bible itself, without any sort of concurrent explanation, is a sufficient guide into its own meaning; I ask whether you are ready to risk something—say the faith of your child—upon your conviction? It is open to any parents who wish to do so to make the experiment. Only they must make it honestly (which in a Christian country it might not be easy to do), and steadily refuse to let the child's mind be biassed by any sort of religious instruction. Neither his mother, nor any one else, is ever to mention to him God or Jesus or the Holy Spirit; he must never be bidden to pray, or have one single word said to him as to what prayer is; nor must he even be told that there is a future state of existence in store for him, the character of which will depend upon his conduct. Yes! if the Bible is really and truly quite capable of being its own interpreter, it can need no more the explanations of a mother, than those of a priest or minister of religion. We will, however, because that was postulated by yourself, give your child a fair secular education, —nay, will even teach him to read Greek, which is the original language of the New Testament, —and we will assume that there is nothing defective in his mental powers, and that he is quite up to the average mark in point of ability. And then, when he has reached his twenty-first birthday, and we may hope that his judgment is matured, is to be made upon this unbiassed, unprejudiced, unprepossessed mind, the great experiment. Then for the first time you are to bring forth the Bible (the name of which he has never heard before), and place it in his hands with a solemn charge; "My son, this is the written Word of God. It contains all truth necessary to our salvation. You know the original tongue, in which the more important portion of the volume was written. Take it, and study it for yourself, and make out the truth from it." ... Can you conceive for a moment that, with the very best intentions, he will succeed? What has he got to make out? What are the most important elements of this "truth," which he is to derive into his own mind by the mere study of the Scriptures? Probably the doctrines of the Trinity and the Atonement. Well; will he rise from the study of the Bible a sound believer in the Son's co-equality and co-eternity with the Father, (a most vital doctrine; for if Jesus be not God, where is the sufficiency of His Atonement?) or in the substitutional character of the Blessed Saviour's sufferings? Do you not see that in order to understand the Scriptures at all, or to any purpose, a certain group of religious ideas must be formed in the mind, which the Bible assumes to be already formed, and to which it appeals, and *which therefore must be obtained from another source?* For example; our unprejudiced youth, on whom the experiment is to be made, opens the Book we have given him, and reads its

[marginal notes: At the age of twenty-one let the Bible be placed in his hands, and let him be exhorted to ascertain from it all religious truth.

Certainty that he will fail to do this, even on the more important doctrines.]

The very first verse of the Bible assumes previous knowledge, not to be gained from the Bible itself.

first words: "In the beginning God created the heaven and the earth." Well; it is only one verse. But even this one verse assumes previous knowledge, not to be gained from the Book itself. It assumes that there is a God, and that you, the reader of the book, grant it. The Bible never proves God, never attempts to demonstrate His existence; it only says that the man who denies His existence is a fool, but does nothing to reason that man out of his folly. I must have an idea of God, then, before I can understand even the first verse of my Bible. And the idea must be

The sources from which we derive our idea of the existence of God.

borrowed from something outside the Bible. As a fact, the idea comes to us partly from our reason and conscience,—but very mainly also from the instructions which we have received when young, and which have put into definite shape the intimations of reason and conscience. We have been assured very early in life that there is one God, of infinite power, wisdom, and goodness; His power and wisdom, we were told, were shown in making the stars and trees and flowers, and His goodness in showering upon us natural blessings, and in sending His Son to redeem us. And we were further assured that this great Being will judge us for our actions, and reward the good and punish the wicked. And thus was developed an idea in our minds, which is necessary to our understanding of the first verse of our Bibles. But it never could have been developed, without some teaching outside the Book itself. And this teaching was that of the Church—first, of a Christian mother, bringing her children up in the nurture and admonition of the Lord, and then subsequently, as the time drew on for our Confirmation, of a Christian Minister.

But possibly some of my thinking hearers are still not quite satisfied as to the necessity of admitting any human interpretation for the right understanding of Holy Scripture. You ask, perhaps, in reference to those doctrines of our Faith to which I have adverted; "Must we not allow that the doctrines of the Trinity and the Atonement are to be found in Holy Scripture?" Most assuredly they are to be found there; and, when found, they are as two great keys, which unlock and open the meaning of the entire volume. But the question is not whether they are to be found there, but *whether they are to be found without any guidance or help.* In the British Museum, or in the Bodleian Library, there are, we will say, at least a hundred editions of the works of Shakspere. So that those grand repertories of books have no lack of copies of our greatest writer;— Shakspere is found there in profusion. But I exceedingly question whether, if you were shut up in the Bodleian Library alone, and left to find Shakspere by the exercise of your own faculties, you would succeed. You would ask for the index, or you would inquire for the librarian. You might and would forget the service they had rendered you, when you had seized and begun to devour your literary treasure; but nevertheless they would have been quite indispensable to you. And similarly a librarian and an index have always been found indispensable to the

That all the doctrines of the Faith are to be found in Holy Scripture, does not imply that they can be found there without a guide.

Fruitless search for a great work in a vast library, unless we have guidance and help.

ascertainment of the true sense of Holy Scripture, the librarian being the Church, Jewish or Christian, and the index that traditional interpretation, which has followed the Word of God down the stream of time, and which has always been a God-given light under which the Scriptures have been read. That we all habitually avail ourselves of this interpretation is a fact, whether we like it or no. And if we were to ignore this interpretation, we should cut ourselves off from a large amount of comfort and edification, and remove the only key we have to the meaning of certain passages. Take one or two instances. In order to light up the narrative of the Fall with any sort of moral meaning, you must suppose that the serpent was not a mere beast of the field, but the devil using the serpent as his instrument. But how do you know that it was so? There is not a vestige of the fact in the sacred narrative itself. If you persist in going by the letter of Genesis, you have no warrant whatever for saying that the devil appeared at all to our first parents. St. John, it is true, in the very latest book of the New Testament, does call Satan that "primeval serpent," from which a believer in and reader of the New Testament might gather that the serpent which appeared at the Fall was something more than he seemed to be. But must we not suppose that long before the Revelation was written, every member of the Jewish and Christian Churches perfectly understood who the serpent was, that plays so very prominent a part in the history of our race? Was St. Paul

Whence did we obtain the information that the serpent in Gen. iii. is the devil?

St. John, the only Scriptural writer who gives a hint of it; and yet surely the Church must have possessed the information before his time.

ignorant who the serpent was, when he wrote, "I fear, lest by any means, as the serpent beguiled Eve through his subtilty, so your minds should be corrupted from the simplicity that is in Christ"? —Whence then did Jews and Christians, and St. Paul among the rest, obtain the information that the serpent was in reality the great enemy of mankind? There is no means of answering that question but by supposing that the Old Testament came down to them, not floating in a vacuum, but wrapped round with an atmosphere of traditional sentiments and explanations.

But we shall perceive the existence of this atmosphere still more clearly, if we proceed a little further in the history. Immediately upon the Fall was issued what is called the first Prophecy. It pleases us to call it the first Prophecy; but, as it stands in the narrative, it is really nothing else than the sentence of the Lord God upon the serpent, in which are incidentally introduced these very enigmatical words of comfort to the woman: "The woman's seed shall bruise thy head, and thou shalt bruise his heel." A preacher, preaching on this text, would, without hesitation, interpret Christ (the Virgin-born) to be the woman's seed—the bruising of the heel of Christ to be the sufferings which His lower nature should undergo from wicked men, instigated by wicked spirits,—and the bruising of the serpent's head to be the crushing of the devil's power by the Saviour's death and resurrection; and his congregation would receive his interpretation as assuredly true, and as the right use to be made of the

Usual interpretation of the Prophecy respecting the Seed of the woman.

not obtained from the Bible itself;

passage. But whence did he and they get it? Certainly not from the letter of the Bible. I am not aware that it is ever said of the woman's seed (though it is of Abraham's) that by that expression Christ is meant. Your son, whom you have brought up with a good secular education, but without any hereditary religious ideas, could by no possibility make out from the document that

nor could a person deriding the usual interpretation be convicted of error from the Scriptures.

Christ was meant. And if, in the perversity of his scepticism, he chose to laugh outright at your idea that the sufferings of Christ at the hands of the devil, and His glorious triumphs over the devil, are enigmatically foretold in those words, and to insist that there was nothing in them at all beyond the natural antipathy which men (all of whom are born of woman) feel for serpents,—an antipathy which leads them, when they see a snake in the grass, to trample on its head, in the endeavour to do which the creature may sometimes turn and sting them in the heel,—you could say nothing at all from the letter of Scripture to disprove his view and prove your own. What *would* you say to him? You would probably say, "You are very perverse; you reject an interpretation which all Christendom has agreed to put upon the passage." And he would not unreasonably reply; "You told me the Book would speak for itself, and be an abundantly sufficient guide into its own meaning. If so, of what service can the judgment of Christendom be to me? I maintain there is nothing here but a saying about serpents and men; true enough, no doubt, but having no moral or spiritual bearing whatever." And he is right. In the letter of the Bible we in vain seek for anything more.

Again; consider how very large a portion of most valuable typical teaching we must consent to forego, and, consequently, to how great an extent the Old Testament must become a dead letter to us,—merely interesting as an antiquarian record, —if we resolve to be beholden in nowise to that traditional interpretation, which, concurrently with the Scriptures themselves, the Church, both Jewish and Christian, has handed down.

For instance, what possible connexion with the great subject of Good Friday has the first Morning Lesson which our Church appoints for that day,— the Chapter of Genesis, which records the offering up of Isaac by his father? A young Sunday-school child would give you a ready answer to this question. "The Chapter is appropriated to Good Friday," he would say, "because on that day God gave up His dear Son to suffer death upon the cross for the sins of the whole world, and Abraham's sacrificing Isaac is a figure or type of God's doing this. And just as the wood, whereon he was to be offered, was carried by Isaac, so our beloved Lord was made to carry His wooden cross to the place of execution, before He was stretched upon it to be crucified." Nobody educated in the usual way, under the light of traditional Christian sentiments, doubts that Isaac is an eminent type, or questions that his carrying the cloven wood is a typical particular; but the Bible itself never tells us anything of the sort. And if any one should choose to maintain that Isaac is not a type of Christ

The typical relation of the sacrifice of Isaac to the Sacrifice of Christ

must be denied, if the Bible is to be strictly self-interpreting.

at all, there is nothing in the letter of the Scriptures to confute him.

Once more, it is unquestionable, because the writer of the Epistle to the Hebrews affirms it expressly, that the old patriarchs looked not for transitory promises,—that Abraham, for example, "looked for a city which hath foundations, whose builder and maker is God." But whence did Abraham derive this expectation, an expectation which is so vital an element in everything deserving the name of religion, that we may truly say religion cannot exist without it? Unless you suppose a communication of the fact of eternal life being in store for God's true people to have been made to our first parents by the Almighty, and handed down in the line of Seth as a thing understood in the Patriarchal Church, and as the revealed basis of all piety, Abraham's grounds for the expectation must have been of the very slenderest. They must have been confined to the translation of Enoch, the memory of which would, no doubt, be carefully preserved, and from which pious men might augur the probability of a future state of blessedness for those who walked in Enoch's footsteps. But surely only the probability. There was this great argument in favour of Enoch's case being in all respects exceptional, that it was markedly exceptional in one particular. Enoch was removed; he never died. Because Enoch was taken to glory, it would not be conclusive to argue that those over whose heads the grave did actually close should pass out of it again, to become sharers of Enoch's blessed-

[Margin notes: St. Paul's direct assertion that the old patriarchs looked not for transitory promises. They had nothing in the Old Scriptures to ground their hopes upon. Insufficiency of the history of Enoch for a well-grounded hope in the case of others.]

ness. And when, in the time of Moses, the written Scripture did at length appear, the hints of eternal life given in the Pentateuch were so rare and so obscure, that without help from some external traditional sentiment, some instinctive consciousness cherished by the people of God, it would have been impossible to decipher them. Bishop Warburton, in his "Divine Legation," makes the silence of Moses on the subject of eternal life one premiss of his rather perverse argument. His object is to prove the indisputable truth that Moses received a divine commission. This he does by showing that every great legislator except Moses found it necessary, in promulgating his law, to appeal to eternal sanctions. Moses did not find it necessary to do this. He therefore must have had something else to fall back upon, in procuring the acceptance and observance of his law. And what he had to fall back upon was the consciousness of the people that God had indeed commissioned him, flowing from their witnessing his miracles. No doubt Warburton stretches a point to prove his minor premiss. But if eternal life had been revealed with any plainness in the Law, it would have been utterly impossible to adopt his line of argument.

<small>Absence of the doctrine of eternal life from the Pentateuch, a postulate of Warburton's argument.</small>

I need not pursue the subject further, except to say that we all, as a fact, deal with the New Testament on entirely the same principles as those on which the Church has always dealt with the Old, accepting it, that is, not in its mere letter, but as wrapped round with an atmosphere of traditional interpretation. Of course it is, in its

<small>Though the New Testament needs explanation less than the Old, yet in many points we are obliged to call in the tradition of the Church, in order to interpret it.</small>

very nature, far more explicit and plain, far less enigmatical and obscure, than the earlier volume; but still we accept very many things in our system of doctrine and practice which, while they may be very plausibly supported by the New Testament, still could never be found in the mere text of it, except with the help of the traditional interpretation, which the practice of the early Church puts upon it. The observance of Sunday (I am not speaking of the Sabbath, but of the Lord's Day), an observance which we rightly prize and cherish,—where is it made incumbent upon us by the law of Christ our Saviour, unless you will admit the general sense of the early Church as throwing light upon the Lord's mind? If you rest *the principle* of the observance (as you may reasonably do) on the fourth Commandment, still you must show some reason for shifting the observance from Saturday to Sunday. "God blessed and sanctified the seventh day," not the first. And the only reason you can possibly show for the change of day is the general sense of the Church throughout the world, that the Lord's Resurrection having fallen on the first day of the week, was a sufficient justification for the transfer. Again, we prize dearly Infant Baptism, as sealing our little ones for the Lord, and bringing them under the gracious influences of His Spirit, before consciousness dawns. But while we may and do support Infant Baptism out of the New Testament, no one can say with truth that he finds it in the letter of the volume. The early Church had an instinctive sense that it was in

The substitution of the Lord's Day for the Sabbath, and its sanctification,

nowhere expressly prescribed in the New Testament.

Infant Baptism also rests not on express New Testament prescription, but on traditional usage, tracing back to the earliest times.

accordance with the mind of Christ to baptize infants; and they did uniformly baptize them. Finding the practice universally prevalent in the first few centuries after Christ, and therefore bearing every trace of derivation from the Apostles themselves, we then go to Holy Scripture, and find there several passages beautifully consonant with it, such as, "Suffer little children," etc., and the Baptism of whole households recorded in the Acts. But we nowhere find any positive rule to baptize infants.

Enough, I trust, has now been said to prove the point, which is, that we all (more or less) do as a matter of fact read Scripture in the light of an hereditary transmitted interpretation, and that, if we are to possess ourselves of its full moral and spiritual significance, we must read it so. The experiment never was honestly made of reading the Scriptures without note or comment, or without such previous prepossession with certain religious ideas as virtually is note and comment; and there is every reason to believe that, if the experiment could be made, it would be a miserable failure as regards the arriving at truth. The Ethiopian nobleman was right. He *could* not have understood what he read, without "some man" to "guide" him. St. Philip the Deacon was to him the representative and accredited agent of the Church of Christ, which, in reference to God's Truth, is a guiding and illuminating pillar, —leading the way, and giving light. And this office the Church fulfils for us, partly by her Creeds and Confessions of Faith, partly by her

No one really reads Scripture without borrowing something from an hereditary transmitted interpretation.

Office of the Church fulfilled by St. Philip to the Ethiopian, when he complained that he could not understand what he read, except some man should guide him.

formularies (which embody a large amount of doctrinal teaching), and still more by that transmitted hereditary meaning of Holy Scripture, which she carries down along the ages, and which is a sort of instinct or conscience, like the Scriptures themselves, widely influential, but very difficult to give an account of.

In what sense Holy Scripture is, in its turn, the pillar and pedestal of the Church.

But we must not omit to remark, in conclusion, that if the Holy Scripture needs the explanation of the Church, the Church still more needs the explanation of Holy Scripture. If in one point of view the Church is the pillar and pedestal of "the truth," in another and no less important one, "the truth" is (as Chrysostom clearly saw) the pillar and pedestal of the Church. I receive the Holy Scriptures in the first instance on the testimony of the Church. I read them under the light which the Church transmits. All this is indisputable. But, on the other hand, how can the Church explain what she is, or what authority she has, without an appeal to Holy Scripture?

The office, authority, history, and existence of the Church can only be ascertained from Holy Scripture.

"You call yourself the Church," the person approached by her might say; "but what is a Church? what account can you give of yourself, or of the authority with which you profess to have been invested? I know nothing about you at present." It is of course utterly impossible to answer such questions *without the Book*,—more impossible even than it would be to understand Scripture without the Church's commentary. The charter and title-deeds of the Church are in Scripture; and if you remove Scripture, you cut away the very pillar and pedestal of the Church.

The sum is, that both the Holy Scriptures and the Church are God's witnesses among men, and that they are mutually necessary to one another, linked in the closest of bonds. The Church is the ordained *teacher* of truth, which must reach us, in order to be influential with creatures constituted as we are, *through a living voice.* The Holy Scripture is the great *criterion* of truth, the only standard of appeal by which every controversy must be tried, so that "whatsoever is not read therein, nor may be proved thereby, is not to be required of any man, that it should be believed as an article of the faith, or be thought requisite or necessary to salvation;" and it has moreover this great prerogative, that it is always pure, perfect, infallible, whereas the prejudices and passions of men, their controversies and partisanships, often grievously deprave the Church, and render it utterly unlike even its primitive model, —far more unlike its ideal in the mind of its Founder. "What God hath joined," however, "let not man put asunder."

The Holy Scriptures and the Church mutually necessary to one another.

Exclusive prerogative of the Holy Scriptures, above the Church.

Let us prize our Bibles above all earthly treasure, reading (or rather studying) them with earnest prayer for God's Spirit. And let us hold fast, while studying them, that clue which God has given us to their meaning in our Prayer-Book, which for us embodies and represents the teaching of the Church, "the pillar and ground of the truth," at once supporting and illustrating it. This signification of the Prayer-Book we shall exhibit in our last Chapter.

Subject of the final Chapter introduced.

Catechism on Chap. IX.

1. *Catechist.*—We are now to consider the ideas yielded by the words, " the pillar and ground of the truth," on the hypothesis that the Apostle, in using them, is alluding to the pillar of fire and of the cloud, which journeyed before the children of Israel in the wilderness. State once again what those ideas are.

   Answer.—That the Church guides into the Truth, and throws light upon it; because the pillar of a cloud led the people the way by day, and the pillar of fire gave them light by night. (See Exod. xiii. 21.)

2. *Question.*—Where do we find a promise of the restoration of this pillar of fire and of the cloud?

   Answer.—In Isaiah iv. 5: "And the Lord will create upon every dwelling-place of mount Zion, and upon her assemblies, a cloud and smoke by day, and the shining of a flaming fire by night."

3. *Question.*—Are we to look for the fulfilment of this promise in Gospel times?

   Answer.—It would appear so. The heading of the chapter, in the Authorized Translation of the Bible, is, "*In the extremity of evils, Christ's kingdom shall be a sanctuary.*"

4. *Catechist.*—The context of this passage then concerns Christ's kingdom, or, in other words, the Church. And probably the Church is meant by the term "mount Zion" in the verse before us. If this be so, what will be the interpretation of the "cloud and smoke by day, and the shining of a flaming fire by night"?

   Answer.—These words will find their fulfilment in the guiding and illuminating functions of the Church, by which she indicates the true sense of Holy Scripture. She not only recommends, exhibits, and defends the Truth, but also guides into the knowledge of it, and throws light upon it.

5. *Question.*—For us, who live since the Canon of the New Testament has been completed, what *is* "the Truth?"

Answer.—The volume of the Holy Scriptures.

6. *Catechist.*—Your assertion is, then, that the Church guides us into the knowledge of the Holy Scriptures, and throws light upon the study of them. But there are some who think and assert that the Holy Scriptures need no explanation, and are best read without note or comment. They suppose that all that is required to gain the Truth from the volume of the Bible is sufficient intelligence and a certain amount of general education, and that, where a person is possessed of these qualifications, he can make out the Truth for himself, or (at all events), make it out so far as is sufficient for his own edification and salvation, without further help or guidance. Scripture, they say, is its own sufficient interpreter. How would you deal with views like these?

Answer.—I should point out that no good and devout person does ever, as a fact, trust the Bible to interpret itself, however much he may insist theoretically upon the position that Holy Scripture is its own sufficient interpreter.

7. *Question.*—What do you mean?

Answer.—I mean that people would not act upon this theory, where something valuable had to be risked in acting upon it, thereby showing that they have no real practical belief in what they maintain. It is said that a divine, who in the year 1860 had made up his mind, from the study of unfulfilled Prophecy, that the end of the world would come about in 1870, afterwards went and took a house upon a long lease for ninety-nine years, at the expiration of which, if his theory of unfulfilled Prophecy were true, the earth ought to have been laid in ashes for eighty-nine years. He cannot really have believed his own prediction, though he may have persuaded himself that he did so.

And, in like manner, no one acts as if he believed that the Bible is its own sufficient interpreter, however earnestly he may maintain that position in argument.

8. *Question.*—What specially are you alluding to?

Answer.—To the fact that every one, in educating children, thinks it right and necessary to give them, along with the Bible itself, that explanation of it which is currently received among Christians.

9. *Question.*—If people really believed that the Bible (with the help of a good general education) is its own sufficient interpreter, what experiment on their children ought they to be contented to make?

Answer.—That of bringing them up until they reach an age to judge for themselves, without instilling into their minds a single religious idea.

10. *Question.*—But why are they bound to go so far as this, if they desire to be consistent?

Answer.—Because, by instilling a single religious idea, they are in fact putting an explanation upon the Bible, and anticipating what the child ought hereafter to get from the Bible for himself.

11. *Question.*—Are these people on their own theory doing something, not only superfluous, but positively mischievous and wrongful, when they instil religious ideas into the minds of children?

Answer.—Yes; because they are biassing them towards certain religious opinions of their own, before the judgment can possibly be matured. If God has not provided us with any living guide or instructor, but wills us to gain all our religious knowledge for ourselves out of a book which He has caused to be written, it must surely be wrong as well as harmful to interfere with His method, by prepossessing the minds of children with any religious sentiments whatsoever, before they come to an age to examine the Bible for themselves. If, on the other hand, God has provided a guide and instructor for both young and old, and has made His instructions necessary for the right understanding of His Holy Word, it must be very perilous to dispense with the services of this guide.

12. *Question.*—As general propositions are often apt to mislead, and as the question before us is a grave one, in which it would be very serious to be misled in either direction, will you mention one or two Scriptural doctrines of the utmost importance, which could not be obtained from the mere letter of Scripture without collateral explanation?

Answer.—I may mention the doctrine of the Holy Trinity, and that of Christ's Atonement.

13. *Question.*—What circumstance would make the doctrine of the Holy Trinity very hard to find in Holy Scripture, without some previous doctrinal training?

Answer.—The circumstance that the doctrine is, if we except the controverted and very doubtful text in St. John's 1st Epistle (v. 7), nowhere explicitly stated in terms in the Bible.

14. *Question.*—But if the Holy Scriptures do not expressly state it, do they contain it?

Answer.—Most assuredly they do: only they give it us piecemeal, and by continual references to it and assumptions of it. There are many passages[1] in which Christ is expressly said to be Divine. Other passages[2] clearly intimate the Godhead of the Holy Ghost. And yet we are repeatedly warned, both in the Old and New Testaments, that there is but one God.[3] The combination of the truths taught in these various passages results in the doctrine of the Trinity. Then again there are many passages which assume and refer to, though they do not expressly state, the doctrine. Such

---

[1] As John i. 1; Rom. ix. 5; 1 Cor. xv. 47; Heb. i. 8, 10 Isa. ix. 6; Acts xx. 28, and many others.

[2] As Acts v. 3, 4; Acts xxviii. 25, 26; with Isa. vi. 3, 9, etc. etc.

[3] As Deut. vi. 4; St. Mark xii. 29; 1 Cor. viii. 4; Isa. xliv. 8, etc. etc.

are the prescribed form of Baptism (St. Matt. xxviii. 19); the Apostolic Benediction (2 Cor. xiii. 14); and the text, " Jehovah our Elohim is one Jehovah " (Deut. vi. 4; and St. Mark xii. 29); literally, "the Lord our Gods is one Lord." So that this grand doctrine may be most clearly and certainly proved from Scripture, though it is nowhere stated in terms there.

15. *Question.*—Can you give any illustration of a doctrine being really and certainly contained in a document, which yet is never expressly stated there?

Answer.—I think I can. Let us imagine some book, which contains all the Acts of the British Legislature for a single year. The doctrine of the English Constitution, and of the respective powers of the Sovereign, the Lords, and the Commons, might be made out from such a book, though it would not be in its province to make a formal statement of the doctrine. We should find that in all cases, after a Bill had passed one House, it was considered (and occasionally altered) by the other, and that, when it had passed both Houses, it was invariably submitted to the Sovereign for the Royal Assent. And thus we might make out, by comparing different parts of the volume, the full doctrine of the English Constitution, and of the checks upon legislative action which it involves.

16. *Catechist.*—If this illustration is just, it would seem that Holy Scripture is designed rather to *prove* the Truth than to *teach* it. Is this so?

Answer.—It is. The Bible assumes the existence of a living instructor in the Truth, who will indoctrinate us into the rudiments of it, and refer us to the Scriptures themselves for the proof of what he teaches. If the instructor is dispensed with, and the disciple thrown back merely on the Bible and his natural faculties, he will be very liable to stumble, almost certain to do so as regards those more recondite definitions of doctrine, which the Church's experience of heresies has shown her to be necessary, and has taught her to make.

17. *Question.*—Why would a person, into whose mind no religious ideas had been instilled in childhood, almost certainly fail to find the true doctrine of the Atonement in Holy Scripture?

Answer.—Because the idea of atonement belongs to a group of ideas, which the reader of Holy Scripture is assumed to have ready formed in his mind, before he comes to the perusal of the Volume. Expiation made by the sufferings and death of an innocent victim for the sins of the guilty, is an idea which we catch, each one of us, from the atmosphere of religious tradition, which wraps us round in our childhood, and we read our New Testaments under the light which that tradition furnishes. If this light were not shining upon us, we should be puzzled to know what to make of such inspired statements as these, which at present are the comfort and joy of our hearts;—" Behold the Lamb of God, which taketh away the sin of the world" (St. John i. 29); " He was wounded for our transgressions, he was bruised for our iniquities; the chastisement of our peace was upon him; and with his stripes we are healed" (Isa. liii. 5); "Christ died for our sins, according to the scriptures" (1 Cor. xv. 3); "Who his own self bare our sins in his own body on the tree" (1 Peter ii. 24); "Herein is love, not that we loved God, but that he loved us, and sent his Son to be the propitiation for our sins" (1 John iv. 10); "Unto him that loved us, and washed us from our sins in his own blood" (Rev. i. 5).

18. *Catechist.*—You say that before a man can understand the Bible, he must have a mind furnished with certain ideas, which ideas the Bible assumes as known and admitted. Show that the Bible in its earliest verse assumes a truth, which must be drawn from some other source than the Bible itself.

Answer.—Let us suppose that a mother, without ever having told her child anything about God, reads to the child the first verse of the Bible, under the belief that the Bible itself will teach him all it is necessary for him to know—" In the beginning God created the heaven and the earth." The child would certainly ask, " Mother, who is God?" And when the mother explains that God is a Being of infinite power, wisdom, and goodness, who holds our life in His hand, and from whom flows our every blessing, an intelligent child might naturally ask, "How do you know *there is such a Being*, as you say you have never seen Him?" And this question cannot be answered out of the Bible. The Bible *assumes* the existence of God, but does not *prove it.* It speaks to those who admit the existence of God, and have an idea of Him already formed in their minds. The Bible seeks to exalt this idea, to elevate it, to purify it, to make it worthier, and grander, and more attractive idea than it ordinarily is (a very large part of the Bible is occupied in doing this), but it never offers a proof of God's existence. It simply says, that to deny the existence of God is sheer folly (See Psalm liii. 1).

19. *Question.*—Whence then, if we are not taught it by the Bible, do we derive the conviction that there is a God?

Answer.—From the intimations of conscience, which assures us of the existence of a Righteous Governor, "who will render to every man according to his works," and from the works of nature, which lead us to the conclusion of a great First Cause. The existence of God proves itself to our conscience and reason, which are so constructed that we cannot but believe in a Superior Being. And these intimations of the reason and conscience are developed and put into shape by the teaching we received in our childhood. That there is a God, all good, all wise, who controls and governs us, and sees all our most secret thoughts, was an idea instilled into us before any other.

20. *Catechist.*—But surely, if the more important doctrines of the Faith are really and truly contained in Holy Scripture, and repeatedly inculcated there, any one will be able to find them for himself, who has a fair amount of intelligence and education?

Answer.—I do not deny that he may find them easily, if he avails himself, or in times past has availed himself, of the appointed guidance. A man brought up in the ordinary way, under the instruction of parents, tutors, and Christian Ministers, one who has always breathed the atmosphere of religious thought which circulates throughout the Church, and which is more or less inhaled by all of us, whether we will or no, will find no difficulty whatever in laying his hand upon the Scripture proofs of the Trinity and the Atonement. But that is not the case supposed. We are imagining the case of one who is thrown upon the study of the Bible, with his mind an absolute blank as to all religious ideas (a case never actually realized to the fullest extent), and we say of such an one that he simply would not know what to make of the Bible, and that, though he might read the texts (among many others), which contain the more vital doctrines, he could not appreciate their importance or central position, nor indeed understand them.

21. *Question.*—Can you compare his dilemma to anything which may illustrate it?
Answer.—It somewhat resembles the case of a man shut up alone in a vast library, to find a copy of a famous author, of whose writings several hundred copies exist, scattered up and down the library.

22. *Question.*—What would such a person want, in order to get at the work of which he was in search?
Answer.—He would want the librarian, or the index, or perhaps both.

23. *Question.*—In ascertaining the true sense of Holy Scripture, what corresponds to the librarian?
Answer.—The Church, which is "the pillar and ground of the truth."

24. *Question.*—And what to the index?
Answer.—The traditional interpretation, which has from time immemorial been current in the Church.

25. *Catechist.*—Many people look with great suspicion upon this traditional interpretation. Why could it not be dispensed with?

Answer.—Because it is absolutely necessary to the understanding of certain passages, and to the profitable understanding of others.

26. *Catechist.*—Show this by giving an example.

Answer.—We read in Gen. iii. of the serpent's seducing our first mother, (and through her our first father,) from her allegiance to God. And in 2 Cor. xi. 3, where the Apostle speaks of the serpent's "beguiling Eve through his subtilty," the same phraseology is adopted. Every child who reads the story of the Fall, is told without hesitation that the serpent, who successfully decoyed our first parents, was the Devil, taking the form of a serpent. And unless we suppose it to be so, the narrative loses its moral, and its consistency with the plan of salvation as developed in other parts of Holy Scripture. But it is never said in the narrative that the serpent was the Devil, nor is the slightest hint dropped to that effect. A traditional interpretation has come down side by side with the narrative, which is absolutely necessary to make it instructive and edifying.

27. *Catechist.*—But surely, without the help of this traditional interpretation, you might infer with certainty that the serpent was the devil from Rev. xii. 9, where St. John expressly calls the Devil the primeval (or aboriginal) Serpent: "And the great dragon was cast out, *that old serpent, called the Devil, and Satan, which deceiveth the whole world.*"

Answer.—No doubt a person possessed of the Book of Revelation, and believing in its genuineness and inspiration, might feel satisfied from that single expression that it was the Devil who, under the form of a serpent, conducted the temptation of our first parents. But the Book of Revelation is in point of date among the latest books of the Bible; and it is quite impossible to suppose that believers, before the Book of Revelation was written, were ignorant who this serpent was, or that the Corinthians did not understand St. Paul to mean the Devil, when he wrote to them about the serpent, "who beguiled Eve through his subtilty." St. Paul, using as he does at all times "great plainness of speech" (see 2 Cor. iii. 12), would certainly have been more explicit, had he felt that there was the smallest chance of his being misunderstood. But every Christian at Corinth was perfectly aware who the serpent in Genesis was, without being told. Side by side with the books of the Old Testament, had come down a traditional interpretation of them, which the Jews unhesitatingly received, and which the Apostles handed on to their Christian converts, when they placed these books in their hands.

28. *Catechist.*—Give another instance, in which we are entirely dependent on the traditional interpretation, for a right understanding of the Holy Scriptures.

Answer.—The explanation which every Christian puts upon the first promise of a Redeemer really comes, not from Scripture itself, but from a tradition which has for ages found currency in the Church.

29. *Question.*—What explanation do you mean?

Answer.—That which is always given of Gen. iii. 15. That by "the seed of the woman" is meant Christ, who was born of a pure Virgin. That "the seed of the serpent" means wicked men, instigated by devils. That "the seed" of Christ means believers in Him. That "the head" of the serpent denotes his chief seat of power. That "the heel" of Christ denotes his lower (or human) nature. That the bruising of the serpent's head denotes the extinction of his power. That the bruising of Christ's heel denotes what He suffered in His human nature from the enmity of men and devils. None of these explanations are given either in the narrative itself, or in any other part of Holy Scripture. Indeed we are never told in Scripture that by "the seed of the woman" is meant Jesus Christ, which is the foundation of the other explanations, and without which key to the meaning the passage loses all its moral and spiritual significance, and degenerates into a trivial description of the instinctive antipathy which men feel for serpents, the way in which a snake injures a man, and in which the man retaliates.

30. *Catechist.*—But all Christians will tell you, with one accord, that this great prophecy respecting "the seed of the woman" speaks of much higher things than the mutual hostility of men and serpents.

Answer.—Or, in other words, the Christian Church assures me that this is the true meaning of the passage, and the meaning I ought to accept. It does so, I know. But as the Bible does *not* tell me so, I find that something outside the Bible itself is necessary for the right understanding of the holy Volume, that it is not, as is sometimes pretended, self-interpreting.

31. *Question.*—Can you show how the principle that nothing but Scripture itself can be accepted in the interpretation of Scripture, and that no traditional comments can be admitted, would deprive us of many edifying types, and evacuate many of the Old Testament histories of their evangelical meaning?

Answer.—Isaac is one instance in point. Joseph would be another. Neither of these patriarchs is anywhere expressly said to have been a type of Christ. But it is abundantly clear, and indeed generally acknowledged, that both of them were so. Every child is taught that Abraham's sacrifice of Isaac is a type of God the Father's giving His Only-Begotten Son to be a sacrifice for the sins of the world; that Isaac's acquiescence is a type of Christ's cheerful and zealous compliance (see St. John x. 18); that the wood being laid upon Isaac is typical of Christ bearing the cross, and that Isaac's being laid upon the wood is a type of the Crucifixion of Christ. None of these things are said in the narrative; nor can we find any text in the Bible which explicitly calls Isaac a typical character. And yet we make no question of the fact. It is a traditional interpretation, which has come down to us concurrently with the Scriptures. And if we reject it, we leave large tracts of the Old Testament without any special Christian significance. Accept it, and those passages are lighted up with a new and beautiful meaning.

32. *Question.*—Is there any warrant for saying that the Church of England regards Isaac as a typical character?

Answer.—Unquestionably she does so. For the Church of England appoints the account of the sacrifice of Isaac to be read as the first Lesson at Morning Prayer on Good Friday. Now, unless the sacrifice of Isaac was typical of the Sacrifice of Christ, there would be no reason or appropriateness in this arrangement.

33. *Question.*—What must pious Jews of old have found in the Law of Moses, which is never clearly expressed there, and which they must have gained therefore from traditional comments and interpretations, handed down with the Law?

Answer.—The great doctrine of eternal life after death.

34. *Question.*—How do we know for certain that they *did* look for eternal life after death?

Answer.—Because the Apostle Paul tells us so in his Epistle to the Hebrews. Speaking of Abraham he says; "He looked for a city which hath foundations, whose builder and maker is God" (Heb. xi. 10). And more generally: "These all" (he has mentioned Abel, Enoch, Noah, Abraham, Isaac, Jacob and Sarah) "died in faith, not having received the promises, but having seen them afar off, and were persuaded of them, and embraced them, and confessed that they were strangers and pilgrims on the earth. For they that say such things declare plainly that they seek a country. And truly, if they had been mindful of that country from whence they came out, they might have had opportunity to have returned. But now they desire a better country, that is, an heavenly: wherefore God is not ashamed to be called their God: for he hath prepared for them a city" (Heb. xi. 13-17). We may say without hesitation that *all* holy men under the Old Testament Dispensation shared in the same expectations, and were lifted above the world by the same bright hopes. As our Seventh Article says: "They are not to be heard, which feign that the old Fathers did look only for transitory promises."

35. *Catechist.*—To begin with Abraham, whom you mentioned first, and who lived before the earliest Books of the Old Testament were composed. Whence shall we suppose that he derived his assurance of eternal life after death?

Answer.—He can only have derived it with any certainty from some Divine communication, probably made originally to our first parents in connexion with the promise respecting the seed of the woman, and handed down by tradition in the family of Seth.

36. *Question.*—Might not Abraham have augured from the fact of the translation of Enoch, that some bright and glorious future was in store for the true children of God?

Answer.—Doubtless he might. But, as Enoch never *did* die, but "was translated that he should not see death" (Heb. xi. 5), his case would not be parallel with that of the rest of mankind; and from it alone Abraham could hardly have augured that eternal life *after* death would be his own portion, and that of other pious and devout persons. Death *seemed* to extinguish the existence of men. Why should it not be as it seemed?

37. *Catechist.*—In speaking of Abraham, we have been speaking of a period before the Pentateuch was composed. But even after written Scripture appeared in the world, and Moses had published his Five Books, was there any *express* revelation of eternal life after death?

Answer.—We seek in vain for any such explicit revelation in the Pentateuch. A future state may be *assumed* by the writer (and indeed it is hard to understand how a system of religion can have any other basis than the doctrine of a future state); it may be darkly hinted; but it certainly is not expressed.

38. *Question.*—What great theological writer of the English Church makes this silence of the Law on the subject of a future state one premiss of his argument?

Answer.—Bishop Warburton, in his "Divine Legation of Moses."

39. *Question.*—What is the argument by which Warburton seeks to prove that Moses must have received a Divine commission, and have been supported by the exercise of supernatural power?

Answer.—The argument is this: All other legislators, in order to obtain influence over the people, have found it necessary to appeal to an eternal recompence of virtue and vice in a future state of existence:

Moses says nothing of this eternal recompence, and yet exerted a greater influence than any other legislator:

Therefore, Moses must have had the support of the supernatural power of God, and must have been really commissioned by Him.

40. *Catechist.*—You have shown sufficiently that the Old Testament requires a collateral interpretation, in order to its being understood aright. But can the same thing be said in any measure of the *New* Testament?

Answer.—The New Testament is no doubt a much plainer and more explicit Revelation than the Old. Things which were only hinted at and obscurely insinuated in the earlier Volume are proclaimed on the house-top in the later. More especially, as to the subject of which we have recently been speaking, life and immortality, which before lay in shadow, are brought to light by the Gospel. But still there are certain points, and those not unimportant ones, in which the

New Testament also needs a traditional comment, in order to the right understanding of it.

41. *Catechist.*—Mention any such points which occur to you.

Answer.—The observance of the Lord's Day is one such point, and Infant Baptism another.

42. *Catechist.*—But surely the observance of the Lord's Day is clearly prescribed by the Fourth Commandment?

Answer.—No. The *principle* of setting apart a certain proportion of our time for direct acts of Worship *is* prescribed by the Fourth Commandment. But the Fourth Commandment orders the observance, not of the first, but of the seventh, day of the week. And no Christian *does* observe the seventh day.

43. *Question.*—But are there not intimations in the New Testament of a special sanctity attaching to the first day of the week?

Answer.—Doubtless there are; but they are only intimations, and all of them put together do not amount to anything like a moral obligation. It would appear that our Blessed Lord appeared to His disciples after the Resurrection on the octave of Easter Day (that is, the first Sunday after Easter). (See St. John xx. 26.) From Acts xx. 7 we gather that on the first day of the week it was the habit of the disciples at Troas to come together "to break bread." From 1 Cor. xvi. 2 we infer that on the first day of the week there was a respite from the week's work, and a quiet period when its gains might be computed. And in Rev. i. 10 we read that St. John, the beloved disciple, "was in the Spirit," and received the Apocalypse, "on the Lord's day." All these passages have their weight in showing that the earliest Christians regarded the first day of the week as sacred. But there is not a line in Scripture which goes to show that the first day ought to be substituted for the seventh, or that the seventh need not be observed, since the first has been appropriated to the purposes of rest and worship.

44. *Question.*—From what source then must this substitution, so uniformly acquiesced in by Christians, have come?

Answer.—From a tradition of the Universal Church. An instinct of the early believers taught them that the day of the Resurrection of Christ deserved to be called the queen of the days of the week, and that even the old legal day of rest must not dispute with it the pre-eminence. And this arrangement has come floating down to our times in the current of tradition.

45. *Catechist.*—But you said that Infant Baptism is another observance which we receive very mainly on the tradition of the Church. How is this?

Answer.—Because the Baptism of Infants is never literally prescribed in the New Testament; nor is any instance of it upon record there.

46. *Question.*—Is there anything to be said from Scripture in favour of baptizing Infants?

Answer.—Yes, a very great deal; but nothing amounting to actual prescription. We may observe that there are several whole households mentioned as receiving Baptism, among which it is improbable that there should have been no children; that St. Paul calls the children of a believer holy (1 Cor. vii. 14), which must at least indicate their meetness to receive Baptism, even if it does not mean, as is supposed by some early commentators, consecrated to God in Baptism by the universal usage of the Church; that the circumstance of our Lord having blessed little children at so early an age that they could be taken up in His arms (see St. Mark x. 16) shows that such children are capable of receiving a spiritual blessing; and above all, that under the Old Testament dispensation children of eight days old were admitted into covenant with God (see Gen. xvii. 12, 13), and that if, under the new and better dispensation, this was to be altered, the Apostles, who had been reared in the idea of a covenant-relationship subsisting between God and the youngest children, would surely have warned us of the change, and called our attention to it. But all this falls short of a literal command to baptize children, and of an example of their being baptized in Apostolic times.

47. *Question.*—How then did the custom of baptizing Infants establish itself so universally in the Church, that no other custom was heard of in the early ages?

Answer.—Because it was in accordance with the interpretation which the early Church put upon the New Testament, and which was carried down along the ages in the current of tradition.

48. *Question.*—Will you now give a brief summary of what it is sought to establish in the Chapter upon which you are being examined?

Answer.—That we cannot fully understand what we read in the Scriptures "except some man should guide" us into the true meaning of them, and that the appointed guide is the Church, in her Creeds and Confessions of Faith, in her Formularies of Devotion (which embody a large amount of doctrinal teaching), and more particularly in certain traditional interpretations and usages, which she hands down to us side by side with, and as a commentary upon, the text of Scripture.

49. *Catechist.*—We have seen in what sense the Church is "the pillar and ground of the truth." But is there not also a sense in which the Truth (that is, the Holy Scripture) is "the pillar and ground of" the Church?

Answer.—Most assuredly there is. If Holy Scripture requires explanation from the Church, the Church still more urgently requires explanation from Holy Scripture. For, if it were asked what is the origin of the Church, what is the warrant for the Church's authority, nay, what the very meaning of the word "Church" is, it would be utterly impossible to answer these questions without referring at every step to Holy Scripture. The Church's title-deeds, charter, and claims, the whole explanation of what she is and of what she professes to be and to do, is to be found in

Scripture, and nowhere else. Cut away Scripture, and you can no longer give any account of the Church's existence and functions.

50. *Question.*—Will you then state with great brevity the respective functions of Holy Scripture and of the Church, as they have been exhibited in this and the preceding Chapter?

Answer.—I will. The Church is the ordained *teacher* of Truth; and the Holy Scripture is the only *criterion* of Truth, by which every doctrine of the Church must be tried, and only accepted if found to be in conformity with it.

CHAPTER X.

OF THE PRAYER-BOOK AS A COMMENTARY ON THE BIBLE.

"Therefore, brethren, stand fast, and hold the traditions which ye have been taught, whether by word, or our epistle."—2 THESS. II. 15.

The necessity of some help from traditional sentiment and observance, for the full understanding even of the New Testament.

IN the last Chapter it was pointed out how the volume of the Holy Scriptures has come into our hands, not, as I ventured to express it, surrounded by a vacuum, but floating in an atmosphere of traditional sentiments and explanations. The proof of this was more largely developed in the case of the Old Testament than in that of the New. But it holds good almost equally of the later volume. Let any one who can do so (and it demands some effort of mind) strip himself quite bare in imagination of all such help towards the understanding of the New Testament as is derived from the sentiments, customs, and observances which have actually obtained among Christians. Let him suppose, for example, that he never had *In the absence of such help, the most well-intentioned man might find himself at a loss in many points.* been taught any Creed, never had been present at Divine Service, is not at all aware how important texts of the New Testament are understood by persons around him,—and he will surely see how almost impossible it would be for him, even with the very best intentions, to find out in what sense a great number of things said in the New Testament were to be taken, and how a great number of things, there apparently prescribed, were to be done. We will suppose his heart to have been touched with the simple and beautiful message of the Gospel, which he finds written with a sunbeam on the pages of the New Testament, and to be sincerely bent on carrying into effect the commandments of Christ, as far as he knows them. He will see that Christ founded a Church, to which he and all men were to belong; he will read much of the early history of this Church in the Acts of the Apostles; and he will find three Epistles of the Apostle Paul addressed to men in the capacity of Church rulers (or, as we should say, bishops), and devoted almost entirely to the subject of Church administration. But surely if he had had no experience of the Church system, but were left to frame a system for himself out of the notices furnished by the New Testament, he would be very much at a loss. He would feel a great blank in his mind as to how several instructions, given by the Apostle in the Epistles to Timothy and Titus, were to be carried into effect, and still more as to what was to be done on sundry points where there are no instructions. Are infants to be baptized or not? That, at all events, is a point of very great interest and importance, on which there seem to be no absolutely conclusive instructions. Did our Lord intend the washing of feet which He practised upon His disciples, and might seem to have enjoined literally, when He

What he would find about the Church in the New Testament.

What he would not find there:—

a definitive prescription on the subject of Infant Baptism;—

said, "I have given you an example, that ye should do as I have done to you," to be a perpetual observance in the Church; or did He merely indicate the spirit of deep condescension and humility, which should animate His followers in their deportment towards one another?—I might mention very many more instances, in which the person supposed would wish for definite guidance; but let the above suffice. What our supposed inquirer would desiderate would be,to know how the Christians who lived nearest to the Apostles understood the instructions given by the Apostles, —what were their customs, their observances, the sense in which they understood many things which the Apostles taught. It is clearly indicated in St. Paul's Epistles that there were customs which the Apostles themselves had set on foot, and which they wished the Churches of their foundation to hold fast by. Thus, for example, we read in the Second Epistle to the Thessalonians, "Brethren, stand fast, and," as if this were a security, a great moral holdfast in times when "strong delusion" was abroad,—"hold the traditions which ye have been taught, *whether by word*, or our epistle;"—so that evidently there were oral as well as written traditions, which it behoved Christians to hold fast, one of them possibly being the Creed or "form of sound words" itself, which it appears from a passage of St. Augustine was purposely not put into writing in those early days, lest it might be used as a ground of accusation against the Christians. From the next Chapter, in which he speaks of brethren in the Thessalonian Church walking disorderly, and not after the tradition they had received from him, it would appear that one of these traditions which he had delivered was of serious practical import, being nothing less than that every Christian should work for his own livelihood, and not consider himself entitled to eat unless he did work.—The First Epistle to the Corinthians furnishes other instances of traditional instructions coming down from the Apostles to the early Church. We there find St. Paul giving a rule for the conduct of a believer who happened to be united in marriage to a party still a heathen,—a rule which he makes imperative on all the Churches of his foundation by the words, " and so ordain I in all churches." Later, he commends the Corinthians for holding such observances as they had received from him, from which it would seem that there must have been a considerable body of them. " Now, I praise you, brethren, that ye remember me in all things, and keep the ordinances " (literally, the traditions), " as I delivered them to you." He then proceeds to issue a new " ordinance " or traditional observance, that men shall not appear covered, nor women uncovered, in the public worship of Almighty God. While he argues in favour of this regulation, he insists that those who are not convinced by his argument shall submit themselves to the universal custom, which had obtained in the Church. " But if any man seem to be contentious, we have no such custom, neither the churches of God." And at the end of this

in 2 Thess. iii. 6, 10;

in 1 Cor. vii. 12, 17;

in 1 Cor. xi. 2;

in 1 Cor. xi. 16;

Chapter, the remainder of which is occupied with the subject of the administration of the Lord's Supper, he refers to several points which needed some authoritative arrangement from him, but which might wait till the occasion of his next visit to them. "And the rest will I set in order when I come."

and in 1 Cor. xi. 34.

It is clear, then, that the New Testament itself recognises certain traditional customs, observances, and precepts as having been handed down by the Apostles, not all of which, however, were embodied in writing. And I think it would be felt by every reverent and devout student, that the being accurately possessed of these traditions, before by lapse of time and unauthorized accretions they had become corrupted, would be a great help to the right understanding of the New Testament. But how is it competent to an ordinary person, with average education and intelligence, but with very limited time at his command, and perhaps very limited access to books, to gain any such knowledge? Such a task might well be the study of a life, and would ask besides powers of research and actual attainments in dead languages, which fall to the lot of very few. How then may an ordinary Christian attain to such a knowledge of primitive apostolic traditions, as shall for him bring out and illustrate the divine teaching of the Holy Scriptures? We English Churchmen have a royal road to such an attainment. Our Book of Common Prayer embodies and represents for us all these traditions,—is a brief but sufficient digest of them. We have no desire unduly

The being possessed of these traditions would be a great help to the right understanding of the New Testament.

Such knowledge can only be obtained by ordinary Christians through the Book of Common Prayer.

to magnify this Book. Doubtless, as being the composition and compilation of uninspired men, it has its weak points. But this is certain, that not only deep devotion, but profound theological learning,—a thorough acquaintance with Holy Scripture and the writings of primitive Christian antiquity,—were called into exercise both in the original draughts of the Prayer-Book and in its subsequent revisions. And surely the result has justified all the pains and all the ability bestowed upon the work. It may be very much questioned whether there is such another uninspired book in the world. For the Reformed Communions have not in general adopted a liturgy, preferring to devolve the great duty of public worship on the Minister exclusively, and to leave him in the conduct of it to the guidance of his own judgment, except so far as a general plan or order of the worship is concerned. The Romanist boasts, no doubt, in his Missal and his Breviary a great deal that is really ancient and Catholic, but it is so laid over with modern and unscriptural accretions, with traditions of a date long subsequent to the Apostles, and with superstitions which wither in the full light of Scriptural truth, that their Office Books have ceased to be fair expositions of the way, in which the Church of the first and purest age accepted the teaching it had derived from the Apostles. In this state the old Service Books were, when they fell into the hands of the English Reformers—men of ripe theological attainments, and who, while they saw that much in these old Offices needed to be cut

Qualifications for their work of the compilers of this Book.

Why the Prayer-Book is probably a unique book of its kind.

Deformed condition of the old Service Books, when they fell into the hands of the Reformers.

away with unsparing hand, saw also an underlying stratum of devotions which traced up to a very early period, and which, since it might justly be regarded as a precious heritage bequeathed to the Church by the Apostles or their successors, it would be a species of desecration to throw away. So they set themselves to purify and simplify the Offices of the Church, thereby not only rejecting much which would not stand the tests they thought right to apply, but also reducing the book to such a compass as to put it easily within the reach of all. Their tests were two: *first*, Holy Scripture itself, the universal touchstone and criterion for distinguishing between the wheat and the chaff, the true and the false. A true tradition, they knew well, could never be at variance with Holy Scripture. Accordingly, all prayers addressed to saints, all the false homage which had gathered around relics, all references to the cleansing away of sin by purgatorial fire in another life, fell at once, like so much rotten wood, beneath their pruning-knife. Their *second* test was Primitive Antiquity itself. So thoroughly were they convinced that the teaching, manner of life, and traditions of the Apostles must have percolated through, and found some expression for themselves among the members of the Churches they founded, and that these traditions might often expand and explain what the written Scripture gives us only in an obscure hint, that they sought in the Fathers who lived nearest to the apostolic times the counterfeit presentment of that Church, which was "built upon the foundation of the apostles and prophets," and endeavoured to construct our Offices on that model. And the result is (to use the language of the late Professor Blunt, who has touched this subject with a master's hand), that "the Prayer-Book is a book *sui generis*. We have no other of the same kind, or like it; it is not an author's, a publisher's, and a bookseller's affair; it is the voice of the ancient Church expressed upon the highest matters; and so, not improbably, that of the Founder of that Church; God's will, not in this instance only, but in almost all instances, having to be sought out of them that love Him, through some difficulty, obscurity, uncertainty, and doubt." But whether or not men agree with the high estimate of the Prayer-Book expressed in this passage, I suppose it will not be denied that it gives a certain tone to the teaching of Holy Scripture, which it professes to represent and expound—surrounds that teaching with an atmosphere of a certain description—throws it into a certain definite mould. No book of Offices could by possibility do otherwise. The spirit of a man's theology expresses itself necessarily in the prayers and praises which he employs, and might be sufficiently gathered from the tenor of those prayers and praises. Moreover, the rites and ceremonies which a book of Offices must prescribe, are not things indifferent. They express and convey doctrine, and win an entrance for it into the mind. Any directory for worship would infallibly do this, whether its spirit was primitive and truly Catholic, or the reverse; and think not that the saving truths of the Scripture could be

Professor Blunt's panegyric on the Prayer-Book.

Necessity of admitting that the Prayer-Book gives a certain tone to the Holy Scripture, and insinuates a certain view of it.

No devotional form, whether for private or public use, could help doing this; for forms of devotion inevitably convey doctrine.

apprehended at all, or apprehended in their true significance, except through some such medium. The atmosphere, which wraps round the earth, is essential to the life and beauty of the forms which are seen on the earth. Earth and earthly creatures have their being in this atmosphere. Remove it, and the earth is made over to barrenness, solitude, and death; the landscape withers; and no more softening tints and hues are thrown over it. But while an atmosphere is essential, it may of course become noxious. It may be charged with poisonous exhalations; it may be obscured, and transmit the light of heaven with difficulty; it may be heavy and oppressive, and wanting in transparency. And such was the condition of the ecclesiastical atmosphere, which wrapped round the volume of the Scriptures at the period before the Reformation. It was rendered heavy and oppressive by old and effete superstitions; it was rendered opaque by a mass of unauthorized traditions, which hindered the blessed light of evangelical truth from streaming through; it was rendered noxious by elements of anti-Scriptural practice and doctrine which did actual spiritual mischief. So our Reformers set themselves to work, not to dispense with an atmosphere altogether (as those well-meaning but unthinking people would do, who plead for the Bible alone without note and comment), but to purify the existing atmosphere, to make it salubrious, quickening, transparent, and transmissive of the true light. The result of their labours is the Book of Common Prayer, which we maintain to be a beautiful, pure, primitive medium for the transmission of evangelical truth, and of which the eminent author above quoted says, in another passage of an admirable sermon called "An Apology for the Prayer-Book;" "The book is to be regarded as a code of primitive tradition, which helps to the full interpretation of the Bible, expressing what may be there hinted, enlarging what may be there succinct, illustrating what may be there obscure, concentrating what may be there dispersed, organizing what may be there promiscuous." It may be, I think, interesting and instructive to give brief instances of the different ways here pointed out, in which the Prayer-Book helps to the full interpretation of the Bible.

The five helps which the Prayer-Book gives to the full interpretation of the Bible.

1*st*, then, *It expresses what is there hinted.* The question about the propriety of Infant Baptism, in favour of which the Scripture gives the three pregnant hints of Circumcision (whereby children were admitted into Covenant with God at eight days old); "Suffer little children to come unto me, and forbid them not," etc.; and the instances of several households being baptized,—is in the Prayer-Book set at rest. The Baptism of Infants, and their speedy Baptism, without unnecessary delay, is there definitively ordered. And the order is in accordance with the most primitive apostolic traditions. Justin Martyr, a heathen philosopher, born at Sichem, in Samaria, who became a convert to Christianity in the earlier half of the second century, and who might nearly have seen St. John, writes as follows in his first Apology:—"Several persons among us of sixty and seventy years old, of

1st. Expressing what is there hinted. Question of the propriety of Infant Baptism decided by the Prayer-Book in the affirmative, on the ground of primitive usage.

both sexes, *who were made disciples of Christ from their childhood*, do continue uncorrupted." Here it appears quite incidentally, that several persons existed in Justin's time who had been baptized as children; for the word translated "made disciples" is the very same as that which our Lord uses in St. Matthew's Gospel, when He bids the Apostles " go and make disciples of all nations, by baptizing them in the Name of the Father, and of the Son, and of the Holy Ghost." Justin flourished about the year A.D. 140; and therefore the persons of sixty or seventy years old in his time, who had been baptized as children, must have received Baptism before the end of the first century, and therefore while St. John (at all events) was alive. Is it for a moment conceivable that this could have been the case, unless the Apostles generally had sanctioned Infant Baptism? And is it conceivable that they could have sanctioned it, if it had not been in complete conformity with the mind of their Divine Master,—possibly intimated by Him so to be in the course of those great Forty Days between the Resurrection and Ascension, during which He spake to them of "the things pertaining to the kingdom of God"?

[margin: Justin's testimony to the Baptism of children in his days]

[margin: makes it almost certain that the practice must have had the sanction of the Apostles.]

2. *Enlarging what may be there succinct.* St. John teaches in the Revelation that all Christians, not the clergy only, are priests:—" Unto Him that loved us, and washed us from our sins in His own blood,"—an allusion probably to the laver in the Tabernacle, in which the priests washed their hands and feet before sacrificing—" and hath made us kings and *priests.*" His colleague, St.

[margin: 2. Enlarging what is there succinct.]

[margin: The priesthood of the Christian Laity recognised by St. John.]

Peter, expands this designation, speaking of Christians as "an holy priesthood," designed "to offer up spiritual sacrifices, acceptable to God by Jesus Christ." And in a somewhat obscure passage, to be adverted to more fully under the next head, St. Paul speaks of one "occupying the room of the unlearned" (strictly, of the private, non-official, unprofessional person), saying "Amen" at the close of a thanksgiving, as if there were some definite part for a Christian layman to play in the Church's worship. Now the Prayer-Book beautifully developes and expands what is stated succinctly in these passages of the New Testament. It gives to the Christian laity a large share in the Services of the Church, thus recognising their priestly functions. Sometimes they are to say words *after* the Minister, as if guided by him; sometimes *together with* him, as if belonging to one and the same family; often they are to respond to him, not merely by the repetition of "Amen," but by distinct prayers and suffrages of their own, intermixed with those which he is directed to offer. So that in our public worship there is "a room" and sphere marked out for the unprofessional private person (or Christian layman), which he is entitled to "occupy." And I should add that this is the case in all the ancient Liturgies, the use of which may be traced back to a period long antecedent to the putting forth of any Papal claims. All give the people a very material part in the Office of the Holy Communion,—a circumstance wonderfully illustrating the slight hint given by St. Paul

St. Peter,

and also by St. Paul.

These intimations expanded by the Prayer-Book, which assigns to the Laity a distinct part in the Services of the Church, sometimes by directing them to join audibly with the Minister in the recital of Prayers, sometimes by putting responses into their mouth.

where he speaks of "the cup of blessing which WE bless;" "the bread which WE break," as if all the congregation, no less than the Minister, had their share and function in the blessing and the breaking. It is obvious that among Christian bodies which provide no *form* of prayer for public worship, there can be no "room" for the layman to "occupy," beyond the mere expression of assent by the final *Amen*.

3. *Illustrating what may be there obscure.* The text about the final *Amen* is by no means a clear one, as it stands in the original, though the difficulty of it is considerably aggravated to a reader of the English version only. St. Paul is arguing against the use of an unknown tongue in public worship, and his words are; "Else" (that is, if thou shalt use an unknown tongue when officiating in the congregation) "when thou shalt bless with the spirit" (pronounce the words of blessing in a devotional rapture, but in language unintelligible to any but thyself) "how shall he that occupieth the room of the unlearned" (the Christian layman) "say the *Amen* at thy giving of thanks?" (literally, at thy "Eucharist," for such is the sound, as well as the sense, of the word in the original). All difficulty is immediately removed from this passage by referring to the account given by Justin of primitive celebrations of the Lord's Supper. He makes mention of the Church's meeting at the same place, on the day called the day of the Sun, and of the writings of the Apostles and Prophets being read, and of a sermon from the president of the assembly, which

followed this reading, and of prayers for all conditions of men,—" after which bread and a cup " of wine and water are brought to the Presi- " dent of the brethren, which he takes, and offers " up praise and glory to the Father of all things, " through the name of His Son and of the Holy " Spirit; and this thanksgiving to God for deeming " us worthy of His gifts is a prayer of more than " ordinary length. When the president has finished " the prayers and the thanksgiving service, all the " people present signify their assent with an audible " voice, saying, *Amen*. Now *Amen* in the Hebrew " tongue means, 'So be it.'" And again, further on: "After prayers, bread and wine and water are offered, and the president, as I said before, sends up prayers and thanksgivings with all the fervour he is able, and the people conclude all with the joyful acclamation of *Amen;* then the consecrated elements are distributed to, and partaken of by, each person that is present." And he adds, "This food is called among us the Eucharist." I need hardly remark how very near the Eucharistic Service of our Prayer-Book comes to Justin's description, in which we have the Epistle and Gospel, the Sermon, the Oblation of the Bread and Wine, the Prayer for the Church Militant (which is certainly a prayer for all conditions of men), and the Prayer of Consecration (still, as in those days, a prayer of more than ordinary length), with its concluding *Amen*, and immediately afterwards the distribution of the elements. Here, then, is an instance in which an obscure passage of the New Testament derives full illustration from a

Particulars of this account.

'Eucharist' a primitive name to denote the Holy Communion.

The order of our Communion Service very similar to that which is described by Justin.

surviving description of the Eucharistic rite, as celebrated in the middle of the second century, the leading features of which description are all reproduced in our own Office.

4. Concentrating what is there dispersed.

4. *Concentrating what may be there dispersed.* I cannot give a better instance of this than the doctrine of the Holy Trinity, a doctrine of supreme importance, as set forth in the Creeds and formularies of our Church. In Holy Scripture that doctrine lies about in scattered fragments, but is never reduced to method or stated systematically. In one place we find Christ addressing His Father in prayer, showing that He and the Father are distinct persons; in another distinctly declaring, "I and My Father are one," showing the unity between these Persons; in a third, promising to send the Holy Spirit, thus establishing another distinction of personality in the Godhead. These and many similar notices of Holy Scripture are pieced together and brought into one view in the doctrine of the Trinity, as it is stated in our Confessions of Faith and Articles; and those who wish to see how each separate position, which goes to make up the great doctrine, is by itself provable from Holy Writ, have only to refer to the very compendious tractate of Jones of Nayland on the subject.

The doctrine of the Holy Trinity gathered from several places of Holy Scripture, which the Church has collected into one focus.

5. Organizing what is there promiscuous.

5. Finally, *Organizing what may be there promiscuous.* Take the Ordinal as an example, which is prefaced thus:—" It is evident unto all men diligently reading the holy Scripture and ancient Authors, that from the Apostles' time there have been these Orders of Ministers in Christ's Church; Bishops, Priests, and Deacons."

Yes! it is evident to persons reading the Scriptures in the light of "ancient Authors;" for at a very early period of the Church's history we find the threefold Ministry germinating and taking shape. Then, looking into the volume of the New Testament, we find what is there introduced incidentally and promiscuously reduced to method. Putting aside terminology (for we look to things rather than to names), we find Timothy and Titus set over the elders (or presbyters) of the Church in their respective provinces, with a charge to censure them, if need were—to reward them, if their services deserved it. Then we have the earlier notice in the Acts of an institution of a subordinate class of Ministers for the lower and more secular functions of the Church, and a reference in the Epistles to some such subordinate class, under the name of "Deacons." And going back still further to our Lord's own lifetime, we find Him sending forth, not only twelve Apostles, but also seventy Disciples, whose mission and powers very much resembled those of the Apostles. The Prayer-Book throws these notices into shape for us. We find little more than the scattered germs of the threefold Ministry in the Scripture; but in the system of the Church, which is or should be a living illustration and exemplification of Scripture, these germs are collected and developed,—"the promiscuous is organized."

The testimony of 'ancient Authors' to the existence of a threefold Ministry.

The Scriptural warrant for which is to be sought in different connexions, in the Inspired Volume.

And now the task, which I have in this work proposed to myself, approaches its completion. I know not what better concluding advice to draw from a summary retrospect of it than that, in these days of fermenting thought and diverging opinion, my readers should take the Holy Scriptures, as interpreted by the Book of Common Prayer, for their guide in controverted points, on the ground that the latter book is really the voice of the Primitive Church, fulfilling her function of a pillar of the cloud and of fire, guiding into the meaning of God's truth, and illustrating it. I would say, with all the earnestness which such a counsel demands;—" If the Bible approves itself to you as the Word of God by the strange unearthly force with which it appeals to your conscience, and the deep chords which it strikes in your affections; and if it has been at all satisfactorily proved to your reason that the Book of Common Prayer does, on the whole, represent with great fidelity that guidance of the Church, which God will not have any of us ignore or dispense with, then let this be to you an end of controversy on all controverted points; and, leaving endless questions, and the strifes which they gender, abandon yourselves to the far more safe and salutary work of quietly growing in grace and in the knowledge of our Lord and Saviour Jesus Christ. You are quite sufficiently secured against serious controversial and doctrinal mistakes by holding fast to the teaching of Bible and Prayer-Book; any religious questions, which Bible and Prayer-Book both leave open, may safely be left open till we arrive at that better state, when we shall know even as also we are known. Too apt are we, far too apt, to take up with controversial subjects, as

[sidenotes: The practical advice which flows from the consideration of the whole subject. / Let an end of Controversy be sought by accepting the Prayer-Book as the interpretation of the Bible. / Questions, which this acceptance does not set at rest, may safely be left open for the present. / Desirableness of an end of Controversy.]

affording an easy escape from those great practical and personal questions which are our only real concern, and as furnishing to our own consciences some sort of evidence of an interest in religion. 'Settle the controversy between us and the Jews as to the right place of worship,' said the Samaritan woman to the Saviour, flinching from the probe which those words of His omniscience had applied to her conscience; 'Thou hast had five husbands; and he whom thou now hast is not thy husband.' How marvellously true to nature! The personal and really momentous is evaded, shunned, put aside for a more convenient season; the conscience shall take up with inquiries about something more on the surface of the field of theology; and interest *about* religion is substituted for interest *in* it. 'Sir, I perceive that you are a minister; tell me—not how I shall love the Lord more sincerely, or follow Him more faithfully, or prize at a higher rate His inappreciable and glorious salvation; but whether the priest should stand, in celebrating the Communion, looking due south or due east, or neither, perhaps, but south-east, and whether the preacher should appear in a black robe or a white one.' Without at all wishing to depreciate reverence in small things, or to put out of sight our Lord's solemn warning that 'he that is faithful in that which is least is faithful also in much,' I still must take the liberty to think that these, and the like of these, are not the questions which should be allowed to occupy much of our time and thoughts. Many of us are far past the prime of

Danger of being drawn off by speculative and controversial from personal and practical questions, enforced by the story of the woman of Samaria.

life; and those who are not cannot count with any certainty on having much time to spare as regards the work of their salvation. Let us put away our controversies (specially as we have a ready means of solving all the really momentous ones), and address ourselves to the work of living nearer to God. We have minds that crave for light; hearts that hunger for love and for solid satisfying good; and there is in Christ's Gospel abundant provision both for mind and heart. Be it ours to endeavour to turn this provision to account, and to study day by day how we may be 'rooted and grounded in love,' and 'be able to comprehend with all saints what is the breadth, and length, and depth, and height; and to know the love of Christ, which passeth knowledge, that' we may 'be filled with all the fulness of God.'"

Let us put away controversies, and address ourselves to the task of growing in grace and knowledge.

Catechism on Chap. X.

1. *Question.*—Upon what are we all dependent for an understanding of many points contained in the New Testament?

 Answer.—Upon traditional explanations, which have come down to us side by side with the text of Holy Scripture.

2. *Question.*—What is the best mode of bringing home to ourselves our need of these explanations?

 Answer.—To imagine ourselves entirely destitute of all such help.

3. *Question.*—What sort of particulars should we have to imagine, in order to put ourselves in the required position?

Answer.—We should have to suppose that we had never learned a Creed or Confession of Faith; that we had never attended a Christian Service; that we were utterly ignorant how persons around us understood the doctrines and precepts given by Christ and His Apostles, and how they attempted to put them in practice.

4. *Question.*—Are there not then sufficient materials in the New Testament itself for forming a judgment on all matters connected with the Church?

Answer.—The New Testament would by itself teach us that Christ founded a Church, and called all men into it. It would also give us all necessary instruction on the Sacraments of the Church. It also records the history of the Church in its earliest period, and the progress which it made under the preaching of St. Paul, until the Gospel was planted in the Metropolis of the heathen world. And moreover we find in it Epistles addressed by that Apostle to rulers (or bishops) of the Church in their official capacity, directing them in many particulars of their administration, and giving an insight into the internal condition of the Churches over which they presided. That these instructions would form in our mind a sufficient idea of what those Churches were, and of what the Apostle would have all Churches to be, must be admitted. But there are many points (and some of no small importance), on which we should be still quite at a loss, if left to frame a system of Church administration for ourselves out of the New Testament, without any help whatever from traditional comments, sentiments, and usages.

5. *Question.*—Will you mention any such points which occur to you?

Answer.—Although, as I have showed in a previous examination (p. 305), we might reasonably gather from the Scriptures that infants should be admitted into the Church by Baptism, and although the whole of the Scriptural evidence leans in this direction, yet on observing that penitence and faith are made by the Apostles and their companions qualifications for this Sacrament,

("*Repent*, and be baptized every one of you in the name of Jesus Christ for the remission of sins" (Acts ii. 38); "*If thou believest with all thine heart*, thou mayest" [be baptized] (Acts viii. 37);) and that our Lord Himself places the preaching of the Gospel and the believing of it *before* Baptism, (" Go ye into all the world, and *preach the Gospel* to every creature. He *that believeth* and is baptized shall be saved" (St. Mark xvi. 15, 16)); a doubt might reasonably arise as to the propriety of administering the Rite to those who can neither hear the Gospel, nor exercise repentance and faith. But when we find that the Christians of the earliest ages baptized the infant children of believers, and that this practice was universally accepted and adopted without question down to a very late period of the Church's history, this traditional usage settles a point which might be otherwise considered doubtful. If Christians of the earliest ages understood the Baptismal precept in such a manner that it embraced infants, it must have been the mind of Christ's Apostles, and therefore of Christ, that they should be baptized.

6. *Catechist.*—Give any other instance of a question which must receive its settlement from something outside the New Testament itself.

Answer.—The account of the foot-washing, which Christ not only practised but prescribed on the night of the Last Supper, might raise such a question. It might reasonably be thought that He meant it to be a perpetual observance or Ordinance of the Church (like Baptism and the Lord's Supper), if it were not that the Church has never so accepted His words; "If I then, your Lord and Master, have washed your feet; *ye also ought to wash one another's feet*. For I have given you an example, that *ye should do as I have done to you*. Verily, verily, I say unto you, The servant is not greater than his lord; neither he that is sent greater than he that sent him. If ye know these things, *happy are ye if ye do them*" (St. John xiii. 14, 15, 16, 17).

7. *Catechist.*—You say that the Church has never so

accepted the words. But has not our Lord's action received a literal imitation in certain parts of the Church?

Answer.—No doubt it has. The Pope on Maunday-Thursday still washes the feet of pilgrims in imitation of our Lord's action. And the sovereigns of England have done the same, even since the Reformation. And it was customary in many monasteries of old for the abbot to wash the feet of the brethren. But the Church has never accepted this precept of Christ as prescribing an Ordinance or perpetual observance, though it has been customary among some great ones of the earth to copy literally our Lord's example.

8. *Catechist.*—You have given instances of questions, which a thoughtful perusal of the New Testament might raise in the mind, but to which it would furnish no answer. What knowledge, if we could obtain it, would set at rest such questions?

Answer.—The knowledge how the primitive Christians understood the instructions given them by the Apostles, and what were the usages and observances, which had sprung up among them during the lifetime, and under the government, of the Apostles.

9. *Question.*—How do you know that there were unwritten traditions, both of doctrine and practice, in the Apostolic Church?

Answer.—Because we read of such traditions in St. Paul's Epistles. In 2 Thess. ii. 15 he thus exhorts his Thessalonian converts; "Therefore, brethren, stand fast, and hold *the traditions which ye have been taught, whether by word,* or our epistle."

10. *Question.*—Why were the traditions here referred to in all probability doctrinal?

Answer.—Because the Apostle had been speaking in the earlier part of the Chapter about " that man of sin," " that Wicked" one, " whose coming is after the working of Satan with all power and signs and lying wonders, and all *deceivableness* of unrighteousness in them that perish; because *they received not the love of the truth,* that they might be saved. And for this cause God shall send them *strong delusion, that they should believe a lie:* that they all might be damned *who believed not the truth,* but had pleasure in unrighteousness" (1 Thess. ii. 3, 8, 9—13). He is putting them on their guard then against doctrinal error, since he speaks of "strong delusion," "believing a lie," "not believing the truth," and so forth. And therefore probably the traditions, which he exhorts them to cling to as a moral hold-fast, were doctrinal,—very possibly the Creed itself, or a summary of the chief things to be believed.

11. *Question.*—Can you give any instance of a tradition of practice?

Answer.—Such a tradition is referred to in the Chapter following that which has just been quoted (2 Thess. iii. 6); "Now we command you, brethren, in the name of our Lord Jesus Christ, that ye withdraw yourselves from every brother that walketh disorderly, and not after the tradition which he received of us." And he then goes on to say that he had set them an example of working for his maintenance, though he had a right, if he chose, to demand a maintenance from them; and that he hoped they would follow his example, seconded as it was by his express precept; "For even when we were with you, this we commanded you, that if any would not work, neither should he eat" (2 Thess. iii. 10). The tradition referred to, therefore, was probably a precept to the effect that no member of the Christian Community should be without an occupation, by which to earn his bread.

12. *Question.*—What other references are there in St. Paul's Epistles, to traditions which he had delivered to the Churches founded by him?

Answer.—There is one of considerable importance in 1 Cor. xi. 2, which has been much obscured by our translators having rendered the word, which really means "traditions," "ordinances." "Now I praise you, brethren, that ye remember me in all things, and keep the ordinances," (in the margin you have *traditions*, as an alternative rendering), " as I delivered them to you" (1 Cor. xi. 2).

13. *Question.*—What do you gather from the fact that he speaks of "the traditions" in the plural number, and with the definite article?

Answer.—That there was a considerable body of these traditional rules and usages, and that they were generally known and recognised by members of the Church.

14. *Question.*—What new "ordinance," or traditional usage, does he then proceed to prescribe?

Answer.—That the men should appear uncovered, and the women covered, in the Public Worship of God.

15. *Question.*—Does he give reasons for this usage?

Answer.—He does; some of which are drawn from the original relation of the woman to the man, as set forth in the Book of Genesis (compare 1 Cor. xi. 7, 8, 9 with Gen. i. 26, 27; ii. 21, 22; and ii. 18), others from a natural sense of propriety(" Judge in yourselves: is it comely," etc.? " Doth not even nature itself teach you," etc.? see vv. 13, 14). But it is very noticeable that he concludes by saying that, if any man is not convinced by his arguments of the propriety of the usage in question, at all events it is one which obtained in the Church of Corinth and in all other Churches. "But if any man seem to be contentious, we have no such custom, neither the churches of God" (1 Cor. xi. 16).

16. *Question.*—What does this language show?

Answer.—First, that there were traditional "customs" in the primitive Churches, sanctioned and set on foot by their Apostolic founders; and secondly, that these "customs" were binding on every rightminded Christian, even if they did not coincide with his own judgment.

17. *Question.*—What other glimpse have you, at the close of the Chapter you are referring to, of tra-

ditional usages authorized by the Apostles in the Churches which they founded?

Answer.—The Chapter ends thus; "And the rest will I set in order when I come" (ver. 34);—words which might be paraphrased, "I reserve, as more suitable to be communicated by word of mouth than by letter, my judgment on the other points submitted to me."

18. *Question.*—What does this manner of speaking show?

Answer.—That certain ecclesiastical arrangements in the Church of Corinth were communicated orally, and not by letter, to the Church.

19. *Question.*—Would not the knowledge of such ecclesiastical usages as really had Apostolic authority, greatly help to the right understanding of the Scriptures of the New Testament?

Answer.—Doubtless it would; but to attain such knowledge with any accuracy would demand long and laborious study, as well as a competent acquaintance with dead languages, which would put it out of the reach of ordinary Christians.

20. *Question.*—How then may ordinary Christians attain to such a knowledge of primitive Apostolic traditions, as may for them illustrate and bring out the meaning of the New Testament?

Answer.—The Book of Common Prayer embodies and represents these traditions, and is a sort of digest of them.

21. *Question.*—Were the persons who framed the Book of Common Prayer qualified to impress upon it this character?

Answer.—They were. For not only were they men of deep piety, whose minds were thoroughly attuned to the strains of devotion which were found in the old Service Books; but they were also profound theological scholars, thoroughly versed in Holy Scripture and in the writings of the early Fathers.

22. *Question.*—Upon what material had these learned and devout men to work, in constructing the Book of Common Prayer?
Answer.—The Ancient Offices of the Church, which in course of time had expanded into large dimensions, and become separate Volumes,—the Missal, the Breviary, the Ritual, the Pontifical,—were in their possession, and formed the foundation of their work.

23. *Question.*—What had they to do with this foundation in the first instance?
Answer.—To clear it with a stern hand of all the superstitious usages, modern traditions, and unscriptural forms, which had gathered over it in the course of ages, and to exhibit it, as far as might be, in the very shape and dimensions in which it came from the hands of the Apostles, and their immediate successors.

24. *Question.*—In this work of clearance, and recurrence to the old lines on which the Primitive Church had been traced, what tests did they employ in order to discriminate the wheat from the chaff?
Answer.—The first test was the Holy Scripture. A true Apostolic tradition could not be at variance with the writings of the Apostles. If then a tradition, professing to be primitive and Apostolic, was not in unison with the New Testament, it was at once discarded.

25. *Question.*—What parts of the old Church Offices would not abide this test, and had to be ruthlessly swept away?
Answer.—All references to Purgatory (a doctrine " grounded upon no warranty of Scripture, but rather repugnant to" such passages as Rev. xiv. 13, St. Luke xxiii. 43); all Worshipping and Adoration of Reliques (repugnant to 2 Kings xviii. 4, and Deut. xxxiv. 6, with Jude 9); all invocation of Saints (repugnant to 1 Tim. ii. 5, Heb. vii. 25, St. John xiv. 6); all references to human merit (or to anything save the Blood of Christ) as having expiatory power (repugnant to

Ps. xlix. 7, Isaiah lxiv. 6, Job iv. 18, Phil. iii. 9). (See Art. xxii.)

26. *Question.*—What was the second test which the Reformers applied to the old Offices of the Church?

Answer.—The test of Primitive Antiquity and the Early Fathers.

27. *Question.*—Upon what principle did they employ this test, in order to determine what portion of the old Offices should be discarded, and what retained?

Answer.—On the principle that the ecclesiastical arrangements made by the Apostles, the rules which they established, and the customs which they set on foot, must have been observed in the Churches which they founded for a certain time after their foundation, and that such rules and customs, if ascertained out of ancient writers, could not fail to throw light upon the inspired writings of the Apostles and their associates.

Catechist.—But you speak as if God's will (at all events on questions of Church discipline and Church organization) has to be ascertained by us with some effort out of ancient documents in a dead language, and is not in all cases patent, lying on the surface of His written Word. Is this in conformity with God's usual dealings with His Church?

Answer.—It is. *The great principles* of human conduct are written as with a sunbeam on the pages of Holy Scripture, so that the blindest cannot fail to see them there. But by allowing some obscurity and doubt to hang over the right path in *particulars* of conduct, God exercises the spiritual instincts of His people, and makes their arriving at a right conclusion a trial of character. This is intimated in Phil. i. 9, 10, "And this I pray, that your love may abound yet more and more in knowledge and *in all judgment; that ye may approve things that are excellent,*" (in the margin, *try the things that differ);*

"that ye may be sincere and without offence till the day of Christ." There can be no room for an exercise of "knowledge" and "judgment," where the pathway of God's will is so clear and plain that it cannot possibly be mistaken.

29. *Catechist.*—You have described the principles on which the Prayer-Book was compiled. When offered to us side by side with the Bible, and perused together with it, what character does it assume?

Answer.—It becomes a medium, through which Bible Truth is viewed, recognised, and accepted.

30. *Question.*—Must any book of devotion inevitably become such a medium?

Answer.—It must. The listening to the extemporaneous private prayers of an individual will show at once what view he takes of Bible Truth; his prayers (if really extemporaneous) will be his private commentary upon the Bible, will let us see how the truths of the Bible present themselves to his mind. The Book of Common Prayer is not the devotional effusion of an individual mind, but of the mind of the Primitive Church. And it lets us see how the Bible presented itself to the Primitive Church,—what sense the Church, when still under the supervision of the Apostles, put upon the Bible.

31. *Question.*—Would it be impossible to compile a Book of Prayers without expressing and conveying doctrine?

Answer.—Manifestly so. The drawing up a prayer at all (with the intention of using it) must imply that the person who draws it up believes that God is a God that heareth prayer, "a rewarder of them that diligently seek him" (Heb. xi. 6).

32. *Catechist.*—But the idea of a medium, through which we look at Holy Scripture, is not altogether palatable to me. I should like to read it quite colourless, without a medium. Would it not be better to let the Bible speak absolutely for itself,

and to read it without any explanations but such as are suggested by our own minds?

Answer.—Thus we come back to the idea of reading the Bible "without note or comment," which in a former examination was shown to be (to the full extent) impracticable. A mother's teaching gives the Bible a certain colour,—is a medium, through which her child is obliged to look at it. Much more so is a preacher's sermon, a religious work, a book of devotions (to whatever school it may belong). And even if we could (which we cannot) make ourselves thoroughly independent of all human comments in studying the Bible, it is in the highest degree unlikely that we should arrive at the true sense of Holy Scripture.

33. *Question.*—To what may you compare the various interpretations of Scripture, which have come down to us in the current of tradition?

Answer.—To an atmosphere which wraps round the Sacred Volume.

34. *Catechist.*—Show the propriety of this image.

Answer.—Whatever may be the case with other planets, an atmosphere is essential to the whole economy of animal and vegetable life in this. All the animal tribes live, and move, and have their being in this atmosphere,—are so constructed as to be every moment dependent upon it. Vegetables too live by the air, and by what they imbibe from it. Remove the atmosphere, and the earth would become a scene of barrenness and death. Similarly, if you were to strip the Bible quite bare of the traditional explanation which has always accompanied it, you would remove the very element which vitalizes the Bible, and makes it such a blessed and comfortable book. If the " seed of the woman " may not be interpreted of Christ; nor Noah, nor Isaac, nor Joseph, nor David, nor Solomon, taken as types of Christ; nor such Psalms as the twenty-fourth understood of Christ's ascension (and all these are traditional explanations, never explicitly given, though some of them insinuated, in Scripture itself), how comparatively barren and profitless does the volume of the Old Testament become!

35. *Catechist.*—You speak of an atmosphere as being essential to life. But may not an atmosphere be vitiated?

Answer.—Certainly it may. It may be charged with noxious vapours, with infectious maladies; it may be heavy and oppressive, and exclude (instead of transmitting) the light.

36. *Question.*—And has this never been the case with the atmosphere of traditional sentiment and usage which encompasses the Bible?

Answer.—Notoriously it has. This atmosphere, at the time of the Reformation, was "rendered heavy and oppressive by old and effete superstitions; it was rendered opaque by a mass of unauthorized traditions, which hindered the blessed light of evangelical Truth from streaming through; it was rendered noxious by elements of anti-Scriptural practice and doctrine, which did actual spiritual mischief."

37. *Question.*—What then had the Reformers to do for the atmosphere?

Answer.—Not to dispense with, but to clear and purify it. They took away the superstitious usages, discarded those traditions which had taken rise in the later ages of the Church; and eliminated from the Offices every unscriptural doctrine and rite.

38. *Question.*—And in what did their labours result?

Answer.—In a Book of Common Prayer, which represents truly the mind of the Primitive Church, and is a beautiful medium for the transmission of evangelical Truth.

39. *Question.*—Will you express, in the language of Professor Blunt, the various kinds of help which the Prayer Book gives towards the understanding of the Bible?

Answer.—" The Prayer Book is to be regarded as a code of primitive tradition, which helps to the full

Y

interpretation of the Bible, expressing what may be there hinted, enlarging what may be there succinct, illustrating what may be there obscure, concentrating what may be there dispersed, organizing what may be there promiscuous."

40. *Catechist.*—Give an instance in which the Prayer Book "expresses" what in the Bible is only "hinted."
Answer.—Infant Baptism is an instance.

41. *Question.*—What are the "hints" which the Bible gives in favour of this practice?
Answer.—They are principally three. First; the fact of the (analogous) rite of Circumcision having been administered to children of eight days old. Secondly; our Lord's words and action, when He took little children into His arms, put His hands upon them, and blessed them. Thirdly; the Scriptural notices of several whole households having been baptized.

42. *Question.*—How does the Book of Common Prayer "express" this "hint"?
Answer.—By affirming, in the twenty-seventh Article, that "the Baptism of young Children is in any wise to be retained in the Church, as most agreeable with the Institution of Christ;" by the Rubric preceding the Office for "Private Baptism of Children in houses," which prescribes that "*The Curates of every Parish shall often admonish the people, that they defer not the Baptism of their Children longer than the first or second Sunday next after their birth, or other Holy-day falling between, unless upon a great and reasonable cause;*" and by providing an Office for "the Ministration of Public Baptism of Infants, to be used in the Church."

43. *Question.*—How did the Reformers ascertain that the Baptism of young children was an Apostolic tradition?
Answer.—Because, by applying their test of the early Fathers, they found there such passages as this from Justin Martyr: "Several persons among us of

sixty and seventy years old, of both sexes, *who were made disciples of Christ from their childhood*, do continue uncorrupted."

44. *Question.*—How do you know that Justin is here alluding to the Sacrament of Baptism?
Answer.—Because He uses the very same word which our Lord uses in instituting the Sacrament of Baptism, and which our translators have rendered "teach" (in the margin, *make disciples*); "Go ye and teach all nations, baptizing them in the name of the Father, and of the Son, and of the Holy Ghost." (St. Matt. xxviii. 19.)

45. *Question.*—When was Justin born?
Answer.—In the earlier half of the second century. St. John the Evangelist, it is generally supposed, lived to see the *beginning* of the second century. Therefore there cannot have been very many years between the death of St. John and the birth of Justin Martyr.

46. *Question.*—What do you infer from this?
Answer.—That the practice of making persons "disciples of Christ from their childhood" cannot have established itself in the Church at so very early a period without the sanction of the Apostles.

47. *Question.*—And what would the sanction of the Apostles imply?
Answer.—That of their Divine Master.

48. *Question.*—Give an instance in which the Prayer Book "enlarges" what in the Bible is "succinct."
Answer.—I give the instance of the laity's having a part assigned them in the Church Services.

49. *Question.*—Upon what Scriptural ground is this practice built?
Answer.—Upon the priesthood of all Christians, which is affirmed in the ascription at the opening of the Book of the Revelation (ch. i. vv. 5, 6). "Unto him that loved us, and washed us from our sins in his own blood, and hath *made us kings and priests*

unto God and his Father." And again (1 Pet. ii. 5);
"Ye also, as lively stones, are built up a spiritual
house, an *holy priesthood, to offer up spiritual sacrifices, acceptable to God by Jesus Christ.*" And again
(1 Pet. ii. 9); "Ye are a chosen generation, a *royal
priesthood*, an holy nation, a peculiar people."

50. *Question.*—What, in all probability, is the allusion
in the words, "Unto him that washed us from our
sins in his own blood"?

Answer.—It probably alludes to the ceremonial
washing of the hands and feet of the Priests in the
laver of the tabernacle, before they offered sacrifice.
This washing is prescribed in Exod. xxx. 17-22.

51. *Question.*—But how do these passages bear upon
the question of the laity taking part in the
Services?

Answer.—They teach us that all Christians (and
not the Clergy only) are priests. And if priests, they
should have a part to play in the Public Worship of
Almighty God.

52. *Question.*—Is there any other passage of Holy
Scripture, which seems to show that the laity did
take such a part in Public Service in the time of
the Apostles?

Answer.—Yes; there is the passage in 1 Cor. xiv.
16: "Else when thou shalt bless with the spirit"
(ἐὰν εὐλογήσῃς τῷ πνεύματι), "how shall he that
occupieth the room of the unlearned" (τὸν τόπον τοῦ
ἰδιώτου) "say Amen at thy giving of thanks" (ἐπὶ τῇ
σῇ εὐχαριστίᾳ), "seeing he understandeth not what
thou sayest?"

53. *Question.*—What is the meaning of the word
"unlearned" in this passage?

Answer.—It means a private man, one who does not
appear officially, an unprofessional person; or, in other
words, "a layman."

54. *Question.*—What do the words "he that occupieth
the room of the unlearned" seem to import?

Answer.—That the layman had a certain "room" (or sphere) assigned to him in Public Worship.

55. *Question.*—What appears from this verse to have been part of the layman's function?

Answer.—To say "Amen," when the person officiating had finished the Thanksgiving.

56. *Question.*—How does the Prayer Book "enlarge" these "succinct" intimations?

Answer.—By assigning to the laity a very considerable share in all its Services. Sometimes by merely directing them to say *Amen* at the end of a Collect or Prayer. Sometimes by requiring them to repeat Prayers *after* the Minister, as in the General Confession. Sometimes by directing them to say Prayers *with* the Minister, as in the recitation of the Lord's Prayer. Sometimes by putting into their mouth distinct Responses of their own, as (specially) in the Litany, as well as in the Morning and Evening Prayer, and in the Communion Service. Thus a "room" (or sphere) is provided by our Prayer Book for the layman to occupy, by the occupation of which he may assert his priesthood.

57. *Question.*—Is there any slight indication in Holy Scripture of the laity's taking part in the Office of the Holy Communion?

Answer.—Yes; St. Paul, speaking of the Consecration of the Bread and Wine in the Lord's Supper, says; "The cup of blessing which *we* bless, is it not the communion of the blood of Christ? the bread which *we* break, is it not the communion of the body of Christ?" (1 Cor. x. 16), as if the act of Consecration (which is the highest of all Ministerial functions), were an act in which the people took part with the Minister.

58. *Question.*—What feature in the ancient Liturgies seems to confirm this view of the Apostle's meaning?

Answer.—The circumstance that response enters largely into all of them; that in none of them is the Office confined to the Priest alone.

59. *Question.*—Give an instance in which the Prayer Book "illustrates" what in the Bible is "obscure."

Answer.—An instance may be found in the text which has been just quoted, and which even in the original is obscure.

1 Cor. xiv. 16.

Ἐπεὶ ἐὰν εὐλογήσῃς τῷ πνεύματι, ὁ ἀναπληρῶν τὸν τόπον τοῦ ἰδιώτου, πῶς ἐρεῖ τὸ ἀμὴν ἐπὶ τῇ σῇ εὐχαριστίᾳ, ἐπειδὴ τί λέγεις οὐκ οἶδε ;	Else, when thou shalt bless with the Spirit, how shall he that occupieth the room of the unlearned say Amen at thy giving of thanks, seeing he understandeth not what thou sayest?

60. *Catechist.*—Give a free translation of this passage, and explain the connexion in which it stands with what precedes.

Answer.—The Apostle is arguing against the use of an unknown tongue in Public Worship, unless an interpreter should be present to explain what is spoken in such a tongue; and he says in the verse before us; "'If thou shalt use an unknown tongue in blessing [the elements at the Holy Communion], executing that Office in a devotional rapture, but in a tongue not understanded of those around you, how shall he on whom devolves the duty of the layman" (the duty, namely, of responding to thy prayers) "say *Amen* at thy celebration of the Eucharist, seeing he does not understand what thou sayest?"

61. *Question.*—But what grounds are there for finding in this passage any reference to the Holy Communion?

Answer.—These in the text itself; that the word rendered "Thanksgiving" is literally "Eucharist," a very early designation of the Holy Communion; and that the word translated "bless" is the same word as that used at the account of the original institution by the two first Evangelists (St. Matt. xxvi. 26 ; St. Mark xiv. 22), when it is said that "Jesus took bread, and blessed it," and akin to the substantive "blessing," which St. Paul uses, when he designates the chalice of the Holy Communion "the cup of blessing" (1 Cor. x. 16).

62. *Catechist.*—These strike me as slender grounds. Have you no better?

Answer.—They would be slender, I admit, if they stood alone. But let us read side by side with the text this passage of Justin, in which he gives an account of the Lord's Supper, as it was celebrated in his time (the middle of the second century). He mentions that a meeting of the Church is held "on the day of the Sun;" that the writings of the Apostles or Prophets are read, and the reading followed up by an exhortation from the President of the assembly, and by prayers for all conditions of men, which being concluded " we salute one another with a kiss."

Justin Apol. 1. ch. 65, 66 (*See also* 67).

Ἔπειτα προσφέρεται τῷ προεστῶτι* τῶν ἀδελφῶν ἄρτος, καὶ ποτήριον ὕδατος καὶ κράματος· καὶ οὗτος λαβὼν αἶνον καὶ δόξαν τῷ πατρὶ τῶν ὅλων διὰ τοῦ ὀνόματος τοῦ υἱοῦ, καὶ τοῦ πνεύματος τοῦ ἁγίου ἀναπέμπει. καὶ εὐχαριστίαν ὑπὲρ τοῦ κατηξιῶσθαι τούτων παρ' αὐτοῦ ἐπὶ πολὺ ποιεῖται· οὗ συντελέσαντος τὰς εὐχὰς καὶ τὴν εὐχαριστίαν, πᾶς ὁ παρὼν λαὸς ἐπευφημεῖ λέγων· ἀμήν. τὸ δὲ ἀμήν, τῇ Ἑβραΐδι φωνῇ, τὸ γένοιτο σημαίνει. εὐχαριστήσαντος δὲ τοῦ προεστῶτος, καὶ ἐπευφημήσαντος παντὸς τοῦ λαοῦ, οἱ καλούμενοι παρ' ἡμῖν διάκονοι,

Then is brought to the President of the brethren bread, and a cup of water and mixed wine. And he, taking them, sends up praise and glory to the Father of all through the name of His Son and by the Holy Ghost. And he maketh at great length a thanksgiving for our having been thought worthy by God of such blessings. And when he has finished the prayers and the thanksgiving, all the people present signify their joyful assent by saying *Amen.* Now *Amen* in the Hebrew tongue signifieth So *be it.* And when the

---

* It is observable that in 1 Thess. v. 12, this very verb is used to describe the Ministerial Office:—

τοὺς κοπιῶντας ἐν ὑμῖν, καὶ προϊσταμένους ὑμῶν ἐν Κυρίῳ, καὶ νουθετοῦντας ὑμᾶς.

Them which labour among you, and *are over you* in the Lord, and admonish you.

διδόασιν ἑκάστῳ τῶν παρόν-
των μεταλαβεῖν ἀπὸ τοῦ εὐ-
χαριστηθέντος ἄρτου καὶ οἴνου
καὶ ὕδατος . . . . Καὶ ἡ τροφὴ
αὕτη καλεῖται παρ' ἡμῖν εὐ-
χαριστία.

President has given thanks,
and the people have signified
their assent, those who go
among us by the name of
Deacons give to each of those
present a portion of the
bread and wine and water
over which thanks have been
given . . . . and this food is
called with us the Eucharist.

Putting this passage of St. Justin by the side of the text from St. Paul, there seems no longer any room to doubt that "the thanksgiving" referred to by the Apostle is "the Prayer of Consecration in the Communion Service," and the "Amen," which it is the part of "the layman" to "say," the *Amen* with which that Prayer is concluded.

63. *Catechist.*—Yes. Justin's description of a primitive celebration does make it almost a certainty that St. Paul is referring to the Holy Communion, and its long prayer of Consecration, and the fervent response "Amen," by which the congregation were wont to conclude that prayer. I see how the writings of Justin illustrate that which in the Bible is obscure. But what has this to do with the Prayer Book?

Answer.—Because the Communion Office in the Prayer Book represents with great fidelity the Order of that Service as it was in Justin's time. We have there the Epistle and Gospel (the former of which is even now occasionally taken from the Prophetical Writings, as on the Monday and Tuesday in Easter Week); the Sermon or Exhortation, the Oblation of the elements, the Prayer for the Church Militant, the Prayer of Consecration, with its concluding *Amen*; and then immediately the distribution of the Elements. Since Justin lived so near to the times of the Apostles, our Reformers felt that the Order of Service then observed must have had their sanction, and emanated from them; and this Order of Service they have retained very faithfully in our present Communion Office, which thus gives the mind of the Apostles as to the method of administration. The Prayer Book, then, taken as representing and embodying the usage described by Justin, does very much "illustrate" what in the Bible is "obscure."

64. *Catechist.*—Give an instance in which the Prayer Book "concentrates" what in the Bible is "dispersed."

Answer.—I cannot give an instance more apposite than that which is furnished by the doctrine of the Holy Trinity. This doctrine is given to us in Holy Scripture, as I have before had occasion to observe, piecemeal, the Godhead of the Son being asserted or implied in some texts, that of the Holy Ghost in others, the distinctness of the Persons being recognised in passages occurring here, their Co-equality and Co-eternity in a different connexion, while the Unity of the Godhead is a doctrine which pervades the whole of Scripture. These various doctrinal statements, which are dispersed over the Sacred Volume, result, when "concentrated," in the doctrine of the Trinity, as it is stated at large in the Athanasian Creed.

65. *Catechist.*—Give an instance in which the Prayer Book organizes what is promiscuous in the Bible.

Answer.—The best instance I can give is the threefold Ministry of Bishops, Priests, and Deacons.

66. *Question.*—What do you mean by saying that this threefold Ministry is to be found *promiscuously* in the Bible?

Answer.—I mean that it is to be gathered from different parts of Holy Scripture. During our Lord's own life there was the appointment of the Twelve, and afterwards of the Seventy (see St. Luke ix. 1 and x. i.), both Orders, it would appear, receiving powers and a commission not very dissimilar. Then, in the Acts, we have the account of an Order designed to relieve the Apostles of the lower and more secular parts of their duty (Acts vi. 1-7). Then, in the Epistles, what we find is summed up thus by Professor Blunt:—

" Timothy was set by Paul in a position of authority even over those who had a control of their own over the flock; for Timothy, on the one hand, was commissioned to receive an accusation against an elder, and, if necessary, to rebuke him; and yet the elder, on the other hand, was commissioned on his part to bear rule; while the deacon, as his very name indicates, was appointed only to minister or serve, and was not to be raised to a higher grade or 'good degree,' till he had given proof that he was fit for it; Timothy, meanwhile, deriving his superiority from no advantage in age, for he was so young that he is cautioned not to allow himself on that account to be despised. Titus is in the same case with respect to years, yet he, too, is commissioned ' to rebuke with all authority;' and both the one and the other are intrusted with the power of Ordination, an exclusive power, for the manner in which the exercise of it is enjoined them, shows that the character of the clergy lay in their hands by the cautious choice which they should make and the previous examination they should institute, a provision which would be entirely defeated, if the clergy in their respective dioceses might be self-appointed, or appointed by other indifferent parties; an exclusive power, too, which was not to be confined to them, but to descend in like manner to those who should succeed to their places; for Timothy was to 'keep the commandment,' that is, I apprehend, the instructions he had just been receiving from St. Paul, ' until the appearing of our Lord Jesus Christ;' an injunction which would imply that they were to be binding on future bishops to the end of time."— Finally, in the Book of the Revelation, we find the Epistles to the Asiatic Churches addressed to their respective " angels " (or presiding bishops), in whom the Church is regarded as being summed up, and who are addressed as representing it before God.

67. *Question.*—How does the Book of Common Prayer "organize" these various notices respecting the Ministry?

Answer.—By assuring us in the Preface to the Ordinal; "*It is evident unto all men diligently reading the holy Scripture and ancient Authors, that from the Apostles' time there have been these Orders of Ministers in Christ's Church; Bishops, Priests, and Deacons;*" and also by assigning to each Order special duties and functions, those of the Deacon being to assist the Priest in Divine Service, but not apparently to stand in the Priest's stead.

68. *Question.*—What is specially to be observed in the passage of the Ordinal which you have just quoted?

Answer.—That it does not assert that Holy Scripture *alone* makes the threefold Ministry *evident*. Scripture only gives *intimations to that effect*, which ancient authors (Ignatius, the Apostolical Constitutions, and others) develope and confirm. Scripture, not by itself, but *read in the light of "ancient Authors,"* makes it *evident*.

69. *Question.*—What practical recommendation flows naturally from the subject to which this Chapter is devoted?

Answer.—That we should accept the Prayer Book, as for us the authorized guide into the teaching of the Bible, on the ground that it is really the voice of the Primitive Church, guiding us into the truth, as the pillar of the cloud and of fire guided the Israelites in their journeyings.

70. *Question.*—What happy effect would this final acceptance of the Prayer Book, as the interpreter of Holy Scripture, have upon our minds?

Answer.—" That we henceforth " should " be no more children, tossed to and fro, and carried about with every wind of doctrine, by the sleight of men, and cunning craftiness, whereby they lie in wait to deceive; but speaking the truth in love," should " grow up into him in all things, which is the head, even Christ, from whom the whole body fitly joined together and compacted by that which every joint supplieth, according to the effectual working in the measure of every part, maketh increase of the body unto the edifying of itself in love." (See Eph. iv, 14, 15, 16.) In short, there would be for us an end of controversy, and a good prospect of quiet growth in grace if we could acquiesce in the Bible, as interpreted by the Prayer Book.

71. *Question.*—But are there not many controverted points upon which the Bible, as interpreted by the Prayer Book, pronounces nothing; and which therefore must still be left open questions?

Answer.—Doubtless there may be such points. But we may be sure that they are not of serious importance. And, although some of them may interest our curiosity, we may be content to wait for their settlement till the day when all obscurities, which at present hang over the counsels of God, shall be cleared up. Here below we may not expect more light than will serve for our practical guidance.

72. *Question.*—What is the great danger of interesting ourselves too much in the *speculative* questions of controversy?

Answer.—That they may draw us off from questions of practical and personal interest.

73. *Question.*—What Scriptural instance is there of a person allowing the mind to seek refuge in controversy from those personal questions, which apply a probe to the conscience?

Answer.—That of the woman of Samaria, who, when our Saviour had charged her with living in sin, took the opportunity of consulting Him on the subject of the controversy which divided the Samaritans from the Jews. (See St. John iv. 18, 19, 20.)

74. *Question.*—How did she evade the home thrust, which our Lord had given to her conscience?

Answer.—Taking no notice of her present sinful life, she answered Him; "Sir, I perceive that thou art a prophet. Our fathers worshipped in this mountain ; and ye say, that in Jerusalem is the place where men ought to worship" (St. John iv. 19, 20).

75. *Question.*—How may we imitate her example in this particular?

Answer.—By allowing much of our time and thoughts to be taken up by slight ceremonial questions, while the weightier matters of the law stir in us comparatively but little interest.

76. *Question.*—What is the great end, from which curious controversies too often call us off?

Answer.—That of growing in grace and living nearer to God; of finding greater satisfaction for the mind in His light, and for the heart in His love. That of comprehending " with all saints what is the breadth, and length, and depth, and height; and " of knowing "the love of Christ, which passeth knowledge, that" we might " be filled with all the fulness of God."

THE END.

www.ingramcontent.com/pod-product-compliance
Lightning Source LLC
Chambersburg PA
CBHW031420230426
43668CB00007B/375